WOMEN'S EQUALITY
A Struggle for Survival

Jaya Arunachalam

GYAN PUBLISHING HOUSE
NEW DELHI-110002

Women's Equality— A Struggle for Survival

Rs. 790

ISBN: 81-212-0842-4

Published in 2005 in India by
Gyan Publishing House
5, Ansari Road, Darya Ganj, New Delhi-110002
Phones : 23282060, 23261060, Fax : (011) 23285914
E-mail : gyanbook@vsnl.com
Website : http://www.gyanbooks.com

Laser Typesetting at : Shree Vaishnavi Creations, Delhi
Printed at : Delux Offset Press, Delhi

"Dedicated
to
Mithila - *my grand daughter*
whom I missed during these travels"

Contents

Foreword

The social progress of the developing nations is evidently being seen largely in the hands of women, who however are suffering from marginalisation and oppression in many communities and countries. A number of initiatives in the world have proven that organisation and empowerment of women can have a decisive positive impact on the lives of women, their families and children and their communities.

Especially today when it is becoming blatantly clear that internationally and nationally the rich get richer and the poor get poorer, the realities of the poor need to be voiced clear and loud. The persistent and growing poverty of hundreds of millions in the rural areas and in urban slums all over the South, and in a big way in the relentless liberalising market economies of South and East Asia, is only leading to massive hopelessness, being often a breeding ground for destructive and/or self-destructive forces.

The way Working Women's Forum has become an instrument of marginalised, exploited poor women, owned by these same women is striking in its simplicity as well in sophistication. There is the immediate importance by women in general and reproductive health and there is the basic importance of access to income. Both around these elements the Forum has evolved with an uncompromising rule to engage, train, and empower the same social group of poor women and adolescent girls as organisers and facilitators. In the Forum one does not find a high profile vocabulary about Adult Education or experiential learning, but the daily practice simply is Adult Education, experiential leaming or Learning through Action. It is one of those rare present day manifestations of Mahatma Gandhi's teachings.

I met Jaya Arunachalam in 1990 during the then mid term evaluation of the Netherlands support to Working Women's Forum. Here was a woman who completely identified herself, without any compromise, with the cause of thousands of poor women. Their struggle for survival being her struggle. Their pains of suffering being her pains. And their hopes for a bit better future being her hopes.

The speeches, addresses and articles in this anthology show the full range of Jaya Arunachalam's rich and full involvement with, and struggle on behalf of the poor, downtrodden and victims of class, caste, gender discrimination and of HIV/AIDS. Its publication is especially welcome at a time when nationally and internationally India stands in the limelight of its achievements in advanced sectors like information technology and growing consumer spending of urban middle classes.

Jaya Arunachalam has never been distracted by middle class- or market hype. She stands in the middle of a movement of poor and exploited women workers in the so-called informal sector, who only want to live with a little dignity in their lives. In the middle of small market vendors, beedi rollers, indebted marginal dry land farmers and landless labourers, where exploitation by the market translates into outright violence in the forms of bonded labour, alcoholism, domestic violence and suicides.

As being presented in these pages, the path from a group of mere 800 women in 1979 to a movement, labour union and credit cooperative of more than 7,00,000 women members in 2004 has been long and winding. Again and again there were occasions on March 8 or others to come out to the streets to underline a burning issue and oppose oppression, to show collective strength and build up confidence. And never an opportunity was missed to present to a national or international audience, be it academics, students, bankers or social activists, press or policy makers, the causes of persistent poverty and most of all give exploited women a voice in India and abroad.

As can be seen from these speeches at a very early stage Jaya Arunachalam has made the link between poverty and dwindling natural resources and growing lack of access or entitlement by the poor to these resources. With forests declining, soil fertility eroding and being destroyed by indiscriminate use of chemicals in agriculture, commons being encroached by or handed over to private interest, agrarian reforms being halted or even being reversed, what remains for the poorest?

Jaya Arunachalam's concerns are with the well being of women and families and communities. She is also one of the most worldly and at the same time down to earth persons that I have ever met. She is too a great healing force, from which I suspect more and more people will draw new-found strength and inspiration.

I am sure the writings of this book will provide a rich resource references for many young development workers who share the same concerns and who are working with various women's issues across the world.

Paul ter Weel
31th July, 2004

Advisor
Rural Development
Royal Netherland Embassy,
New Delhi - 110 021.

एम. वी. राजासेखरन्
M.V. Rajasekharan

योजना राज्य मंत्री
भारत सरकार
योजना आयोग
योजना भवन, संसद मार्ग,
नई दिल्ली– 110001
MINISTER OF STATE FOR PLANNING
GOVERNMENT OF INDIA
PLANNING COMMISSION
YOJANA BHAWAN SANSAD MARG,
NEW DELHI-110 001
TEL : 011-23096561, 23096562
E-MAIL : mvraja@yojana.nic.in

Dr (Mrs) Jaya Arunachalam who is the present President of Working Women's Forum (India) is one of the outstanding social activist and has done tremendous work in organizing the poor women workers, who have been working in the informal sector and putting their hard work, through which they try to earn income to sustain their livelihood

Her contribution in the field of organizing the women workers has not only got recognition within the country but also all over the world including the United Nations Agencies. She has received largest number of awards both within the country and also outside India. She has made extensive studies with regard to promoting poor women workers in particular and as well as the role of voluntary organizations in the country. Because of her deep knowledge in this field she has been invited from time to time to participate in the various seminars and workshops held both within the country and also in different countries from all over the world. She has distinguished herself as one of the first women leaders from Asia and has occupied a number of high positions in some of the well-known international agencies. She has also been providing leadership in the field of social service organizing Farmers Movement and as well as organizing different women groups empowering them to shape their own destiny. She has also been responsible for developing the concept of Micro Credit for women workers to pursue their own small enterprises.

Her contribution for building very vibrant and sustainable Working Women Movement in India has got worldwide recognition. At a time when we think about active participation in a civil society we always look towards eminent women leaders like Dr. (Mrs) Jaya Arunachalam.

Acknowledgements

The task of pooling together the several speeches and talks delivered at the various National / International Conferences, on many important occasions, was no doubt a herculean task. However, the inspirations for this effort, at the outset had come from the poor women of the Working Women's Forum (India), who never failed mention in any forum if and when they were given a chance to speak, on my visit both within and outside the country, saying I go there only speak on their struggles and trials. Thus my women in the first instance gave me the courage that required to publish this book, therefore my thanks to them. My deep sense of gratitude to Mr. Paul-Ter-Weel, the development Donor / Partner for seventeen years, from 1989, Advisor Rural Development from the Ministry of Development Co-operation Netherlands, who used exceptionally excellent language to provide this book the preface to initiate the process to move forward. I owe a debt of gratitude, to Hon. Minister of State for Planning, Dr. M.V. Rajasekaran, a well-wisher and an old friend on his liberal use of superlatives, on his note on the author.

It is pleasant task to acknowledge my deep sense of gratitude to several friends in many institutions around the world, who have given me an opportunity not only to present these papers and share my views on the various aspects of work in the Working Women's Forum also heard them attentively. I am particularly thankful to Global Institutions such as Asian Institute of Management, Philippians, Ryfeission union Germany, Ministries of Development Co-operation Belgium and Netherlands, U.N. conferences such as World Summit for Social Development, as Copenhagen, IFAD, ILO, Citi Bank and other development outfits. Also, my thanks to institutions such as Sri. Vaikunta Metha Co-operative Institute, Pune, Gandhi Labour Institute Ahmedabad, and other institutions of national repute.

I owe my deep sense of gratitude to Ms. Egammai, Secretary WWF, who travelled along with me all these twenty-five years on the development path shared tears and laughter. My thanks to Vidhya Rajagopalan and Kamakshi, both coordinators of the Working Women's Forum (India) for interacting with me in preparing many of these articles. My thanks Ramesh, Nandini, Janaki and Yesho for intellectual inputs, to several of my speeches before they are finally done. In general thanks to my family, if they had not been liberal I would not have been able to achieve what has been possible today.

I thankful to Mrs. Akansha Goyal for her patient editing of the whole script and the unstinted support of Mr. Goyal for the same. My thanks to our typists who took special attention make it ready for publication. Above all I will be failing in my duty if I don't place or record the innumerable women of the Working Women's Forum (India) and my collegues who provided an opportunity for me to work with them these 25 years. It is they who made these speeches possible.

I am thankful to the Gyan Publications Mr. B.P. Garg and Amit Garg who took very special interest with patience even when I was sending the articles in bits and pieces.

1

Indian Study Mission to China-Observations*

The population of China is one-seventh of the world's population and it occupies one-fourth of landed area. A high powered Indian Delegation recently had its study tour of China and Hongkong, sponsored by UNFPA. The team was led by the Health Secretary, Ministry of Health, Government of India. The duration of this study tour was 10 days, i.e., from 14th to 24th December. The team was composed of 11 officials and 1 non-official. The team visited Beijing, Nanjing in Jiangsu Province, Guangzu province (Canton) and finally, FPA at Hongkong, a voluntary organisation.

The Learnings

The study tour was an appraisal of China's efforts to contain her population in the following directions:

1. Chinese (National) Government's policy on birth control and its political will or commitment to carry through the policy with conviction.
2. Education and motivation through intensive publicity programmes. The role of the National People's Congress and Media.
3. Restructuring of research in support of State's policy on Family Planning and Population Control.
4. Orientation and training to suit the need to prepare cadres to work for the success of State's policy on birth control both at administrative and grassroot level.

---

*As member of Indian Inter-Ministerial Team to China and Hongkong Ms. Jaya Arunachalam's observations of population incentives of Chinese Government - 14th to 24th December 1985.

5. Linking up Family Planning with employment - strategies of incentives and disincentives.
6. Effective implementation mechanisms for the follow-up of the programme of the Family Planning from the National, Provincial, County and Township level, even in remote rural area.

Visits Discussions

During the course of the visit, the team met the officers of the State Family Planning Commission, Beijing's Publicity and Education Centre for Family Planning, visited the National Research Institute for Family Planning measures adopted for workers. The team visited rural areas to study Family Planning Programme at Provincial, County and Township level. Team had an opportunity to observe the implementation mechanism and effective delivery systems from national to the grassroots level. Team studied the training methodology adopted to train cadres to work at different levels, and monitoring of such training programme at the sub-centres at county level.

Discussion and interactions during the visits were with people like Vice-Ministers, Personnel incharge of publicity programmes, Doctors, Research Scholars, Training Personnel, Leaders from National People's Congress and so on. The following information on population programmes and implementation strategy in mainly elicited from discussions with these personages.

On the first day, 16th November, we visited the State Family Planning Commission and the Vice-Minister of SEPC, Dr.(Mrs.) Peng-Yu, gave us a brief introduction of their programme. While extending all courtesies to the Indian team, she referred that both our countries - India and China - face a similar population crisis. Further, both countries have another similarity in having large numbers of people living in rural areas.

At present China pursues a vigorous policy of family planning, in order to adopt the pace of nation's social and economic development. Therefore, practicing family planning is one of the basic tenets of national policy. The nation pledges to work hard to control the country's population to 1.2 billion by the end of this century. In order to achieve this goal, they evolved a national birth control and family planning policy and restructured the entire country's planning mechanism in pursuance of the same.

Pre-revolutionary Era and Population Trends in China

To understand China's present population policy, one has to understand the problematic China in the pre-revolutionary era, when there was a very high birth rate and a low natural growth rate. According to 1936 statistics, 38 per cent was the birth rate and 28 per cent was the death rate per 1000. But since 1949-1970, the economy has improved, birth rate being 18 per cent and death rate being 7 per cent per 1000, with the growth rate of 10 per cent. Due to an alround economic improvement in the country, the population has been growing faster in rural areas and has doubled since 1949, and during this period China faced several birth peaks.

At present, younger people under the age of 30 are 65 per cent in China and middle-aged are about 23 per cent, from 1962-75 about 25 million children were born each year. All these young people now have attained marriageable age. China's fear is that in the next 15 years, 12 million more young people will attain marriageable age.

Problems of Uneven Distribution of Population

Uneven distribution of population is another problem faced by the Chinese. Eighty per cent of the Chinese population is rural. Ninety per cent of this rural population cover 50 per cent of China's landed area, which is approximately 1002 per sq. mile, 3.5 times larger in density than the world's average.

Apart from the Han nationality which constitute the majority of Chinese, a total of about 55 groups of multi-national minorities make up for 6.7 million people in the country. Though their population is small, they live scattered in many autonomous areas across the country and occupy 62 per cent of the total land area. Besides the economy, the development of China is under the threat of lack of cultivated land area now. The cultivated land is 3.4 Moo in some area, which amount to 1.5 Moo per person on an average (15 Moo is hect).

Inspite of a high improvement in country's health and hygienic status, contagious disease are still common in the countryside. Illiteracy is another problem, 12 million Chinese still cannot read and write. Average number of birth rate is 14 per 100 in rural areas. Fearing the fast growth of people that would become double by 2000 A.D. The Chinese have adopted a vigorous policy of family planning and population control and felt it an important compulsion and urgent task of the nation to contain the population to 1.2 billion by 2000 A.D.

Policy of "One Couple One Child"

To promote this family planning programme in pursuance of their socialistic ideology and state policy the Chinese Government, advocated in 1979 the ideal of "One Couple One Child" as a fundamental task to control and improve the quality of population. They also adopted severe changes in the upbringing of children, making parents pay more attention to the physical and intellectual development of children and improve the quality of the future generations. With the result, the government has been able to achieve 20 per cent of their target in major cities. The marriage laws were amended to suit the state policy of family planning. The minimum marriageable age for men is 24 and women is 22.

The publicity and information wing of the government were given complete guidelines for effective publicity and mass campaigns on family planning both in rural and urban areas.

The government along could restructure the clinical research in the field of medical sciences to suit a mass family planning programmes. A series of employment, health, education and other incentives and disincentives to promote family planning to parents of single children entering kindergarten and primary schools. Mothers of single children were given longer maternity leave.

Media and Mass Campaigns

On December 17th, in the morning the Indian team visited Beijing's Publicity and Education Centre for Family Planning. This centre receives guidelines from the State Family Planning Commission from time to time for printing and publication of propaganda material. They produce audio, video materials and TV films to popularise birth control methods as well as intellectual scientific knowledge of family planning. Film-tapes are telecast on many channels of TV through a network, disseminating the message of family planning countrywide. TV stations alongwith mobile vans, fully equipped with audio and video systems go to villages for education and motivation. They have 60 such publicity vans to move about throughout the state. They also have other educational agencies who are engaged in publicity work apart from the TV units and government departments.

The leaflets, pamphlets and posters seem to have effective themes of population control, and could persuade the most difficult people that have strong traditional views.

The state education and publicity department has various sub-centres through which publicity materials are sold at low prices. The publicity materials also are of varied kind, i.e., producing of materials, like handkerchiefs, fans and bags with family planning matter printed on them.

Yet another important aspect at this publicity centres is that they also promote consultancy service on family welfare matters by associating experts and activists, who are respected by people. The centres also train people to be sent to their sub-centres to carry on family planning work.

The National People's Congress is closely associated with publicity work of this centre, since 1980. Experts from abroad are often associated with this centre for professional guidance.

The themes of publicity centres are mostly to enhance the status of women and decry men who discriminate women. The TV films are produced on themes, such as, harmful effects of marriage between close relatives, some are educational materials for genetic excellence and better upbringing of children. Some films are supposed to be for older people to persuade them to change traditional ideas. The publicity centres make people think on calculative and comparative methods to understand better, and to have less number of children.

The most important focus of publicity centre in urban areas is to have only 'one child' as these city areas are not suited to have more than on child.

Centres make their annual publicity plans according to the need of the people, since pre-formulated plans help smooth working. Their emphasis is to cover more rural people who live in the countryside.

National Research Institute of Family Planning

In pursuance of their new thrust in the birth control programmes, the medical research in modern China has achieved a new dimensions. After the revolution, government having adopted the policy of 'one child', the task of the research was to divert its attention to restructure the methodology to make its result and benefits reach 80 per cent of the population in rural area. The family planning methods have grown faster and major towns like Beijing and Shanghai are examples of such high technological advance, where birth control targets were achieved faster. Medical research and medical education departments became specialised units and affiliated to State Family Planning Commission.

Production of contraceptives was carried on warfooting in collaboration with UNFPA. Throughout the country, 30 factories have been established for contraceptives and 20 kinds of contraceptives were produced. There has been alternatives for oral pills as it has side effects on its use.

IUD is the most popular method used by large number of women. Earlier in China, Japanese IUDs were much in use. The most important IUD is a special type of steel ring produced recently and locally in China and has become very popular, as it is devoid of any side effects. The Chinese Government spends lot of time and resources to help continuous research to prevent side effects of IUD. The clinical research on family planning in China in the recent years have advanced much in preventing side effects, which is very important for any effective adoption of methods.

In China, according to the findings of the National Research Institute of Family Planning, at present there are 240 million couple in child bearing age and 130 million couple have accepted different kinds of contraceptives.

The contraceptives are supplied free of charge even in rural areas. The research institute has its own personnel to distribute the contraceptives even at the grassroots level.

Training Priorities

Nanjing College of Training

Training was completely re-oriented in Modern China to suit the need of State's Family Planning Policy. The 'activists' and 'paramedics' are trained to meet the needs as per family planning requirements of large rural population of country at the grassroots. Training as such has played a great role in assisting to achieve the target and has been given very high priority. This was evident when the Indian team studied the training methodology and *priorities at Nanjing College of Training* in Jiangsu Province. From the State Family Planning Officers down to the Grassroots cadres, family planning personnel go through suitable training courses before they enter their work.

There are five types of training programmes taking place in this college:

1. For family planning cadres to work at various levels both in the urban and rural areas including 'activist' at the 'grassroots'.

2. Training in pre-evaluation work in a given area for field work.
3. Training to be a good task force.
4. Train them to be good family planning administrators.
5. Train them for research in family planning.

The training programmes are conducted not only just to impart knowledge on family planning, but also to raise the level and quality of those workers to be good task force for the family planning programmes. The workers learn alongwith family planning methodology, psychology and administration.

Apart from administration, psychology, family planning methodology the training also includes MCH Education, protein and nutrition in the curriculum. Most kindergarten teachers are trained continuously on protein and nutrition so that they can enhance the quality of population.

The college takes up training of personnel to work in different sub-centres in various countries and townships, who, in turn, train part-time workers and 'activists' to work in rural areas. A low cost multiplication effort is evident here.

Study of Family Planning Measures Adopted for Workers in Beijing Textile Factory

The team visited Beijing Textile Factory on 18th December. The factory, which was started during 1954-55, was the project of First Five Year Plan of China after the revolution. The team could observe, manner in which the Chinese Government has re-oriented employment policies by providing a series of incentives to parents of single children. The factory with a capacity of 700 thousand spindles has more than 9,000 workers, out of which 70 per cent are women, 60 per cent are young people below 28 years. Both factory's administrative section and family planning section are handled and headed by two women. Mrs.Chou, the head of the family planning division of the factory, reported that the factory moulded itself is in response to country's policy and took up on themselves publicising contraceptive methods and to advise and pursue workers on 'one couple one child policy'. They counselled and educated mothers about the need to have genetic excellence and better upbringing of children. Though their family planning programme was started in 1965, positive results were produced only in 1980. In 1985, the factory turned a-new by appointing three full-time workers to promote family planning, who, in turn, have promoted 18 workshops among 670 working groups, each promoting an "activist" to cover large number of workers. Much has been done by these working groups in their workshops for promotion of family planning adoptions and training of young mothers to bring up healthy young children.

Incentives

1. If a female worker of the factory promises and gets into an agreement with the factory authorities that she will have only one child and will remain with the same, she gets the advantage of her maternity leave extended even upto six months. She can also abstain from work a month before her delivery.
2. If a female worker postpones the birth of her child upto 24 years of age, she also gets the same benefit.
3. If a female worker marries at an age of 28 years, she gets maternity benefit alongwith extra 10 days of honeymoon and gifts by the factory.
4. Every single child of the factory workers get free books, uniforms and health coverage till they attain the age of 14 years.

The contraceptive coverage of couple in reproduction age in the factory is 100 per cent. The details with reference to number of children among this factory workers.

The couples who have only one child are 59.9 per cent. The couples who have 2 children are 19.2 per cent. The couples who have 3 children are 2.8 per cent. Nobody marries before 24 years. Some of them marry even after 28 years. Some of them are young people who are single and who carry on their studies in the Open Universities, they total about 6.61 per cent.

The couples who have 2 or 3 children are those who have joined this factory before 1949, i.e., the pre-revolutionary days.

Visit to Jiangsu Province

The team visited Jiangsu Province to study the rural population programmes of China. The province has 11 cities, 64 countries and with several villages. This smallest township has 20 villages. The population varies in each of these townships anything between 15,000 to 40,000. 25,000 "activists" work on family planning work in Jiangsu Province, who are paid by the local committees at the county level. The township of Jiangsu Province have 15 full-time workers who are paid by the Family Planning Commission. Jiangsu Province, with a population of 6,17,10,000 and with a per capita cultivated land of 1.12 moo, per person has the highest density of population in the whole of China. The population density in this province is 602 persons per sq.mile and rated as having the seventh place in the whole of China in its density. 58.4 per cent of the population in Jiangsu Province are young people, and therefore, it is a challenge to carry on family planning programme within this province. But the Province had been very successful in bringing down the birth rate with a growth rate of 1.2 per cent. The total number of workers are 3,800 and help in covering 70 million people with all kinds of contraceptives. The strategy utilised in propaganda was to compare the family expenses in having few children as against families with large number of children.

Mechanism for Implementation and Supervision

Judging them from the effective manner in which the birth control methods are pursued both by the government and the people making concentrated efforts in one common direction, one feels that China's prospects of controlling their population is very bright. In the major cities, as we have already read the strategies have started producing positive results. This is because of effective administrative mechanism alongwith reinforcement of above strategies.

The Implementation Mechanism

The family planning programme is a political commitment in Modern China. It is a basic national policy. The government thus, stresses that this policy is the most fundamental to Chinese socialist construction. The Chinese Government apart from other administrative measures, periodically publishes handbooks and other reading matters through the publicity departments, specially designed to disseminate knowledge on methods of birth control and abortion. Not only these publicity materials were disseminated, but were also accompanied by extensive educational mass campaigns in the densely populated areas.

Restructuring major research policies, definite and concrete guidelines to publicity and education campaigns among the masses and alongwith motivational work in the field of family planning, are being carried out in progressive stages. The beginning is with the most densely populated urban greas and in rural provinces like Jiangsu.

The National People's Congress call upon their members from time to time to take lead in implementing the party's commitment to family planning policy of 'one child one couple' policy. The factories and other employment situations have been very closely linked up with incentives and disincentives for family planning adopters, in the rural areas. There is a wide network of 'activist' and 'paramedics' who are made responsible for the implementation of the programme. For instance, a small township has 11 activists, who are voluntary workers. There is one paid worker by the government for every 10,000 people. The much needed resources for effective implementation of this programme not only comes from the government, but also comes from the people. The Chinese experiment shows that grassroots initiatives at the people's level and political commitment to support the same are two important aspects for the success of any committed policy.

In rural areas, three or four villages are classified as clusters and one worker is put incharge of such cluster. The local leaders (NPC) live in and around the area though they don't have control over the area, but do coordinate the family planning workers, government workers, the rural activists, paramedics as well as assist the rural doctors. Nintyfive per cent of the babies are delivered in the hospitals as this prevent a high rate of infant mortality.

How Successful is the 'One Child Norm'

In 1984, 80 per cent of the families in major cities adopted the one child policy. Out of this, 85.18 per cent of the children are first child. Incentives and disincentives are not same in all cities but they differ and they do play a decisive role in achieving targets. In some cities, families with single child, get 40 Yuans from the government as living expenses upto the age of 14. If they break this rule of one child and have another child until this first child completes the 14 years, 5 per cent of the salary of both parents will be cut for three to five years. Sometimes, both parents have to pay 300 to 500 Yuans as fine annually for five years for an additional child. In some rural areas, they collect upto 700 Yuans. But they feel that such disincentives are not good methods to implement a long-term programme. The 'one couple one child' is a policy evolved for historical reasons and after 2000 A.D. the Chinese feel that they may have to revert back to normalcy.

It is evident, Chinese are not able to implement this policy fully in rural areas and among the minorities. They are flexible with these communities since there is 'male child phobia' among these communities. Sometimes, parents with single child are allowed to have another child. Suitable guidelines with effect to enforcement of this concern have been given to authorities of implementation accordingly.

Problems Faced by Chinese

1. There are problems of traditional values and literacy, such as preference for male child.
2. Traditional and superstitious beliefs are the main reason for high rate of infant mortality in the rural areas, which is being reduced to 6 per cent.

Till few years ago, women preferred to have their children delivered at home. Now, they go to the hospital several days before the delivery and are sent only after they have accepted a permanent or temporary family planning methods after the delivery of the child.

3. The attitude of minorities is impediment in the way of family planning programme work in the rural areas. Female children are still looked down upon in the rural areas.

They are fighting these challenges by giving more preferences to women in jobs and making the boys to live with girl's family after marriage and many other such efforts. Managers have still preference for men in factories for their management programmes, mangers are trained in training workshops to avoid such practices. Also, the Labour Department takes up such matters seriously and regularises them.

Accomplishment of Modern China

China's present GNP is about $800 per annum. Through extensive mass educational and motivational campaigns, they have now achieved a birth rate of 17.2 per cent per 1000, death rate of 6.6 per cent and the national growth rate of 10.8 per cent. There has been a steady decrease of 5.81 per cent in 1981 in the fertility rate of women, 86 per cent of women in reproductive age have been able to adopt one or the other of family planning methods. In 1950, average child bearing age for women was 19, now it is 22.

Both in the urban and rural areas, 92.2 per cent of children are brought up using modern techniques. In 1984, the infant mortality in the urban areas was 10 per cent per 1000. In rural areas, 34.8 per cent per 1000 the average life expectancy is 68 per cent and such expectancy is better for women in the urban areas than in rural areas. In Beijing and Shanghai, people live for 70 years. Widely prevalent anti-natal and prenatal health care for women, improved their health in general. Health education among the younger people have improved the motivation and knowledge of youth in the country. The general aim of this population policy of China is to improve the quality of life among its people so that they can enjoy the fruits of economy.

Impressions and Reflections

During the team's visit both in urban and rural areas, the team had to rely mainly on the introduction and briefings of the personnel of the information departments. As the visits were mostly conducted in a team, we could not visit even a hospital or kindergarten in the rural areas as we desired.

In their attitudes, whether among officials or political leaders everyone is more concerned about number of babies being single child in their families and the total number of babies being prevented from birth every year, other things are only complementary. For instance, in the Jimling township of the Jiangsu Province, authorities quoted that, "In this year 324 babies born. Out of which 300 are first born, 17 are second born and the rest are third born".

The Chinese have now slowly started realising that they are not successful in their policy of "one couple on child" among minorities and in rural areas as in major cities. They feel they could not reach hilly areas and due to enmass-illiteracy superstitions and traditional ideas being rampant in those areas and it is difficult to change attitudes. While the majority believe in communism, there are still areas where people believe in religions, such as Buddhism. It is perhaps prevalence of poverty in remote areas that denies access to visitors such as us. However, wherever we visited, we could see remarkable improvement and one could presume that the Chinese are trying to reach a stage where people can get the basic requirements, such as food, shelter, clothing and basic employment. There does not seem to be any kind of inflation in the economy. Food, clothing and minimum requirement in China are very cheap. This we enquired at the Chinese shops. We also found in private conversation from friends that the house rent is also cheap. This is because of the austere living to which Chinese are compelled to pursue. The roads are clean, the country's health and hygienic status is being kept up very well in all the places the team happened to visit. Food was plenty, abundant and nutritious. People move about only in cycles. We did not see much cars, even on Beijing's broad roads. Many of the old buildings were pulled down and new modern constructions are rising up. Much of the resources of the country must be ploughed in back into the development programmes to create more factories, collectives and other infrastructure in which poor and needy could be employed. Cheaper consumer items could be produced for the consumption of common people. Build up exports to bring in foreign exchange. Thus, austerity is the current key note of modern Chinese life style in the People's Republic of China.

Some Interesting Statistics

The research highlights of Institute National Research for Family Planning, about the Family Planning Coverage of couples in reproductive age.

- 240 million couple are in child bearing age

- 130 million couple have accepted different kinds of contraceptives
- 12.6% Vasectomy - 38.2% Tubectomy
- 3% IUD - 5.3% Pills
- 2.4% Condoms - 0.6% Herbicides
- 1% Natural methods

The coverage of Family Planning among Factory Workers - Beijing Textile Factory

- 19.41% Sterilisation - 30.3% IUD
- 21.4% Condoms - 3.61% Pills
- 3.21% Other methods

The other details in the same Factory : Those who have passed child bearing age in the factory are 7.12 per cent and those who are just married are 12.1 per cent.

- 19.22% married couple using contraceptives - 1.1% Abortion
- 77% Long users contraceptives- 100% Late Marriages

Jimming Country in Jiangsu Province : This country is situated to the South East of Nanjing City.

- Total population - 7,40,000
- No. of women in reproductive age - 1,29,000
- Couple protection rate - 96.6%.
- No. of married women - 1,32,000
- No. of women using contraceptives - 1,20,000

The contraceptive methods used in Jimming Country : (Jiangsu Province)

- IUD 61,000 - 41% Pills 10,000 - 89%
- Female Sterilization 47,000 - 33% Male Sterilization 7,000 - 69%
- Spermisyed 5,000 - 5%

In 1985, upto the end of December, 6,390 children have been born out of which 3,200 are boys and 3,140 girls. The sex ratio is 10.3 per cent. They expect 7,700 children according to our calculation in this area. But only 6,390 children were born. The infant mortality rate is 5 per cent per 1,000 birth rate of 10.4 per cent and growth rate 4.8 per cent.

Visit to Other Areas of Tourist Interest in China

As part of sight-seeing tour in China the team visited places, like the Great Wall of China and Ming Tombs. The Great Wall of China at Badaling is China's traditional defensive line to prevent the northern people entering China and to save them from the severity of Siberian cold winds. On December 15, when we reached the Great Wall of China, it was minus three degrees, one could experience the severity of Siberian winds on a cold day. A true wonder of the world, the Great Wall of China, stretches along the mountains 3,700 miles long, reportedly it is said to be the only man-made structure visible from space. It has been rebuilt and renovated many times by the Chinese emperors.

The team, then visited Ming Tombs. Outside the tombs, there are huge gigantic animal figures in stone, to guard the tombs. Externally and internally the tombs occupy several acres of useful land, with underground shelters where the actual tombs have been dug. The digging of tombs have been kept secret in Ancinet China as these tombs were meant to have all facilities, imitating the living palaces of contemporary emperors and kings, whose organised everything to bury themselves with the wealth, jewellary and other valuable belongings alongwith their family members. Probably, emperors in Ancient China prepared themselves for a life death in the same style as they have lived on earth.

The team visited Mao' Moseleum in Beijing, Sun-Yat-Sun memorial in Jiangsu Province and Goat's Park in Canton. The silence at Mao's moseleum was impressive. The Yangtsee river and the triple arched-stone bridge on this river were included in the visits. The towering tomb of Huangshan (Buddhist monk visited India during Hindu period) on the Yellow Mountain in Jiangsu Province reminded us, historically, how India was close to China early as that when Husanshan visited India in search of Buddhist knowledge.

Shopping was done in Friendship Stores everywhere, which could sell quality things for moderate price, such chain of Friendship Stores were found in Beijing, Nanjing and Canton (Guangzu Province).

Hongkong Family Planning Association

Within its five million people (with mostly a fishing population), Hongkong is in the core of the Far East. The Family Planning Association of Hongkong, a voluntary agency, carries on birth control and family planning services with the assistance of government. Hongkong has also adopted single child policy but not in the strict sense as in China. Till 1956, Family Planning Association received full assistance from the Government. But from 1977, it has promoted a "help yourself project" to raise funds. During 1977, the government was assisting 90 and to the FPA Hongkong in 1982 – 39 per cent and in 1983 only 15 per cent.

The Association is pleased to announce the drop in birth rate from 20 per 1000 in 1974 to 14.4 per 1000 in 1984 the lowest ever achieved in Hongkong. The total FPA cases has also increased to 110,426. This is the first time it has passed the 100,000 mark since the Association handed over 32 of its clinics that were in Government Health Centres to the Government in 1974.

The year 1984 was a very busy for the Association with growing popularity for its services and increasing demand for speciality services in family planning. There was a remarkable increase of 40.7 per cent in pre-marital checkup service and of 46.6 per cent in the seminars for newly weds.

Innovative campaigns to promote the concept of male responsibility in recent years helped to boost the number of vasectomies to 632 (37.1 per cent) but may have caused a slight drop (7.4 per cent) in the demand for female sterilisation. A team of specially trained volunteers made the extension of service hours of the Youth Hotline possible resulting in a significant increase in enquiries from 8,791 in 1983 to 11,197 in 1984.

Suggestions and Recommendations

The author was included in this delegation to visit China and Hongkong, as the President of Working Women's Forum, a grassroots organisation of poor working class women, initiated in 1978. The objective of the Forum is to empower women workers and strengthen their economic roles. The forum has achieved this empowerment through credit assistance and by strengthening such production requirement through intensive family planning programmes to enhance their economic roles.

The family planning programme of the WWF is an innovative methodology where the clientele and cadre belong to the same class, (from the urban slums and from the landless women). WWF adopts a low cost innovative methodology to reach large number of poor working women with an inbuilt employment potential in the programme itself.

Recognising the importance of such a programme among the poor women, the Union Ministry of Health and Family Welfare has included me as the representative of voluntary agencies in the field of health and family planning.

The following suggestions to improve the implementation of the programme of family planning in this country as a whole, is offered herewith as a member of team:

(a) After visiting China, the author propose to suggest to our health workers, in the third phase of this project, to record in their books the number of babies expected in a year and the actual births that took place in each of their areas. This would be a critical data to be filled in by government health workers too.

(b) The author suggest that government should include certain items of tangible benefit to help those backward areas and that take up this programme of family planning vigorously. These women can be considered for trade loans by commercial banks on a priority basis.

(c) The present programme of inventivates do not reach many adopters of family planning directly and voluntary agencies must become watchdogs of such programme implementation.

(d) The results of Working Women's Forum is evident that grassroots initiatives produce effective results among the poor target group.

(e) Government in its effort must not only encourage voluntary effort but must also consult them from time to time as partners in development.

(f) While our voluntary efforts are mostly motivational, referred and educational, the government must coordinate and support us in carrying on this work of health and hygiene in and around the slums in cities and in rural areas.

(g) The efforts of Municipal Corporations in keeping up the surrounding clean at present are far from satisfactory. In the same manner, health authorities in the rural areas are very complacent in their attitudes, in serving poor clientele.

A commitment from all concerned is necessary for effective implementation of any programme benefiting large number of poor women living in a state of backward economy.

Managing by Value and Vision*

Development Priorities for Human Survival

Human survival faces peculiar problems in terms of development priorities. The major questions before us are whether creation of wealth or distribution of wealth is a priority for development. Should the development approach be a relief approach through projects or a more concrete, long-term approach, through substanting strategies for sustainable development of the human race? Further, what should be the priority for development planning? Its growth rate or human resource development? Time has come to set out priorities to accelerate the development process.

Constant decline of natural resources alongside rapid increase of population in all the developing countries poses a major threat to human situations. Therefore, the only option left with us is the empowerment of the available human resources, to help achieve speedy poverty alleviation and accelerate the development process. Many of our earlier efforts failed due to the non-participation and exclusion of actual participants. Hence, the critical need is to review such earlier strategies and add the component of human dimensions to all our efforts. Promotion of people's participation at all levels becomes necessary and there is a need to identify new ways of effective delivery mechanisms to reach the poorest and the most deprived.

Human Resource Development

Whom should these development strategies related to and that sort of approach to development necessary? Are we to make a segment approach or sectoral approach? Should it be a short-term relief approach, or a long-term sectoral approach aiming towards a sustainable development for people?

Most of due are certainly aware that the vast majority of the world's poor remain as an unorganised group, i.e., in the informal sector, who form a major resource potential at the grassroots. Hence, when our priorities of development efforts shift from production of wealth to equitable distribution, this emphasis becomes all the more important. Such a process of human resource development is a process of empowerment - a process which creates conscious, capable, receiving mechanisms at the grassroots. This empowerment aspect becomes even more necessary, since the kind of human resource potential available in all the third world countries are

---

*At the Asian Institute of Management/Manila, Philippines. April, 24th-28th, 1990.

the powerless poor. Dispossession of productive assets, suffering in poverty and squalor, facing conflicts at the hand of local power structures make than totally weak and invisible at the grassroots.

The Details of Working Population in India

To understand the inter-sectoral situation within the context of India and South Asian countries, one should know their background of working population in statistical terms. Let us take the case of India. There are about 292 million workers in India, out of whom only 25 million workers are organised, 6 million of this organised group belong to central trade unions and the rest of the 19 million workers belong to regional and indigenous unions. The remaining 267 million workers do not have any formal or informal unions. 25 million of these workers get Rs.250 to 500 per month. The rest get only Rs.60 to 300 per month. 150 million are construction workers, 17 million are child labourers and 6 million are beedi workers, while 48 million are unemployed. 89 per cent of the total unorganised sector are women. Therefore, any programme of assistance of help women and child workers, becomes a target oriented programme in this sector towards poverty alleviation.

Women as Workforce in the Information Sector

Let us take a look at the women workforce which forms 50 per cent of the total human resource. Women are not only denied visibility in the inter-sector linkages but are also 'nil' in statistical terms, their working conditions are harsh, wages are low, caste and class discrimination undervalue their valuable economic roles, making them totally invisible in the market economy. Mostly these women are either from the slums or belong to landless families, often continuously indebted to moneylenders, traders, and middlemen who supply them with credit for raw materials, daily needs, and social needs on exorbitant rates of interest. Besides, they go through a number of social disabilities, both at home and at the workplace being a worker and being women. (lack of basic healthcare, desertion, common law marriages, large families).

They pursue different occupations as follows: hawkers and vendors, providers of urban services, home-based petty manufacturers, and petty traders among others. Further, the nature of goods and services distributed could be classified under (1) distribution of food items; (2) vegetables and fruits; (3) clothing and household necessities and accessories; (4) petty home-based producers of craft and consumer items; (5) fish trading and (6) dairy farming and so on.

Rural Unemployment

Why do they go through such constraints? Most of our working population of the third world live in rural areas, and with all the thrust on major or minor irrigation schemes, programmes to help dry land agriculture, the employment possibilities to rural population is afforded only for 5 to 6 months. No non-farm employment programmes have been made available for the rest of the months in these areas. Such acute unemployment situations are but common features in rural areas and thus most women (50 per cent of rural labour force) leave the villages, often to cities as potential workforce in search of lucrative employment.

NGO's - Partners in Development Process

The next question is who should handle this empowerment of the human resources? Is it government or the voluntary sector? Undoubtedly, experiments in the third world show that the voluntary sector or non-governmental organisations have potential and the capacity to transform these poorest at the grassroots into a powerful resource potential to face, the struggles or conflicts and have been made to achieve the desired objectives of economics and social emancipation. In recent times, innumerable NGOs have become credible and cost effective delivery mechanisms, helping emancipate lower income groups in the third world countries. They have already land the ground work and set themselves as viable sectors for development interfacing largest systems in our society, such as, government, bureaucracy, private sector, and market forces.

Experiment of Working Women's Forum – NGO's in South Asia

Thus, the major effort of the WWF as one of the largest women NGO's in the third world had been aimed to relieve the poor women from the vicious circle of indebtedness, exploitation, and social disabilities. Strategy adopted by WWF was encouraging formation of neighbourhood solidarity groups or unions at the grassroots to help themselves from the social or economic disabilities faced by them in their daily survival.

Illiterate and unaware of their rights, exploited both at home and workplace, having had no access to formal or informal union, WWF faced numerous obstacles in its early days in their unionisation effort.

Objectives of WWF

In this connection, it is necessary to analyse the four main objectives of WWF as it closely relates to this mobilisation strategy and restructuring of the socio-political and economic dimensions at the grassroots.

Mobilization for Collective Consciousness

Regarding the mobilisation effort, WWF's strategy of organising women workers on trade lines facilitated the women's economic roles using credit as an entry point for such mobilization of women. This is in turn used women as an entry point for the development process. Secondly, WWF adopted a structure in which large number of poor women could be reached in the quickest possible time, using the grassroots structure as an effective delivery mechanism. Thirdly, WWF made it a point to keep the organisation as a women intensive unit, since in India 89 per cent of women workers belonged to this working class. Finally, WWF addressed itself to the critical needs of these women through credit, employment and training, which ultimately enhanced the socio-economic status and decision-making power of women. Though started modestly with 800 members in the year 1978, today WWF has over 1,40,000 women as members. This is just the result of the decentralised structure and the mobilisation process adopted by WWF for collective consciousness and action.

Structure/Innovative Easy Delivery Mechanism

It will be interesting to know that how the programme strategy and the organisational structure in WWF generated new spirit among women for conscious participation in collective action for combat other issues affecting their work and lives. While individually the credit intervention relieved women engaged in subsistence occupations from the drudgery of interest burden, collective consciousness and collective action generated by credit intervention had established the real organisational base at the grassroots. The core of the organisational structure consists of its members formed into groups in the neighbourhood, a group leader nominated by themselves. The leader in this group reports to the organiser of WWF who takes full-time responsibilities on all matters within her area of jurisdiction, relating to the WWF. All these are purely a local initiative in the neighbourhood. So, the entire credit intervention system revolves around this neighbourhood loan groups. Thus, even when an individual woman approaches the Forum for credit, she is always encouraged to form groups in her neighbourhood and meter into group process for the purpose, aiming at collective strength. This is so, together as a movement they can fight authority and discrimination, bargain for their rights and privileges.

Role of Group Leaders

The group leader is encouraged to build up collective consciousness among her members. She is expected to come close to the families of all her members and share both the struggles and happiness, respectively. Therefore, leaders are very much aware and conscious of the problems, such as desertion, dowry harassment, sufferings from drunken husband, wife beating and other crimes against women in those families. The group leaders often bring this to the organiser and then the organiser brings it to the Forum's office for solutions and corrective actions.

Role of Organisers

While we have assessed the role of the group leader in the above paragraph, the tasks of the organisers are equally well-defined in guidelines of WWF in order to extend the activities of the Forum either to other argon slums or to rural areas. They also help to form new groups, highlight the rules and regulations of the Forum to those new groups, assess their genuine credit needs by probing into the viability of their occupations and negotiate with credit authorities. Thus, this organiser serves as a vital link between the groups and the Forum. The majority of these organisers do belong to the same working class households with prior occupational experiences in the informal sector economic activities. Only small portion of these organizers do not belong to this cadre. But there, other women too have reasons due to personal crisis in their own lives for building up solidarity with working class women. Often, deserted women, dowry victims or orphans are women who are willing to work with Forum, to help the working class. It is very interesting to note that women started to perceive their own specific oppression in relation to caste, class and patriarchal society. The entire office bearers in WWF are mostly from the poor working class families or belong to the workers' family engaged in informal sector.

The Office Bearers

The following are the individual examples of women office bearers in WWF. Vice-President of the Forum is a harijan woman, had been a hawker, a diary woman, and had carried on many such occupations single handedly as her husband had always been unemployed. The Secretary of the organisation started her life as a teacher in the nursery class in the slums for a small sum of Rs. 60 though educated upto school final within the slum household. All the other office bearers of the organisation are promoted from the ranks of group leaders or the organisers. WWF thus provides an example of how leadership is built-up form within a demonstrated commitment to others who are equally poor; and all the Forum's group leaders being ex-office members of the governing body of WWF. The Forum is not administered from the top-down approach as many other NGOs. Strikingly different in the WWF is the decentralised participation structure facilitating the growth of women's consciousness, group systems, and grassroots community leaders. It is presented in the organisation chart (Appendix). Members and office bearers are at the top and in the various hierarchies, the President is at the bottom. As described by Dr. Chambers, this is the "style of operation that manifests an ideology of reversals".

Forum's Branches

Working Women's Forum from its modest inception in Madras city in 1978, both through the credit intervention and mobilisation activities has grown intensively and extensively covering a vast area of women in the informal sector in three southern states of India, namely, Tamil Nadu, Karnataka, and Andhra Pradesh, and recently, to a small extent in the slums of Lucknow city in the northern state of Uttar Pradesh. Earlier paragraphs of this paper had highlighted the unique organisational structure and the heightened collective consciousness of women ensuring both solidarity at the grassroots and promoting leadership through a process of self-initiatives. Let us further try to analyse the activities of the Forum branch-wise and effects of such mobilisation, credit intervention, and collective consciousness. WWF adopted in this connection multiple strategies to combat different situations in different branches.

Urban Slums of Madras City

In Madras, 1.5 million people live in the city slums who form one-third of the population of the city. 4.5 million is the city population of Madras. WWF's members in Madras slums are 44,060. These are women who are either casual wage labourers working for low wages or intro entrepreneurs with marginal working capital, low skill resulting in a marginal subsistence income. Due to lack of fixed vending place, most women squat along the road sides and carry on their business even today. Low working capital requirements made these women petty vendors, often depend on the moneylenders who demanded exorbitant, but daily or weekly interest payments. Roadside vehicles damaged their wares. Constantly, the police harassed them with the threat of eviction. Therefore, process of mobilisation for women for credit programme by WWF provided the necessary collective consciousness to these women both to counter the police pressure and fight municipal authorities. Actual money provided for working capital by WWF relieved them from moneylenders and providing necessary capital for business helped them scale up their operation. In some cases, it cleared the old debts. The direct effect of such profitable economic activities had been that women enjoyed self-confidence and a new status both at home and outside thus, making credit as an instrument of social change.

Dindigul Landless Women

In Dindigul, the membership of WWF is 11,831. In this branch, two kinds of women were benefitted by the credit programme, women traders in the rural market and women labourers from the landless agricultural households. Women mostly work about 60 days scattered during a year. Being a drought prone region lacking irrigation, agriculture largely depends upon rainfall in the Dindigul area. The wages are paid both in kind and cash but are minimum and low. Fodder for the cattle is equally scarce, the region being dry. Therefore, when they are paid in kind, with reference to paddy, 2 kgs. of rice were given and for cutting sugarcane crop, sugarcane leaves are given as wages to use them for cattle, for cotton plucking, inferior rejected cotton was given as wages. At the time, when the organisers went there to organise, none of the women were aware of the social legislation provisions of minimum, equal wages law. Continuous non-availability of agriculture work in those areas posed major problems and often landless women workers, fell into debt situation in the hands of moneylenders and landlords, sometimes even went through the system of debt bondage to landlord families. In this context, the Forum launched its branch for these rural women by assisting them with productive assets, such as cattle. However, the Forum found it very difficult to continue this process due to landlessness among women. Privatisation of owing government lands by landlords and other political party members have totally denied women access to land ownership. Also, women, engaged in the looking after the cattle as productive asset, did not opt to go for agricultural work for low wages as before. On the contrary, the landlords during the time of peak labour demand in sowing and harvest times, were forced to draw labour from the other hamlets. The only option for these women workers has been not to go for the agricultural work for low wages, but on the contrary, their other counterparts from other village are being exploited and are brought to work in the same field. While their personal bargaining power has improved through economic empowerment still they have improved in overcoming the class situation. Also, credit assistance to sandy women vendors in villages around Dindigul and others who have been assisted with dairy cattle, provided an alternative income earning opportunity. Being a drought prone area, even this had only marginal effect on women, as the income generated was enough make both ends meet in a low productive area like Dindigul. All the assistance of the form has eased the survival constraints to a significant extent for women workers in this areas.

Though direct effect have been marginal still, indirect effects were striking. The process of unionisation did empower them, as women could speak out and articulate their needs and problems as they were trained so in the numerous discussion meetings, organised by the Forum. Further, they came out from their closed and immobile situation and are able to move out and visit larger cities like Madras (Headquarters of WWF) and Madurai which the women valued as a tremendous experience and exposure to them to the world at large. The conscientisation made them understand functioning of political parties, express option on such matters, and also understand the power relationship they have with the administrative or power systems, such as the bureaucracy, moneylenders. In a way, they could perceive on their own their weak position and how bargaining power relation to those powerful structures. They did not with ignorance accept their powerlessness as something as before as fate has bestowed on them. Rather, they became aware of their own powerlessness with resentment. Hopelessness has given way to attempt solidarity building among themselves against powerful and oppressive structures.

Adiramapattinam Coastal Fishing Villages

In Adiramapattinam, in and around 80 coastal villages in Tanjore district, WWF has 12521 members. In this branch, Forum has formed credit groups to help women engaged in fish marketing. In this connection, the role of women in fish marketing has to be understood in the overall fishing economy in that region. Fisherman, as a caste, do formulate decisions within their villages. In all those fishing villages, individuals can't sell fish directly but it has to be handed over to the village auction system. This prevents each fisherman from giving away to his wife his own catch of fish and allowing her to sell the product in the fish market. With introduction of a common auction system (an exploitative system), even women from each fishing village also have to buy the fish from the auctioneers and sell in the fish markets of rural shanties. This new village auction system created a need for cash requirement among women to buy fish at the auction. Women borrowed from moneylenders for the same and get into a debt trap of exorbitant rate of interest. However, this common auction system adversely affected to women fish marketers, though in way women themselves have agreed to this common auction system as those who belonged to the cultural social systems of rural society. This provides an ample example of gender dimensions and biases even in the work roles that women pursued.

Forum's credit intervention here has enabled them to carry on their occupation to some extent by-passing moneylenders. However, even in this case the credit intervention led to collection consciousness leading to collective action. Women engaged in fish vending started helping other women who are peripherally engaged in the fishing economy, such as basket makers, salt sellers, hawkers and others who worked near the fish vending or auctioneering spot.

While their margins were probably only marginal, the indirect effects of credit intervention and group dynamics of WWF were that women became more and more aware of the prevalence of class-conflicts between large launch owners and traditional fishermen or between traditional fisherman and small boat men.

Women Beedi Workers - Vellore

Vellore in North Arcot district has 11,600 members in the WWF's branch. Here, a large number of women and children are engaged in beedi rolling work both with the town and in the surrounding areas. While women work in beedi factories, women mostly work at home as home workers in beedi rolling under middlemen or contractors. Despite the provisions of government's law on equal/minimum wages, the correct wages have never been paid to women. Further, employers always practiced exploitative methods in the supply of raw materials. Such short supplies in raw materials ends up in women facing either cut in their wages or getting into debt traps of moneylenders. In many cases, women borrowed at exorbitant rates only to compensate such shortages. Thus child mortgage is another common feature in the beedi industry as most children being drop outs from school are involved in beedi rolling work. For small sums of Rs.200 to Rs.500 taken by their parents, children are mortgaged and have to work 12 hours a day just to repay the interest, only. Left to themselves these children on their own have the capacity to roll 4000 beedis. Children are beaten up by employers when they refuse to work. During the monsoon period the "mundis" or beedi factories do not give any work and the workers go hungry or get into the loan trap.

Thus, credit interventions as in the earlier cases helped them to ease their position, of acute indebtedness. Also, women as a group could sharpen their collective consciousness and became aware of the exploitative nature of this piece rate, contract labour system. One can now observe the resentment of Muslim women against Muslim mundi owners about their refusal to give raw materials to women on par with men, an act which reinforces the culture subordination of women in the domain of home-base work. Women complained also about the ineffectiveness of labour inspectors, they felt it is due to men employee's biases on women's economic roles that these labour inspectors totally failed in enforcement front. It is but a vicious circle that helped the employers to continue their oppressing and exploitative trade practices.

Women Agarbathi Workers - Bangalore

Trade practice of agarbathi industry in Bangalore is just similar to the lines of beedi industry of Vellore. This is also an industry highly characterised by co-existence of small and medium factories and the prevalent different production systems engaged women as home-based producers. Women had been totally depending on the exploitative merchant capitalists for procuring raw materials as in the previous cases. As in other cases, the credit intervention of the Forum has transformed home-based women workers to become independent-entrepreneurs. When credit became available women purchased raw materials and sold the finished products directly. However, even entrepreneurship did not increase income as expected by them, probably they were out of marginal or survival conditions. However, when once the initial struggles are eased out, women become conscious of what is happening around, and started to probe into the situations in which they are caught up.

The special disadvantages these agarbathi workers suffered is that the most of them are migrant women who originally came and settled in Bangalore slums from nearby Chittoor village (Andhra Pradesh) and Vellore towns (Tamil Nadu). Women have gone through the trials and tribulations to adjust due to this ethnic situation. However, WWF played a major cementing role in unifying these three different ethnic groups into one on the issues of backwardness and poverty that affected them adversely. Women effectively have merged into viable credit units and often they recall situations where suspicion and hostility dominated their mind about each other. It has been a tremendous success and a valuable learning experience for women to come together and build a bridge of communication and an enduring solidarity despite caste, language, and other differences.

Women Artisans – Narasapur (Andhra Pradesh)

Some of our most well-meaning progressive technological advances too, are counter-productive in some cases. Similarly, in the case of the rural landless women of Andhra Pradesh, the green revolution made them become more poorer than they already were. East and West Godavari districts in Andhra Pradesh have witnessed major transformation agriculturally over the past few decades. The pattern of share cropping and tenancy that prevailed in the early days, had been replaced by capitalist agriculture, reducing the share-croppers and tenants to a position of landless labourers. Women in these families have always been confined to domestic work at home. However, in the late 19th century, few Irish settlers, probably Christian Missionaries, came to West Godavari district and taught the women at home the art of lace making. This lace industry has now become a flourishing export trade in the area. The lace industry is totally monopolised and dominated by the exporters. A system of middlemen and contractor has been created at several interventions to deal with women lace artisans; to go round the villages both to distribute the reels of thread alongwith export orders etc. The repayment is based on the highly exploitative piece-rate system of wages - a marginal amount of Rs.4 is paid per reel of thread. It is very interesting as well as surprising to note that the Communist Party which made an attempt to unionise the agricultural labour in that region apparently failed to notice the extremely harsh working conditions of the women lace artisans as lace making is usually perceived as a leisure time work of women. Thus, this had been the story of women lace artisans of Narasapur who are enmeshed in the multi-pronged web of various oppressive structures at the time when WWF had been asked to help lace makers at Narasapur. The three-fold activities of the Forum in Narasapur benefited the women artisans. Firstly, credit assistance to independent lace artisans helped them to buy raw materials to produce their own product and sell it in the shandies where exporters came and bought the same for export. Secondly, attempt of the Forum had been to establish production units with the help of ILO and make women learn new designs (which higher-to had been not taught to women artisans) and export them directly with the help of the Madras office of the Forum. Thirdly, in their own productive unit, WWF paid higher wages to expose the exploitative mechanisms of the merchant and exporters. Women artisans became aware of such exploitative trade practices, started demanding higher wages and started negotiating both directly and through the Forum. The result is that the women are able to receive higher wages as much as upto Rs.10. Lastly, the Forum's credit assistance helped many other unproductive lace making women to shift over to other occupations like weaving or rope making that provided more lucrative income.

Bidar (Rural Karnataka)

On the invitation of Karnataka Government - UNICEF, Working Women's Forum agreed to visit Bidar, a drought prone district of rural Karnataka and initiate an analytical study on the existing project of the UNICEF - Government of Karnataka. Accordingly, a team of grassroots women from WWF's headquarters went to Bidar and made of the reasons for the total failure of a project like this. The wrong choice of the rural cadres to monitor women's programmes contributed to its non-functioning totally. The cadres themselves suffered from biases of caste and class situations and had failed to evoke any response from the grassroots. The project was totally managed by government workers, imposed on women without any understanding of the requirements of women at the grassroots. As mentioned earlier, the study team comprising of grassroots women workers made very valuable suggestions to improve a programme that had totally failed. On the basis of the recommendations made by this study team, the Forum was invited to Bidar district of Karnataka and took up the Bidar project as one of branches of WWF. WWF has been able to establish its credibility as a community-based organisation and continued the project with the help of the community, while the government have failed.

Jawahar Shramikiya Mahila Union Lucknow (Uttar Pradesh)

Recently, WWF has been able to expand its activities to help women workers in Uttar Pradesh. A union has been initiated for women workers engaged in chicken embroidery in the slums of Lucknow city. Most of the women belong to the Muslim community. Oppressed both by class and gender situations, women of Lucknow find the union as a boom to them to express their difficulties. The union in U.P. is called the Jawahar Shramikiya Mahila Union. However, WWF is trying to establish a trade union and a cooperative society for these 1000 women who jointed this union.

Credit as an Instrument of Social Change

We have seen how the credit option in WWF has helped women to come together, as a force to reckon with. Originally, WWF played the role of an intermediary between the women and the Nationalized Banks in India. Later, as the conventional banking systems women of the Forum as it involved lot of red tapism and delays in the sanction.

To get over such conservative proceedings of Banking, women in the WWF established a series of Working Women's Co-operative Credit

Societies, a banking system of their own, both informal and easy to operate. Though initiated in Madras in the year 1981, these informal Banking Centres of WWF soon spread to other rural and urban branches, totally managed by workers. Thus, during the period of 1981 to 88, WWF rapidly promoted a number of such cooperative credit societies in Andhra Pradesh and Karnataka.

Working Women's Cooperative Societies soon had become a model of social banking operators for effecting replication and an instrument of social change resulting in the economic empowerment of very poor women. Women experienced better quality of life in the matter of basic needs, children's education, savings, access to land a productive asset become a reality in the lives of many women. Women learned to hold the custody of their income. Changes in the attitudes of women created alternative leadership within the household.

This leadership at the grassroots is not very usual but an experiment with experience, i.e., leadership that is born in the phase of struggles and conflicts. This leadership that will survive even if the promotional leaders retire from the movement. This further demonstrates the fact that leaders are not born but are evolved through a process under circumstances and opportunities. It is possible to multiply them.

Impact of the Credit Programmes

A retrospective study and a critical analysis of credit programme of 10 years in WWF shows that apart from the abstract aspects of empowerment of poor women, such as optimism, confidence, courage, and their vision to change the static situation in life, there are also tangible results which emerge clearly from credit options.

The study reveals that above 76 per cent of the members have relieved themselves from the continued indebtedness through WWF's credit programme. 90 per cent of the respondents felt that they saved in the form of cash, few others reported other form of investment both movable and immovable. 89 per cent of the respondents reported that they were able to own necessaries of household. Some of them have invested in livestock. 75 per cent have invested their savings on housing and 60 per cent of women have invested in the renewal or extension of their house. This included adding of civic amenities to their household. 92 per cent reported that they are able to eat two square meals in their families, 40 per cent of women have diversified their business or started new and additional business.

The study further shows nearly 84 per cent of the women members of the Forum are sole contributors to their family income and hence have to bear the economic burden of their families. The experience of economic responsibilities also made women to become aware of the social and community responsibilities.

About 80 per cent of the respondents became aware of the oppressive elements in the community like dowry, untouchability and anti-social elements opposing women's education, inter-caste marriages, widow remarriages and women's rights movement. Women felt the need to fight the same.

Grassroots Health Care Project

WWF provides employment to over 400 slums and rural landless women as health workers in their Health, Nutrition, and Family Welfare project. This Health, Nutrition, and Family Welfare Programme had been carried among the poor women as a package deal. They worked to help 90,000 families (over 5,85,000 population) in the city slums; similarly worked in 30,000 rural families in more than 110 villages in Tamil Nadu. The cadres chosen had been from slums and from the landless communities. This choice of community health workers from the same class and neighbourhood to the clientele belonged to, is a innovative strategy which has bridged the communications gaps and helped to achieve a coverage of 71 per cent in family planning methods within the targeted areas. In all these places, earlier the government progammes and services were very mach under-utilized.

Inter-caste Weddings

The large-scale inter-caste weddings are one of the special features of this union to fight caste and dowry oppression. WWF(I) continuously makes an effort to stand firm to help those who believed in such inter-caste wedlocks, especially in the poor communities.

Child Labour Rehabilitation Centres

Child labour is yet another curse in the poorer sections in many families. These children are denied the very basic right of normal childhood, as they are made to work from the age of seven. Millions of poor boys and girls belong to this category in India and Asia. Hence, this is common in the families of WWF members too.

Given the option, 90 per cent of these children want to study and learn. Only very few children express their option to wanting to work. To make these working children to have access to some education, WWF has started a number of child labour rehabilitation centres. In these centres, the classes are run for these children between 6.30 p.m. and 8 p.m., i.e., 5 days in a week. Nutrition and health coverage are also included. These centres are promoted both in rural and urban areas in few of the WWF's branches.

Training and Research

Training in WWF is ongoing continuous event. Training includes organisational and mobilisation skills for credit group leaders, group organisers and health workers; consciousness raising for members of co-operatives; and participatory planning for organisers. Training modules include feminist/class conscious-inputs, group mobilisation skills, technical skills in management, leadership skills, health/credit issues and so on. Participatory methodology is the most critical aspect of WWF's training. Apart from the on-the-job training, training for locating local resources and for effective coordination to deal with sources of power are part of the training process.

Learning from the Visions of Poor Women

Extraordinary motivation behind this mass membership in WWF is a class-centred ideology of a common background, common oppression such an ideology transcends barriers of caste, language and culture. The Forum, therefore, is neither an NGO (in its precise definition) nor a union, but a movement marked by motivation, voluntarism, and class objectives of its members. Prominent development experts of the world feel the "Forum is a counter-culture aiming at the priorities of poor women works only for the poor, promotes leadership from below and exercises clout to get their right". Therefore, the Forum can be perceived as a political process to empower poor women. This empowerment is far superior a substance to keep its members together, than credit, health orally other material programme. Hence, the ideology explains the massive growth and continuity of the Forum.

The Forum understands its role to the pressure groups, relating to government and other power structures. Two very different functions combined in the activities of the Forum are the flexibility of an NGO and the political character gives it the material support, the trade union character gives it political ideology to sustain its membership and fight for equal opportunities.

As mentioned in learning of the WWF, in all developing countries, there are mounting obstacles for women's development. Equally, the social and physical environment are not very conducive for such women's progress. Hence, there is much to share in the rich experience of these poor women. It is sensible not to ignore their vision, wisdom and collective consciousness that resulted in their present state of empowerment and transformation, accomplished in long struggles. As a disadvantaged group, women in this case have visualised their real need as a self-managed union for themselves with ample scope for collective survival through collective action. It is only this long-term vision more than the material inputs that helped them to combat the inequalities and discriminations they underwent. Together, collectively they were able to perceive the class, caste and gender dimensions behind those discriminations and hardships they inherited for generations.

The following incident provides that how on special occasions they come together as a united force. On 8th March, 1988 being an International Women's Day, about 5000 women members of WWF in the city slums, prepared a long memorandum and a charter of demands and presented the same to the Governor of Tamil Nadu (India). The memorandum contained the abysmal conditions of slums in which these women members lived, without roads, electricity, housing facilities, pattas, drinking water supply and so on. They also demanded that all the liquor shops in the vicinity of slums be closed immediately to end the alcoholism of men in the slum communities. Women could achieve about 70 per cent of these demands in 9 months.

WWF and the Groots - International A Networking Process

Working Women's Forum, is a founder-member of a global network on women called the "GROOTS" (Grassroots Women Organising Themselves in Sisterhood). It is a past Nairobi women's action group born out of the "Forward looking strategies" of the U.N. Decade closing conference. WWF attended the Planning Committee meet held last year at Jamaica and invited "GROOTS" to come to India to visualise a definite plan of action to guide or help grassroots women all over Asia, Africa and Latin America. Accordingly, this conference took place at Bangalore this year from 12-13th March, 1990. Alongwith the Planning Committee meeting of Groots International, there had been a concurrent workshop on Leadership Development among the Grassroots Women's Organisation in South Asia including India. Nearly 42 South Asian NGOs and 19 other International Organisations from USA, Europe, Africa, South East Asia and Latin America participated. The objectives of the Groots Planning Meeting in India had been as follows. (1) To create regional networking groups of women's organisation in the North and

South; and (2) To gain and strengthen the knowledge base on successful models, such as the WWF and assist women and the organisations to replicate such models in other areas. At the end of the conference, the South Asian Groots International has been established. Groots South Asian International will facilitate networking within the region, equip other women's organisations with skills to mobilise and train other women, and build in them the leadership capabilities. WWF, as a movement of women in India, through the establishment of Groots South Asian International has initiated networking process of mutual learning, sharing the values and visions of people's organisation within the region.

References

Jaya Arunachalam - A Decade of the Forum - Working Women's Forum (Indian)-A Movement of Poor Women of Self help and Social Transformation,Published by WWF (I).

Jaya Arunachalam - Credit needs of Women Workers in the Informal Sector, Case Study of Working Women's Forum (India), submitted by Appropriate Technology International, USA, September 1987.

Jaya Arunachalam - Towards Sustainable Development, Empowerment of Poor Women paper presented by 19th SID World Conference on "Poverty Development and Collective Survival;" March 25 - 28, 1988, New Delhi.

Dr. U.Kalpagam - WWF A Concept and an Experiment in Mobilisation in the Third World paper presented at the Wenner Gren Symposium on a Decade of Women's Collective Action Anthropological Perspectives held at Mijas, Apin Nov. 85.

Dr. U.Kalpagam - An Evaluation Report prepared by "Solidarity, Strength and Success" Working Women's Forum (India) Points the Way.

Loes Schenk Sandbergen - Poverty and Survival : Ramesh Jain, Published by Manohar Publications, Delhi.

Mahabab Ul Haq - Poverty and Curtain - Choices for the Third World, Published by Columbia University Press, New Delhi.

Nandini Azad - Empowerment Women Workers, The WWF Experiment in Indian Cities, Published by UNICEF, New Delhi.

Ponna Wignaraja - Women, Poverty and Resources, Working Women's Co-operative Society, An Indian Experiment 1988.

Rachael Kannel - Growing Together Women, Feminism and Popular Education, Produced by ISIS International, Bank Series 1988/1, Rome.

Credit Needs of Women Workers in the Informal Sector Case Study of Working Women's Forum (India)*

Powerlessness of the Poor

Dispossession of assets, insufficient means of subsistence and degrading living conditions leave the poor in all the developing countries in a state of acute powerlessness resulting in persistent poverty. Millions of such poor lack means of livelihood, in terms of access to credit, productive assets, technology and other basic services essential for productive activity. Almost two-third of South Asia and one-fifth of Africa (South of Sahara) provide glaring instances of large numbers of such persons living in absolute poverty, particularly in rural areas where over 90 per cent of the population lives.

Planners and experts have debated and discussed various strategies to be pursued for eradication of poverty. One view is that by increasing economic capabilities and activities, poverty can be alleviated. Others have observed that an increase in economic growth would automatically lead to the eradication of poverty. Another view pointed out that the eradication of poverty depended on domestic policies pursued by respective governments. Many programme strategies were thus pursued by governments such as minimum needs programme, non-farm employment programmes and small farmer-development agencies aimed at greater visibility for the informal sector with no real success. Some governments also pursued vigorous rural development policies and considered encouragement to small-scale projects as an important strategy for development. In all these programmes and projects, variables such as the application of science and technology and need for environmental protection were considered vital support. In the absence of an effective delivery mechanism to reach the poorest, the above said strategies failed to provide distributive justice to the poor. Evidently, planners and policymakers did not take into cognisance, the fact that governments had limitations with lack of sensitive bureaucracy acting as a major stumbling block.

The strategic importance of self-reliance, sustainability and people's participation were not part of policies, programmes and projects in developing countries until Non-Governmental Organisations, NGOs emerged. These NGOs armed with innovative delivery mechanisms and

---

*At the Asia and Pacific Development Centre / Kuala Lampur, Malaysia – September 15th – 21st, 1991

outreach systems have been able to successfully confront poverty at the grassroots. They also reached large numbers of the poor rapidly. They have empowered the poor and provided an opportunity for choice and design of strategies.

As the majority of the poor in the developing countries live and work in the unorganised and informal sectors, an examination of their percentage in the country's working population, their contribution to national economies have to be examined by way of analysing few experiments such as the Working Women's Forum (India).

Informal Sector

The informal sector has long been viewed a transitory phase in the economics of developing countries. However, today it is clear that the informal sector is here to stay and a permanent feature of national economics. Further, concern for this sector has been heightened by the burgeoning number of female entrance that have far outpaced the male workers in the sector. The alarming conditions of work and life of women workers in this sector has also increased attention of NGOs, practitioners and policy analysts to this sector. As a result of low visibility, non-recognition, low legal legitimacy, poor investment and resources, low capital formation the contribution of the informal sector has been invisible, leave alone female workers contributions to this sector.

Invisibility of the Informal Sector

Policy options have either overlooked this sector or have had different rate of success with varying strategies. Of the poverty alleviation strategies pursued, the following have had low or poor impact; Enhancing mere economic capabilities, targeting the informal sector in various programme or influencing domestic policies in alleviation of poverty (minimum needs programme, non-farm employment, small farmer development agencies, etc.). The casualty has been heavy due to the neglect of the operational strategy, namely, the delivery mechanisms or rather lack of involvement of the programme participants. Further, blueprint and centralised approaches rather than process-oriented approaches; utilisation of one time, one type of service rather than multi-period, integrated package of services has also led to the high rate of failure. Further, the lack of political will, poor sensitivity levels of the bureaucracy to development issues, particularly gender issues has worsened the implementation of the programmes, leading to more marginalised condition.

NGO and the Informal Sector

In contrast, mass based NGO's in developing countries have fared effectively in the informal sector, especially with women workers. This has been due to the fact that have 'initiated a process' rather than a project in many cases; empowered and armed women with self-reliance and sustainable capacities rather than just economic development; and crucially understood that poverty and powerlessness are related and have to be tackled simultaneously.

Working Women's Forum (India)

The case study of the Working Women's Forum is thus a glimmer of hope in which poor women have demonstrated the capacity and will to shape their own destinies. As we trace the origins of the WWF, we clearly see that each need arose from a special constraint the women faced. Similarly, each of WWF's branch addressed a different issue. Yet, in retrospective the first need at all branches was their need for immediate cash for trading or as a relief their indebtedness. In the following table, the constraints faced by WWF members are listed with the corresponding services offered. Followed by a table listing issues faced by women workers at different branches.

Issues in the Informal Sector Worker; The Case Study on WWF

A description of the issues at the different branches is given below:

(a) Urban petty traders in Madras city were provided low interest credit loans, as an alternative credit option to moneylenders and wholesalers. The health project linked up health and family planning services for an integrated approach to basic services.

(b) Landless women in the Dindigul area (rural) were provided alternative employment options to low wages through creation of continuous employment, such as rearing cattle for milk. In the second stage, due to drought and the lack of grazing land, loans for shandy vendors (selling at local fairs) were provided simultaneously with cattle loans. Now, health services have been provided at this branch.

(c) Fisherwomen in Adiramapattinam were provided the means for eliminating the exploitative hold of the middlemen and wholesaler through credit loans. Health services have been provided at this branch.

(d) Lace artisans in Narasapur were organised to pressurise for higher wages with lace exporters and to strengthen self-employment through small credit loans. Marketing and production centres were part of the second stage of development.

Service Offered by the WWF Addressing Constraints of Women

Sl. No.	*Constraints*	*Service offered by the WWF*
1.	Credit, technology, training and markets.	Small credit loans at understandable terms and conditions; appropriate technology for idli sellers, washer women, etc. marketing for the lace makers in the rural branch at Narasapur.
2.	Lack of social legislation (legal aid, day care, maternal health, minimum wages and other worker benefits)	Creation of legal cells that pay lawyers fees for evicted vendors; conscientise workers on legislations; provision of day care centres.
3.	Basic amenities of housing (sanitation, light, water supply, land, toilets, etc.)	Though the Forum does not have access to low-income housing nor does it provide basic amenities, the WWF provides a forum that helps women fight for civic amenities.
4.	Harassed social conditions (caste; dowry for marriages, wife beating, alcoholism, low-incomes contributed by males, working children)	Register common law weddings; conduct inter-caste weddings; undertake processions against dowry/prohibition of alcohol; prepare women for collective action in the case of wife beating or low-incomes contributed by males; run child labour centres.
5.	Poor health conditions (continuous child birth, lack of aftercare, low nutritive levels, health of the child, hygiene environmental sanitation, etc).	Family planning information; linking up with family planning clinics; free distribution of contraceptives; immunisation for children through vaccines; facilitate prenatal and postnatal referrals at clinics, hospitals; consciousness raising in hygiene, environmental sanitation (through the use of soak pits), use of low cost locally available foodstuffs for bettering nutrition.
6.	Lack of worker consciousness	Organisation of women, consciousness-raising workshops.
7.	Lack of visibility at the local and national level.	Representation of the President on national boards, committees and advisory bodies

(e) Incense stick makers in Bangalore have been organised to pressurise for higher wages from the supplier buyer. By provision of credit loans for self-employment alternative options have been created for women workers.

(f) Similar to Bangalore is the case of the cigar rollers (beedi) in Vellore. An alternative credit option to the middlemen has been provided through loans, crucial in a situation where children are bonded to middlemen. Health services have been provided in the area. The three common issues that were identified in the first phase of the organisational development were lack of access to credit, economic exploitation and lack of consciousness among women workers.

Analytical Framework

The analysis of the WWF experiment is organised around questions such the following: (a) Can lending to the poor be a viable proposition? (b) Can the poor be entrusted with the responsibility of taking care of their own situations? (c) Are illiteracy and ignorance serious handicaps (or barriers) for the poor to participate in the development process? These were some of the issues that were confronted during the initial stages of the WWF experiment based on self-reliance and self-management as prerequisites for the empowering and participative development process.

At the outset, before dealing with the banking systems for the poor, a brief introduction to the informal work opportunities available for the majority of the poor in the urban slums and rural areas is necessary.

In most developing countries, there are large segments of unorganised and informal sector labour and they possess some special characteristics. In fact, around 90 per cent of the labour force work and earn in this rural and urban informal sector in all the poorer countries. These workers, who usually do not possess any specialised skills have no permanent workplace or employer. They continuously move from one place to another in search of new work opportunities for their basic day-to-day needs. The temporary nature of work opportunities has resulted in the invisibility of these workers in the statistical counts in many developing countries. This invisibility of productive roles in turn has led to almost no policy action by the government. Thus, the informal sector labour continue to remain as the "working poor" in "low paid" occupations.

These workers, unorganised as they are, face continuous exploitation, discrimination and harassment in their daily lives. Usually, they reside in squatter settlements in the urban slums or as the landless poor in rural areas. They live in near total poverty and their working conditions are very harsh. Their wages are very low and discriminatory. In rural areas, the peculiar feature is that once the agricultural season is over, most of them migrate to the cities in search of work opportunities. Thus, they create new slums in the city and further deteriorate the already poor environment conditions.

Most NGO's in the developing countries choose their clientele from this growing sector. They have attempted to meet the needs of these poorer clientele by generating alternative employment opportunities. The major problems in this sector ensue from the non-recognition of the informal sector workers by the labour ministries of respective governments resulting in the non-implementation of social legislations and lack of enforcement of protective measures for them. Overall, the invisibility of the informal sector leads to an under-valuation of the output from this sector and also results in underestimation of the womens work contribution to and in this sector.

Clearly, poverty alleviation would be rapid and more effective if the informal sector was recognised and the workers are provided access to basic services and infrastructural facilities, such as credit, technology, productive assets, health and related services, training and non-formal education, and better environmental conditions.

The Indian Formal Sector

It is alarming to note that the majority of the working population of India live and work in the informal sector. India has a total working population of 292 million. Of this, only 25 million belong to the organised sector. The remaining 267 million belong to the informal sector and they remain unorganised as they are not affiliated to formal or informal unions. Of the 267 million informal sector workers, about 25 million earn Rs. 250 to Rs. 500 per month and the rest get only between Rs. 60 to Rs. 300 per month. Regarding their occupational status, about 150 million are agricultural labourers, million are construction workers, and 6 million are beedi workers. Further, 48 million of the unorganised labour are underemployed. Critically, women constitute 89 per cent of the unorganised labour force.

In the last few years, the NGO community in India has mobilised workers in this sector into unions and often also represented to governments the major economics and legal issues confronting these workers. They have also been pressurising governments to recognise these workers as trade unions of occupational groups especially in the context of women workers.

It is in the context of the informal sector mentioned above that the Working Women's Forum (India), a mass based NGO in India mobilised and organised poor women workers from the urban slums and rural areas.

The Working Women's Forum

Origin and Growth

The Working Women's Forum, which provides development

assistance at the grassroots, started operations primarily as a credit group providing assistance to poor and destitute women with neither financial nor social standing. Since its innovative beginning in 1978, the Forum has now grown into a large organisation of over 1,40,000 poor women. It has established branches in Tamil Nadu, Andhra Pradesh, Karnataka, and Uttar Pradesh and also initiated several programmes to cater to the specific needs of its members in these different states and cultural contexts. The major programmes are credit assistance; health and family welfare services; training programmess; supportive services like childcare and child labour rehabilitation centres, and so on.

Target Clientele

WWF's members are street vendors, hawkers and service specialists in urban centres and beedi workers, agarbathi rollers, handicraft workers, landless labourers, fisherwomen and agricultural labours in rural areas. Recently, WWF extended its operations to Northern India, where it has organised chikan embroidery workers of Lucknow and migrant workers and children in the Kanpur industrial belt of Uttar Pradesh.

Demographics

Regarding the demographic characteristics of WWCS' members, 35 per cent are urban and 65 per cent are rural. The WWCS comprises only of women. Over 99 per cent of the credit assistance goes to individual members who belong to loan groups. About 56 per cent of the members are illiterate with 7 per cent of them having studied between class IX to XI. 15 per cent of them having studied upto class VIII and 22 per cent of them having studied upto class V.

The clientele belong to different age groups ranging from 22 to 50 years. About 37 per cent of the members are in the 22-30 years category, 18 per cent are in the 31-40 age group, 34 per cent are between 41 and 50 years of age, and only 11 per cent are 51 years and above.

Occupational Characteristics

Regarding the occupational characteristics of WWCS' members, 815 of women are retail traders operating in groups, 16 of them are service specialists and only 3 per cent belong to the manufacturing sector. Further, 61 per cent of the women entrepreneurs are 'sole traders' about 14 per cent of them have their entire family helping them in their enterprise and 25 per cent have two household members working in their business.

In qualitative terms, WWF's members are : (a) Women who are exploited, discriminated and harassed on the basis of gender, caste and class factors; (b) Women who face the double drudgery of managing the home apart from trying to provide for it; (c) Women who live in extreme conditions of poverty; (d) Women whose working conditions are very harsh and whose wages are discriminatory and very low; and (e) Women who do not have access to basic services, such as credit education, housing, health, family welfare and technology.

Objectives

The objective of the Working Women's Forum are:

- To provide visibility to the valuable economic role played by the poor women workers;
- To devise a grassroots delivery system and organisational structure so as to effectively reach large numbers of poor women;
- To develop an effective credit and employment strategy to address the critical needs of the poor women;
- To implement an intensive health and family welfare programme to strengthen women's productive roles;
- To provide support services to the poor women;
- To help the women perceive the discrimination, exploitation, and harassment inherent in their living and working environment;
- To create awareness concerning their basic rights and also to provide them the leadership skills, confidence and courage required to fight for these rights;
- To make them realise their state of powerlessness as well as the scope and power of their empowerment;
- To make them understand the need for the strengthen of collective action among so as to overcome the gender, class and caste oppressions;
- To provide them the skills, experiences and knowledge that can provide alternative employment opportunities, increase and regularise their incomes, improve their living and working conditions and social status, and lastly, facilitate investments in productive assets; and
- To ultimately enable these women to help themselves in improving their overall quality of life.

WWF's Development Strategy

The Forum's development strategy involves encouraging self-management, having a flexible organisational structure and participative leadership style, and using an integrated approach to service delivery. Further, its mobilisation approach and the class characteristics of its members help in generating community or local involvement and social acceptability. In fact, what is unique about the Forum is the fact that almost 99 per cent of its staff are illiterate. Yet, their participation in the project identification, design, implementation and evaluation is very high. The individual components of WWF's development strategy are briefly highlighted below as they are likely to place WWF's credit programme in proper perspective.

Self-Reliance and Self-Management

The strong leadership role of these women is visible from the fact that they take strategic and operational decisions for managing their own institutions. For instance, when the Nationalized Banks, because of their cumbersome procedures and bureaucratic delays, failed to extend credit to the poor women, the women members of WWF themselves (through their collective consciousness and wisdom) established an informal banking system that would be easy to operate and extend credit to the poor in an innovative and sensitive manner. Thus, beginning in 1981, a series of Working Women's Cooperative Societies, were initiated as separate legal institutions, each operating in different states and cultural contexts under the norms of the respective government cooperative departments. The societies are completely managed by the poor women themselves with their rights and responsibilities as shareholders. Given the high efficiency and volume of operation of these units, the credit for such management certainly goes to the poor women.

Integrated Delivery of Services

Like many formal institutions, governments and official programmes; the WWFs service have exceeded the mere provision of credit. Rather, it has evolved an integrated approach which in principle attempts to cater to the total development needs of the poor women. Thus, WWF does not view the development of women synonymous as with monetary services in the form of credit. Rather it emphasises a holistic approach to meet other emerging needs such as health, family planning, nutrition, environmental sanitation, training, shelter, and awareness raising.

Flexible Organisational Structure

WWF's organisational structure has the ability to avoid class elitism and the caste hierarchies which are usually dominant in India. 99 per cent of the staff of the WWF are from the same poor socio-economic class as the participants of the programme. This compatibility of class background has helped in identifying other poor working women effective and also fulfilling their needs to a great extent. Further, it has facilitated greater outreach and replicability, thereby ensuring that large numbers of the poor are reached and served rapidly.

The President and a few staff in the training department and the credit society are the only staff who do not belong to the target group. Even among these staff, most belong to lower middle-class families. They have been recruited primarily for their research and/or accounting skills. Further, several of these women are single women themselves, mostly deserted, divorced and widowed. Their own personal experiences, social oppressions and other struggles have hardened their attitude towards male dominating systems and the patriarchal culture.

Thus, it is poor women in large numbers, who have provided WWF with strong leadership. They have acted as effective role models so as to help, shape and spread the ideology of the WWF, thereby enabling it to expand from its small base in the Madras city slums to a multi-state organisation with branches in urban and rural areas.

Formal and Informal Banking Systems in India

Prior to introducing WWF's credit programme, a brief overview of the formal and informal banking systems in India is essential to understand the conditions that led to the initiation of need based, flexible, participative and yet effective banking. In India, formal banking still requires collaterals and securities. It is dependent on the deposits collected invariably from the rich and also on lending to the rich at high rates of interest. The banks use the interest collected to pay interest to depositors as well as meet their own establishments cost which are often very high. This type of formal banking system seldom assists the development process and hence, cannot be expected to meet the needs of the poor. In fact, the staff and employees of most government banks have been trained primarily to deal with formal situations, such as lending to large corporations and/or well-to-do individuals.

Under these circumstances, the only alternative option open to the poor are the moneylenders or the 'loan sharks'. This informal borrowing system is disastrous as it charges very exorbitant rates of interest, thereby making the poor enmesh themselves in a vicious cycle of indebtedness and poverty. Nonetheless, this exploitative system remains the only informal source of credit for the poor. In most cases, the poor have pawned their land, house and/or jewels for small amounts of money borrowed at high rates of interest. Usually, pawing small assets to moneylenders implies that the assets are lost once and for all.

Banks were nationalized in India in 1969 with a view to extend credit to large numbers of the poor. Yet, they have made no serious efforts to participate or assist in poverty alleviation programmes. The Differential Rate of Interest (DRI) scheme introduced by the banks to help poor has reached only a negligible number of poor women at the grassroots, with recovery being very poor. Politicisation of these loans has led to loss of credibility in the DRI scheme. Statistically, a mere 1 per cent of the total profit of the nationalized banks has been channelised for this purpose, leaving almost 99 per cent of the poor in the country untouched.

The limited success of the low-interest schemes (DRI) lending in nationalized banks was evaluated in 1982. The failure resulted from lack of identification of the right borrowers, the inflexible structure of the scheme, and the resulting rate of high default. Lack of consumptive credit as well as a supportive infrastructure including healthcare, technical services, training and consciousness also precipitated high default rates. Finally, lending to individuals rather than the groups removed all pressures, such as group or peer pressure for individuals to repay loan instalments.

On the other hand, the success of the WWF clearly show "how a number of needs, strategies, services and mechanisms absent in the lending schemes of government banks were incorporated in the credit cooperative that is the alternative loaning system it evolved".

As the WWF expanded, the women faced problems with nationalized banks in obtaining credit. Therefore, the women through their own collective consciousness initiated their own informal banking system in 1981 with a small revolving fund. Thus, the first Working Women's Cooperative Society was born. It was registered as a separate legal identity as per the norms of the government cooperative department in the states.

The WWCS - The Process of Initiation Origins

Having registered the cooperative with the governmental

cooperative structure (according to the by-laws of the Government of Tamil Nadu) the WWF had to wage a long and hard battle on rules and regulations. The regulation that disturbed the organisation most was the high rate of interest (13 per cent) compared to the 4 per cent DRI loans. Similarly, group loans were not possible through the government cooperative and each individual member was responsible for her own loan. This meant the overhaul of the basic organisational mechanism of the credit group. The Forum uses two sets of ledgers to overcome this problem. The first ledger records loans to individual members as stipulated by the cooperative rules. The second ledger records the loans to groups. This is essential to ensure the group guarantee system (peer pressure) which would not be operative, if the loans were recorded on a individual basis.

Further, the Working Women's Credit Cooperative could not borrow resources at 4 per cent rate of interest from commercial banks according to the cooperative by-laws of the Government of Tamil Nadu. The option before the Forum was to procure resources from donor agencies through its sister organisation, the Working Women's Forum (India). The organisation also had to accept the audits and inspections of the Cooperative Department of the Government of Tamil Nadu.

An interview with loan officers of the intermediary and direct loaning systems of the WWF highlights their perceptions of the difference between WWF's small borrower lending to women as against that of nationalized banks.

At nationalized banks, women sometimes have to bring their children. If the children are dirty or women wear torn sarees, lack oiled/combed hair, bank officials treat women in a low manner. Further, if children pass urine (by mistake) the women members are sent out of the office. Pregnant women have to utilise toilets quite often but nationalized banks sometimes do not even have a urinal for women clients. But on the other hand, when women wear decent sarees (sometimes borrowed from neighbours), they ask "your saree seems worth Rs.300/-, Why do you need a loan at all". So, poor women are treated shabbily whether badly dressed or well dressed. But this is not so at the Working Women's Credit Cooperative. As it is their own forum and a familiar office, women can walk in any time without fear or shyness. All of us are also women and many of us live in the same area as the women. We make it a point to explain all their questions patiently.

At the nationalized banks if one member of a group is not able to come (due to pregnancy, child birth, illness, death in the family) on the appointed day, she cannot get a loan. On the other hand, at the WWCS even if they miss a loan day, we provide them their loan on a convenient day. At nationalized banks, our women are regularly asked about ownership of land, jewels and property. The question is how can these poor women that build houses on encroached land own houses? At the WWCS we only ask them their enterprise, productivity, check their repayment pattern, verify with the organiser that introduced them as well as the integrity of the group leader in collecting loan instalments. The husband's names are not required.

Further in our experience the amount of the loan at nationalized banks is fixed. If you borrow once, twice or thrice, the loan amount does not increase; it just remains at one size (for example, a member who initially got Rs.200 or Rs.400 might get only that amount each time). At the WWCS, we have experience in guaging need and many studies on the credit required for different occupations. We are therefore, flexible depending on the requirement. Giving a bigger loan to a member who has done better, is an appreciation of her work. But, this does not mean that we give bigger loans without a basis. A field visit is always undertaken by the WWCS staff to inquire into the productivity, when providing members large loans.

At the nationalized banks though the officers are educated people, they have no patience to fill in the loan application forms of our members. This work is done by the Working Women's Forum loan officer (under the intermediary lending systems). At the WWCS, our staff patiently fill in loan forms, even though we have not received college education (all the staff are only educated till high school and are trained at the cooperative institute). The difference is that we treat members as one of us. That is why the WWCS office is full of noise, shouting, children and so on. We have only six women on staff and have provided 6,714 women with Rs.32,33,051 as small credit loans in Madras City within four years. The average loan size is Rs.200 to Rs.400. The repayment rate is 96.4 per cent. The WWCS also has service counters in Dindigul (landless women, shanty vendors), Vellore (beedi workers) and Adiramapattinam. In total, the three rural counters have provided 1887 loans worth Rs.3,45,2000 in three years. Further, because of the rules regarding compulsory savings, women have begun to save. The insurance schemes (with the LIC) also guarantees at least Rs.1000 during times of distress or tragedy among women (death, illness, accidents etc.). Since 1984, we also have a sister cooperative in Karnataka state.

Objectives of the WWCS

The objectives of the Working Women's Cooperative Societies have emphasised a long-term solutions to the problems of poor women workers. It has helped them to increase incomes by (a) improving their existing skills; (b) providing access to credit or working capital; (c) introducing technology and (d) imparting training, apart from providing other kinds of support. The credit facilities of the WWCS has not limited itself to merely providing cash credit. Often, WWCS has made arrangements for raw materials, skills training and even marketing of the products with the long-term goal of providing upward mobility for the poor women.

The WWCS

Credit Model

In the WWCS, organisers of the WWF who live in the slums help in identifying and selecting loanees, guaranteeing repayments, and supervising the end use of loans. They also take responsibility for the collection and repayment of the monthly instalments. The highest responsibility of these local leaders is that they create an environment 'peer pressure' so that the defaulting members are made to repay the loans. This aspect is weak in the formal banking systems, such as nationalized banks. Thus, the rate of recovery in all the branches of WWCS is uniformly high, ranging between 90 to 95 per cent. The major factors that have contributed to the effectiveness of the credit model is (a) low processing costs, especially psychological costs (b) high levels and layers of supervision with short span of control (i.e., the members, group leader, area organisers etc.) (c) creation of an environment whereby effective group dynamics has been possible.

Preparing the Member

An integral part of the WWCS' operational strategy is the comprehensive electric training for members, group leaders, organisers and others. These training programmes are of great importance as they provide the women the opportunity to come out, speak and share their experiences. Such training programmes have been replicated in various contexts after adaptation to suit the local conditions. They instil confidence and provide worker, gender, cooperative consciousness at different levels.

In a year, there are 48 training programmes conducted by the cooperative societies. About 1440 women leaders are trained every year (at the rate of 120 per month) at the Madras WWCS branch alone. Likewise, in all WWCS branches, there are atleast two training programmes every month. Thus, about 720 leaders are trained in each of the WWCS branches every year to make a total of 6480 leaders in all the nine WWCS branches. Another training that must be mentioned is the one day training that all women receive prior to their first loan.

The Credit Group

WWF's credit group of participatory in nature; the members live in a given street or locality and come together and elect their own leader. Often it is built on familar and intelligible social forms of existing collectivities (indigenous local groups). The group leader is pivotal in serving as a linkage between the members and the organisation. She is responsible not only for assisting in loan processing and recovery, but is in effect a catalyst that helps members perceive exploitation and denial of rights and services at the local level. The group also provides a base for solidarity from which collective action is initiated and bases of grassroots leadership formed for water, electricity, landtitles, wages, confronting police harassment. The internal dynamics of the group undergoes changes with the increase in loan-cycles that are backed by the organisation with awareness training and other services. Often, defaulting loan leaders have been overthrown and replaced by some other member. Some other times, members have left to initiate groups in areas they have moved to geographic proximity is an important variable in WWF's group dynamics process as it heightens the 'peer pressure' strategy. The supervision of the groups and their leaders is done by a area organiser reporting to one of the secretaries of the organisation. Their is a high level of supervision and checks and balances.

Loan Sizes and Instalments

The first loan is invariably around Rs.200 (about US $18). Usually, the second loan is between Rs. 400 to Rs. 800 depending on the increase in trade volume and the loan absorption and repayment capacity of the individual member. The maximum loan that the society offers is Rs.3000 (about US $125). All loans between Rs.200 and Rs.2000 are payable by members within 10 monthly instalments. For loans above Rs.2000, the members are given 20 months time for repayment.

Loan Uses

Most of the members use their loan partly as working capital and partly for the purchasing small productive assets. Findings from a recent study on the WWCS' revealed that 72 per cent of the women invest their loans in business, 4.5 per cent of them invest on equipment and 17 per cent invest on household utensils which are also used for cooking purposes, in the case of food service specialists. Only 6 per cent of women had used the loan to clear other earlier loans and a very neglible group (0.5 per cent) had used it for education, legal expenses, and contingencies like health treatment etc.

Loan Procedure

The loans are normally secured by the members based on the guarantee given by group leaders and local organisers. The screening of loan applications and the subsequent sanctioning of the loan takes about a month in the case of first loans. Since this is the time that is required by the busy banking staff of the society to make their field visits and other enquiries. For repeat or second loans, the time taken for processing is very quick. It usually takes between 7 to 10 days.

The field officers of the cooperative always visit the work site of the loan applicants alongwith the respective group leaders and organisers. After a thorough on-the-spot assessment of the nature and volume of business, the field officers help the women in working out the quantum of loan required. Sometimes, such field visits help in eliminating women who try to obtain a second loan after having already received a loan through other credit programmes, such as chit funds or nationalized bank schemes. The field visits also help in weeding out women who planned to use the loan for various non-productive purposes.

Savings

All the members of the WWCS' are expected to participate in the savings programmes. However, in the WWCS saving has never been a pre-condition to receive financial assistance.

Interest Rates

Regarding the interest charged, while the rate is 15 per cent per annum, in reality, it actually out to be very low (i.e., 8.25 per cent) as it is computed on the decreasing capital. The prevailing market rates of interest elsewhere in the country (including other cooperative societies) are mostly 18 per cent per annum. While DRI loans in nationalized banks charge 4 per cent, they are very limited and cater to a very small group. Further, the traditional moneylenders charge 3 per cent to 5 per cent per month which translates to 36 per cent to 60 per cent per annum.

Loan Recovery and Default

Regarding the arrears in the WWCS, 30 per cent of the arrears are recovered within a period of three months. 50 per cent of the arrears are recovered in three to six months time and only 17 per cent are repaid over a six month period. As far as loan recovery is concerned, the WWCS rely only on 'peer pressure' through group leaders and members.

The total percentage of loans that are written off in the WWCS' is very negligible, just 2.61 per cent. In the WWCS', despite the clientele being the poorest, failure to repay the loan occurs only when the members are caught in disastrous situations, such as floods or fires in the slums and settlements.

In all, only 1.25 per cent of the WWCS members are default members. This group consists mostly of members who migrate to other places because of failure to reconstruct themselves from their loses due to natural calamities like floods, fire and/or family difficulties such as death, sickness and unexpected accidents (Please see Table 1).

As expected by the WWCS, the loan repayment rates are uniformly high as given below:

Madras	95.7 per cent
Bangalore	95.4 per cent
Dindigul	97.8 per cent
Adiramapattinam	96.5 per cent
Vellore	95 per cent
Narasapur	99.9 per cent
Bidar	94.9 per cent

Impact and Performance of the WWCS Credit Model

With staff and clientele from the same background, the simple credit group model of the WWF is not only efficient and effective, but also suited for replication in other contexts. Thus, the WWF has been able to replicate much faster both in terms of members and areas covered. Further, it has been able to retain its grassroot character throughout its replication and expansion efforts.

The performance of the WWCS have been uniformly the same in all branches. Appropriate staff selection and training, efficiency in operations, accurate record keeping and a low percentage of bad debts are all pointers of the exemplary work done by the WWCS' workers and staff.

Assessing Empowerment in WWW - Some Findings

Evaluation studies have been conducted in the WWF and WWCS' from time-to-time assess, both the empowerment process of the women and also the progress of the various programmes including credit assistance. These studies have revealed valuable insights of which are highlighted below. The parameters used in these studies have not only helped in assessing the actual tangible changes in the life style and living standards of the members, but also thrown light on the high level empowerment process that these women have gone through. The degree of optimism, hope, confidence and courage that these women have gained has heightened their awareness about the static situation in which they live and work. That they desired changes to reshape their future was very evident.

Further, such studies indicated some of the direct effects of credit assistance.

- Nearly 84 per cent of them happened to be sole contributors to the family income.
- The poor women could seek alternative employment opportunities because of the availability of credit.
- 92 per cent of them were able to be sole contributors to the family income.
- 76 per cent had relieved themselves of their continous indebtedness from moneylenders.
- About 40 per cent of them had diversified their business or started new but additional businesses.
- 89 per cent of respondents had been able to own necessities required for the household.
- 96 per cent of them had saved their profits in the form of investments (both movable and immovable), such as livestock.
- 75 per cent had invested their savings on housing and 66 per cent of them had invested in the renewal or extension of their houses or added civic amenities to their existing households.

The studies further proved that women wanted to move from marginal and subsistence level trading to higher options. This finding corporates with one of the primary objectives of the WWF and WWCS' which is to help the women in their advancement and upward mobility. Consequently, the WWCS' plan to increase and intensify the volume of credit to enable women both to increase the volume of their business and earn better profits as well as have access to productive assets, technology and training. The studies also brought out the fact that the women also desired education and training for their girl children, so as to have additional incomes for their families. This is a marked change in the attitudes of the poor women and should constitute a positive step towards the postponement of marriage for adolescent girls, thereby preventing them from being pushed into early motherhood. Thus, WWF's endeavour is to help and facilitate women to take such positive and forward steps, increase their level of empowerment and improving their overall quality of life.

Lessons from the Experiences WWF/WWCS

1. The Working Women's Forum and Working Women's Cooperative Society considered credit as an important issue. However, this focus on credit did not prevent other important needs, such as gender and worker consciousness, training, housing technology, health and family welfare services from being addressed. The small homogenous groups, which are used as conduits for credit assistance, have also acted as support systems and forums for tackling or discussing other problems of significance to the local context.
2. WWF/WWCS has always started with small, short-term loans. Such loans, apart from testing the willingness of the borrower to repay has also provided her the opportunity to ascertain the usefulness of low-interest credit.
3. WWF/WWCS has extended credit in a cost-effective simple way and quickly. First time loans are usually sanctioned within a month. This 'lead time' of a month is for group action on local issues, solidarity building, training and administration. Repeat (or second loans etc.) loans are processed in 7 to 10 days.
4. WWF/WWCS has charged interest at the prevailing market rates, i.e., 15 per cent per annum. However, in reality, the interest rate works out to 8.25 per cent as it is computed on the decreasing capital.
5. WWF/WWCS has utilised less formal mechanisms for administrative purposes rather than complex and bureaucratic

records found in nationalized banks. For example, photographs are used in place of signatures for identification.

6. WWF/WWCS has not demanded security deposits and/or collateral - both of which the poor cannot provide. Rather, the group itself became the substitute for material collateral.
7. WWF/WWCS has encouraged a group approach where loans are given only to persons belonging to groups. The groups, which provided solidarity and collective consciousness, have also acted as social mechanisms for the repayment of loans through 'peer pressure'. Further, it is the poor who will decide as to be members of their respective groups. Thus, membership decisions are based on mutual trust and respect.
8. WWF/WWCS has strongly emphasised mutual responsibility and trust between group members, leaders, organisers and other credit programme staff.
9. WWF/WWCS has encouraged communication and information exchange between the group members, group leaders, organisers, WWF staff and other stakeholders, which are very vital. Collection and dissemination of information involved the ability to listen as well as to speak and react effectively without dominating. Thus, the groups become an area which provided the poor women the opportunity to learn and express themselves.
10. WWF/WWCS has always considered experience as the best teacher. Thus, group learnt by sharing ideas and exchanging experiences with other groups. Likewise, field and credit programme staff also learnt through practical work and direct interaction with the poor although formal and informal training have been utilised as back-up support.

WWF - Groots Networking Process; Transfer of Expertise in WWF

Innovative experiments, such as the WWF are a response to the global need to empower the power. Having collected significant experience in the field for over a decade, it now proposes to transfer its valuable experience to a larger number of NGOs and create similar movements.

An experiment of Leadership Development Workshop 1990 at Bangalore (India) through the joint effort of Groots India Taskforce and WWF, where 42 South Asian NGOs and 19 International NGO participated, provided an opportunity to strengthen the knowledge and solidarity among the national, international NGO community which WWF will continue through the process of networking.

Conclusion

The Forum can be perceived as a political process for the economic empowerment of the poor. Such an empowerment process is far superior to keep these members together than any material programmes. Thus, the ideology explains the massive growth and continuity of the Forum.

References

Arunachalam Jaya : A decade of the Forum - Working Women's Forum (India) a movement of poor women of self-help and social transformation; published by WWF (I).

Arunachalam Jaya : Credit needs of Women Workers in the Informal Sector, Case Study of Working Women's Forum (India) submitted by Appropriate Technology International, USA, Sept. 1987.

Arunachalam Jaya : Managing by Value & Vision Lessons from the Working Women's Forum (India) presented at Asian Institute of Management, Manila, Phillipines, April 24th - 28th 1990.

Arunachalam Jaya : Sharing Poverty or Creating Wealth? Access to Credit for Women's Enterprises, presented by Royal Tropical Institute, Netherlands 7th – 9th January 1991.

Azad Nandini : Empowering Women Workers, The WWF Experiment in Indian Cities, Published by UNICEF, New Delhi.

Azad Nandini : "Creating Bases of Women's Solidarity"; A study of the Grassroots Credit Groups of the Working Women's Forum (India) submitted in partial fulfillment of the requirements for the degree of Doctor of Philosophy in Anthropology in the Graduate School of Syracuse University, August 1987.

Chen Marty : The Working Women's Forum; Organising the Credit and Change Seeds No.6 1983 New York.

Chambers Robert : The Working Women's Forum - A Counter Culture by Poor Women Workers, Published by UNICEF.

Nico Schrijver & C. Pavlien Vanden Tempel : Solidarity Against Poverty - A Socialist Program from Hollans Published by Evert Vermeer Foundation.

Sara K. Gould : "A Working Guide to Women's Self Employment" prepared by Economic Development Administration of the U.S. Department of Commerce.

Wignaraja Ponna : Women, Poverty and Resources, Working Women's Cooperative Society.

Report : A Case Study "Women's Access to Credit in the Dominician Republic", published by UNIRTIAW.

Management Challenges in Population Programmes:* Issues and Opportunities in the 1990s

India's Problem of Population

India with 844 million people, adds more numbers to world's population than any other country in the world. Despite having adopted a National Family Policy in 1952, even one-third of the country's eligible couple are not covered by family planning service schemes. Health services are not only meagre in many rural areas, but almost non-existent in remote places. Over-dependence on government results in an over-emphasis on surgical methods of family planning, to the veritable exclusion of other contraceptives. The virtual absence of temporary methods lead to frequent pregnancies among women, who are left without any spacing options of child births. Large-scale female feoticide and infant mortality continue to be the bane of Indian Society.

Girl Child in India

Even if a girl child manages to survive these ordeals, she is never given a due place in traditional families and faces discrimination right from childhood. Most of them are drop outs at the primary school stage itself. Consequently, they are forced into early marriage or motherhood in their adolescence, with some destined to die while delivering their first baby in conditions of abject poverty and neglect. Low status of employment and poor status of health leading to large families for which women alone have to assume greater responsibilities are the direct results of the denial of educational facilities to women.

Lack of Awareness for Community Responsibilities

Powerlessness of the people living in extreme poverty push them to a state of helplessness. They are totally ignorant of their community responsibilities and privileges. Their indolence and apathy are taken for granted by the government and other power structures. For instance, India had the tradition of each community having its own female birth attendants. This system could have been improved upon to take care of safe motherhood, preventive and promotive healthcare in many rural areas. It would have also supplemented the much needed requirements of basic healthcare among the poorer communities in remote areas of the vast country where even basic healthcare is denied today.

---

*Speech Delivered at International Seminar at Nanjing, China, May 3-7, 1993.

Case Study of the Working Women's Forum (India)

Driven by such concerns and circumstances, Working Women's Forum, one of the largest of NGOs in the third world, has taken upon itself the responsibility to innovate 'an experiment in leadership in grassroot healthcare' preparing the poor women for a process of self-help or self-management. WWF's first effort, towards this end was to organise women in the most unorganised sector, to provide them with economic assistance, aquiant them with health or family welfare services and prepare them for the much required support services. Initiated as a small union with 800 women in 1978, WWF today is multi-state union of over 2,00,000 women in the three southern states of India.

Forum was established in 1978 in the city of Madras as the grassroot union of poor woman workers who until then had no experience in any formal or informal union.

The case study of the Working Women's Forum is a combination of women's enhanced economic participation and social empowerment. The experiment has demonstrated that increase in women's income in combination with their enhanced economic participation and social empowerment.

Experiment in Leadership - Family Planning Project of WWF

Characterised by grassroot orientation, a feminist approach, and leadership roles among the poor working class women, the WWF's credibility lies in its large scale outreach system, shaping itself into a mass movement. It's objective moves beyond a mere material assistance to members and envisages collective action for social change to empower the poor women.

A Grassroot Initiative

In its early days, WWF's core action initiated around credit provisions to its members as most of them were entrepreneurs from the urban slums. Later, in 1980, women of WWF in their heightened awareness, felt that their need went beyond credit, i.e., family welfare service, training and orientation for leadership and other support services to improve their working as well as living conditions. In a period of two years, poor women were able to identify on their own that 68 per cent among themselves were heads of households. As many as 70 per cent of their children in the slums were working as child labourers. Living in private or government land in the congested slums of Madras in abysmal living as well as working conditions with little or no amenities, made them come together and fight for the same. Further, they could identify their own requirements, such as family welfare services, sanitation or civic amenities, house sites and electricity, fuel and water. There was a growing feeling that solutions must be found even if one had to resort to several protest demands to the government and other local authorities after marching on the main streets of the cities and villages in which they lived. The family planning project was thus launched as on such "Need based Experiment in Leadership Development in 1980", in the field of health nutrition and family planning.

Informal Banking Effort of WWF

In 1981, to ensure a smooth flow of credit to the women entrepreneurs, women of WWF established a bank of their own which was both informal and easy to operate. The establishment of this informal credit system was a compulsion on their part as they faced innumerable difficulties in dealing with nationalized banks. The latter felt that the poor women are not bankable since they were illiterate and a powerless group who could not be expected to manage their own affairs. Thus, WWF women on their own promoted a series of Working Women's Cooperative Societies in a number of places in the three southern states of Tamil Nadu, Karnataka and Andhra Pradesh.

Goals and Objectives of WWF's Family Planning Project

The long-term goal of both the Credit and Family Planning Programme of WWF is to improve the status and quality of life of poor working women. Also, achieve the target reproduction rate in all the project area by the year 2000 A.D.

The immediate objectives of the family planning programme are: (a) To increase the couple protection rate by 25 per cent over the current rate of 46.3 per cent; (b) To encourage family planning acceptance by couples at lower ages; (c) To improve the income level of Working Women in the poorer communities; (d) To integrate family welfare education and activities into all the ongoing programmes of the Working Women's Forum; and (e) To create leaders within the community from among the working class women who in turn will train other grassroot workers. The strategy includes promotion of income generation programmes complemented by family planning motivation, education and referral activities through a community based family welfare programme.

Development Sensitisation of WWF

What has contributed to their success? The significant achievement of the family planning programme is due to the effective mobilisation of clients by WWF's well trained grassroot health workers, and a comprehensive approach to the total development to communities total health care, integrated credit/family welfare and other services has contributed to a higher level of family planning acceptance among the poor clientele.

The training of the field workers through a comprehensive sensitisation process on gender issues, i.e., providing the much needed linkage between women's productive and reproductive roles has also enhanced the success of the programme. The significant increase in the immunisation of children under 5 years old in the four rural project areas of Tamil Nadu from 43.3 per cent to 70.7 per cent is a clear indicator of the acceptance of this programme among the poor women. Every woman who wants to adopt any one of the family planning Services has inevitably felt secure when her children are immunised.

Selection of Cadre in WWF

Great importance is attached to recruitment of field workers or supervisors from the slums and villages in the project area, to develop community leaders who can identify with local women and act as catalysts in such changes of perceptions. The criteria laid out are that the candidates must be able to read and write, should have married with one or two children, should have adopted any one of the family planning methods and be skilled in inter-personal communication in a neighbourhood of 500 families. Of course, WWF gives preference to widows and deserted wives, who under compulsion have to support their families. The intensive training of field supervisors is not only in the area of family welfare and population education, but also in gender sensitisation, communication strategy, project management, implementation and monitoring. The training also covers subjects, such as preventive health, social issues, record keeping or reporting systems required for effective management of the project. The field workers and field supervisors are trained to provide the much needed linkage between the under-utilised governmental health infrastructure and the target clientele in slums and villages.

Training Modules in the Family Planning Project

The classroom training is followed by 30 days field training, where the field workers collect basic household data within the 500 families which have been selected as their targeted area. This data collection effort by the cadre helps them to familiarise themselves and interact with their clientele more meaningfully. After the completion of training period, other outreach strategies begin with a programme of house visits to 25 to 30 families a day, motivating and educating family members on mother and childcare and family planning immunisation and gender and other economic issues. During the visits, the field workers usually establish rapport with the families and their potential clientele through interpersonal communication strategies. Not only they advice, but also refer the clientele to appropriate health or family welfare and immunisation services, they also accompany them when necessary. Sometimes, they facilitate access to credit assistance in WWCS for those clientele who need economic assistance in poorer families. The cadres in their interactions in the target areas not only emphasise the need for family planning and health consciousness, but also convince and argue with mothers-in-law and husbands of the clientele to bring them round to become part of the decision-making process to adopt family welfare practices.

Health Cadres - Schedule of Activities

As a follow-up of their counselling, health workers supply contraceptives to the motivated clients. Critical situations arise in many cases, when there is no domestic help to those women who desire either surgery or IUD insertions. At home in the slums, women have little or no help in household chores, little access to water, fuel or even sanitation and civic amenities. The family welfare workers, then sometimes undertake on their own these household chores also. The field workers ensure that every female client who opts for surgery is assured of the incentive payment of Rs. 200 from the government. Every field worker achieves atleast a target of three to five acceptance of each method of family planning, both temporary and permanent.

The health workers record the details of their daily work in a diary and transfer them to their work register every week, which is again monitored by supervisors. The performance of their motivational/ educational programme is classified and rated by supervisors into four categories as excellent, good, average and poor. The latest reports from Madras show that 9 per cent of field workers are excellent, 25 per cent good, 45 per cent average and 20 per cent are poor. In rural branches, the figures are - 60 per cent excellent, 24 per cent good, 38 per cent average and 22 per cent poor.

In addition to referral services, the health workers conduct monthly demonstration on various issues of general health programmes, such as AIDS and other epidemics, family planning and nutrition. Often discussions are held in small groups on socio-economic and gender issues. The periodical review meetings in WWF bring doctors and nurses from the local clinics and hospitals to hear WWF's health staff and supervisors, on their grievances and concern with respect to their dealing with hospitals and government clinics. These, then become basically problem solving sessions. In each of the 500 families, every family welfare worker holds regular monthly meetings with 20 to 25 local women and prepare them for becoming communication leaders. This effort of WWF is an exemplary approach to develop leadership skills among poor women at the grassroot level.

Health Cadre - Network at the Grassroots

WWF fulfils one of the major requirements of the poorer communities in developing countries, i.e., building up a health cadre in grassroot communities and infuse in them the much-needed health care consciousness. Trained in communication skills and emerging from the same community, these cadres have a very high social acceptability in their neighbourhoods, due to their high sensitivity of the problems of the poor. On completion of this project, most of the cadres may not be paid by the WWF project, but would continue to serve their respective communities, building up themselves as a network of health personnel in their own neighbourhoods, looking after uncovered families and new arrivals. Unlike the traditional female birth attendants, these workers have gone through a training of modern methods of health care will take care of their own community needs and their salaries will be compensated by local incentives.

Other Services Towards Population Control in WWF

WWF also operates child labour rehabilitation centres to hold night classes for working children and vocational training classes for female children who are school drop outs. Issues of population education, marriage, small family norm and gender equality are part of the general educational syllabus.

Target Clientele of WWF

The programme of health and family welfare is now being implemented in 232 slums in Madras and 133 villages in four districts of Tamil Nadu. The target of the project area is about, 1,50,000 households with 1,20,259 eligible couples. WWF has recruited 300 trained family welfare workers, 13 supervisors, who are assisted by a number of nutrition demonstrators and gender activists from WWF as volunteers.

Results

Heartening results have been achieved in WWF's projects reflected in the increasing number of couples using temporary methods. During the baseline survey of the projects in 1990, the permanent method accounted for 94 per cent of total acceptors in all the five project areas.

By September 1992, the percentage of permanent method had declined to 70 per cent, clearly indicating the increase in use of temporary method, i.e., oral pills and IUDs. The projects are, therefore, reaching out to more and more younger women and young couples.

Lessons

From the credit side, women feel that credit made available from WWF has increased their income for reinvestment in business, household expenditure, savings or in children's education. Women now feel that they have control over their own income achieved through their own ability. This, in turn, strengthens their role in household decision-making. With their growing status in some cases, they have been able to have a say on their husband's income too. Undoubtedly, WWF's orientation on gender awareness, mobilisation strategy coupled with credit provision have led to women's economic and social empowerment both at the household and at the community level.

Women included in the credit groups have a high level of awareness on family planning issues and methods reflecting a very high rate of acceptance. This has provided the ideological base and a strong conceptual link between the women's productive and reproductive role, a link that is well understood by the WWF's staff and members. Thus, credit has provided an effective entry point for group mobilisation, conscientisation, promotion of family welfare and other related activities. The lengthy discussion and direct interaction with the health workers reveals that it is easier to introduce family planning issues to poor women, by motivating them to accept this through an organisation which has established its credibility at the community level. The feminist orientation of WWF, in addition, is a positive and reinforcing influence on the members.

Conclusion

The uniqueness of India like China lies in its diversity - a kaleidoscope of cultures nurtured over several millennia. Women in both countries, have always played important role of national significance but rarely got their due. In both countries, efforts initiated as microcosms have contributed to larger movements of democratic values. WWF from India is one such microcosm in its early initiation and has grown into a mass movement of 200,000 women today, who control their own destinies through the decision-making process.

Individual Case Studies of Women in WWF

Case Study : Madras

Name : Meenakshi

Meenakshi is a health worker from Working Women's Forum. Mr.Ansarbai and his wife Mumtaj belong to a Muslim community and live in my neighbourhood, i.e., near Pappumasthan Dharka in Triplicane area. Mumtaj is my client. They already have two children. The family suffers in extreme poverty. After the third child, when I advised his wife to adopt family planning practice, he was opposed to it. After explaining both of them about the problems of having many children in crowded households, he reluctantly agreed to adopt family planning practice because he was not able to provide all of them even basic necessities. Surprisingly, after this Ansarbai married again. When asked why he remarried despite having wife and two children, he said that according to the Muslim religion he can marry four times.

Soon after his second wife Nazima had two children, had to advise her too on family planning practices. When she underwent tubectomy, Ansarbai married for the third time. This time became very angry and approached the high priest of mosque and told him about the problems faced by his three wives. But the priest also said, that there is nothing wrong in marrying thrice, however, he would prevent Ansarbai from marrying the fourth time taking his abysmal living conditions. The high priest of the mosque highlighted this problem of Ansarbai on a Friday, during the Namaz time, before the other people of the community. Ansarbai felt sorry and not only changed heart but these days he joins me in family planning campaigns.

Case Study : Vellore

Name : Dhanalakshmi

My name is Dhanalakshmi. We are three in the family. My mother died, when I was 10 years old. My sister helped me to study upto class IX. At the age of 20, I was married to a beedi worker (Country Cigarettes). I learnt to roll beedis from my husband and started earning through beedi work. My first child was born, after a year I had twins. By then, my health showed signs of deterioration and I had to go for family planning surgery without consulting doctors.

In the meanwhile, family business broke down and my husband had to borrow heavily to continue the business. As the debt burden increased, suddenly my husband deserted me one day and disappeared. I had to answer the moneylenders, who insulted me and abused me in public.

Despite my poor health I had to work to survive and to repay the debts of my husband. One day the moneylenders finally caught hold of my husband and presented him in the local Panchayat meeting, where he was asked to live with me and repay rest of the debts. We found it difficult to repay the debts with our meagre income.

In a critical situation as this, through women organisers of Working Women's Forum, I came to know about WWF and then joined this Forum as a health worker. With the salary I received I was able to run the family. My husband's income was used to repay the debts. If I had come across WWF earlier in my life, I would have saved my children. I went through two pregnancies and had three children but none of them is alive today. In my present work, special attention to pregnant mothers is my great concern as I do not want them to face the same situation as myself. Now I face life with confidence.

Case Study : Kancheepuram

Name : Sundari

My name is Sundari and I am the fifth daughter in the family. My mother died when I was five years old. My father struggled-hard to bring up all of us. He married some of my sisters with great difficulty and finally he arranged my marriage with one of my distant relatives, who was a daily wage earner.

Driven by ignorant circumstances, I gave birth to eight children. As the earnings of my husband were very meagre, we were not even able to feed our children. So, we decided to go back to our native place, Kancheepuram, with the hope of getting at least some work on daily wages for both of us.

At Kancheepuram, we had to mortgage our daughters one at a time until they reached the stage of puberty to other silk weavers (bonded workers). My husband and myself continued our daily wage work to take care of other children. Meanwhile, I came to know of the union known as Working Women's Forum from my neighbours. I just approached the Working Women's Cooperative Society, asking for loan so that I can buy a loom to use my weaving skill and earn our livelihood. But at the WWF, women asked me to join as a health worker since I had studied upto class VIII. After that, I attended a training of Health and Family Planning Workers at the Kancheepuram branch.

In the early stages, acceptance in the neighbourhood was very difficult. People being poor in our areas, they wanted monitory incentives from us like from the government. When I explained to them that WWF is a voluntary effort, they refused to attend the health classes. Also, when I tried to acquaint the people with the various methods of family planning, objections came across from the family members.

However, through continuous motivation, and after citing the example of my own case through beneficial schemes of WWF, I was able to succeed in my neighbourhood. I am now able to lead a better life and could relieve my bonded children from weavers families one after another. Women accepted me as their friend, as one among them and followed all that was explained to them.

Case Study : Adiramapattinam

Name : Gunabhushani

Born in Eripurakari village in an agricultural family, I am a fisherwoman by occupation. We do not belong to the category of extremely poor but have an average life of comfortable living. I have studied upto S.S.L.C. After the stage of puberty, I was married to a person who was a drunkard. During my early pregnancy of first child, my mother-in-law deprived me of nutritious meal saying, if the child becomes fat, child birth will be difficult. So the child was born weak. She never believed in immunisation and prevented the same, then the child became a polio victim. During my second pregnancy, I gave birth to triplets. In the belief that triplets are bad omens to families my mother-in-law killed the babies by covering them in the cowdung's basket and keeping a light on the top. During the third pregnancy, she calculated the child to be born in an inauspicious month. This time she aborted the pregnancy by providing me with poisonous herbal treatment.

Then, during the last pregnancy, I was furious and went back to my mother's place so that the child can be safe. This time I gave birth to a girl child, adopted family planning by tubectomy. My husband was disappointed for not having a male child and my mother-in-law advised him to marry again for the sake of a son.

I came in contact with a person who belonged to Working Women's Forum's union. Due to my educational qualification, I was invited to work as health worker in WWF but my husband objected to this. He even made an attempt to kill me with a knife but I survived. I was very happy to attend the training classes and to learn about health and family planning which I was not aware of in my early days. Now I can stand before anybody and speak to anyone, explain them about my struggle in life which provides a lesson for others. Above all, I have been able to change the attitude of my husband who has stopped drinking these days.

Case Study : Dindigul

Name : Thamarai

My parents were agriculturists. We are five children at home. I got married to a person living in my area. He was also an agriculturist. We had two children.

It was at this time that organisers from Muthanampatti areas told me that they were recruiting staff for the Working Women's Forum Family Planning Project, as field worker. My husband at first objected to my going for work. I told him about the financial problems at home and convinced him. I then attended the 15 days classroom training and 30 days field training. I was given 300 families as target in my neighbourhood.

The criteria in WWF's Family Planning Project is that a worker should be using one of the family planning methods, if she has to convince the clientele in the neighbourhood. Then I started using the loop without informing my husband. Accidently, the loop moved away from its original position, so I became pregnant again. The doctors said, that I should undergo tubectomy after my delivery. Again without informing my husband, I underwent the tubectomy operation. My husband did not come to the hospital to see me because he knew that I had undergone family planning surgery. Only the organisers and supervisors from WWF were present to support to me. My husband did not let me inside the house after I was discharged from the hospital. He caught me by my throat and pushed me out of the house. For one whole day, I was sitting in a corner of the road starving.

The next day, when the WWF staff came to know about my situation, they took me to my mother's place. After one month, my husband realised his mistake as the WWF staff spoke to him in detail. The WWF gave me moral support at the time when I needed such a support system.

Note

All these individual case studies of WWF health workers highlight the social-environment against women in traditional societies, in India (also in all developing countries) even in modern situations. The case study in Madras, is about religion, in the case of Vellore, it is ignorance to practice safe-motherhood, in the case of Kancheepuram, it is extreme poverty and prevalent feudal-conditions where women have to mortgage their girl children to weavers families, figure as major obstacles. In the case of Dindigul and Adiramapattinam, it is the oppression of husband and mother-in-law being major impediments. While providing physical environment of better doctors, health clinics and family planning orientations, it requires a mass movement, such as WWF to counter the obstacles of social environment of massive nature against women to improve their health and economic status in all the developing countries.

Women in Transition*

It is evidenced world over that, whatsoever the situation be, i.e., civil war, military regime, colonisation or political anarchy, women are the first vulnerable targets. This popular reflection is reinforced by the unfathomable hardships faced by the women of the former USSR currently undergoing transition. The demand of these long suppressed women for control over all aspects of their lives in their society is far from reality. The problem of combining the socialist values and the old mode of production with the need for social and political equality to all human beings is conflicting and still unsolved. This has tremendous implications on all the former Soviet societies.

Women from Ukraine, Belarus, Russia, Moldova, Estonia were bold and forthcoming to share their plight and relentless struggle with their sisters from world over at the Groots workshop in Kiev, Ukraine held between the 2nd and 11th of April, 1995. The author, Regional Coordinator, GROOTS South Asia, reports on the situation of women during the transition period.

Reflecting on the situation in Moscow they said, "Our life was so stable and there was nothing we needed until "Prestorika" was announced. We started hearing suddenly about unemployment, inflation, war and concentration camps in Ukraine. In the new social order, we were completely excluded. Professional and intellectual women became unemployed. 73 per cent of the women, alone were unemployed. During the closure of defence industries our salary was US $10. It is the self-confidence and strength of our past that has helped us in trying to overcome our struggles."

Faina from Ukraine said, "At the governmental level, it was impossible to trust. They misused our ability and trust. I participated in two agitations. I can stand up for what I hold important. Even now some of the old group of political people are in good positions. They practiced double standards. We do not like Russia, we hate them. They forced on us their culture and decisions. With the help of the Swedish, we now make decisions more easily and are now more social in attitude, but the difficulty is in moving forward."

Ella, the OWEN representative from Ukraine at the GROOTS workshop highlighted the situation in Ukraine. "This country with

---

*Ms. Arunachalam reports from Kiev, U.S.S.R. to GROOTS, 11th April 1995.

22 million people with varied ecological fauna became independent through armed struggle in 1991. Subsequent to the promotion of a national political party, the national women's movement "OLENA TELEGA" was also revived. Severe imbalances in resource distribution between Russia and Ukraine has led to acute economic crisis. Having a high composition of indigenous people, it was impossible to manipulate political affairs. After the October Revolution in 1917, Soviet tradition started dominating Ukraine culture.

Their standard of living, is four times less than that of Russia with an average salary of US $9 to US $20 per month. In the villages, people receive no salary. Since all their resources had to be spent on food, shelter and clothes, nearly 80 per cent of Ukraine people currently live in poverty. In spite of the above situation, Ukraine has the highest number of educated intelligentsia. Renaissance of women's movement is now intensified. Some of the good traditions of Europe are still maintained here. Majority of their lives after the communist party took over, was spent in strifes and civil wars, especially on the land question. Women outnumbered men because most of the men died during World War II. The women's movement OLENA TELEGA, is an example of the historical role of women in the political struggle that is now being revived. The movement is called after, Olina Opasiwich, a writer who wrote a book on her 30 years of imprisonment.

How Do They Percieve the Change?

Nadia, a professor from Kiev University, reports that, "Our idea is to respond to this great change. Since there are no economic ties with Russia, we will never get ourselves pledged back to Russia. We have initiated a women's movement to empower women. Women are interested in taking care of the younger generation and in practicing democratic values. Women definitely feel sorry for the days of communism and feel that communist ideas were wrong, although most of them were committed to communism earlier.

Women are only 10 per cent in Parliament, it was so even in communist regime. In the communist regime, the position of women was not totally bad, the party used to fill up places of women, even if they were less educated, but now women have to struggle with men to get into Parliament. This organisation of OLENA TELEGA is fighting for women to get into the political process. Women have started initiating small organisations in 17 districts of Ukraine. We are also often having discussions on improving our status and conditions of poverty.

As Ukrainian women, we have organised again to relocate ourselves in Ukraine, which is 111 years old. The oldest women's organisation is in Ukraine, which attached great importance to the spirit of cooperation. The women's community here is a long-standing one. Although educationally very forward, they now strive hard to move from totalitarianism to sovereignty."

Most women were proud of Ukrainian history which was surrendered to Russia. It was a matriarchal society with the major objective of democratisation of socialist structures. To help women in the current situation, to gain self-confidence after having been totally brainwashed by the communist party, women are in need of social security, especially in their old age.

Twilight of Hope

Most women involved in reconstructing Ukraine felt that, since their disparities were high, the world should understand them. Women's programme should facilitate women to join to the mainstream economy but with proper support for human values. Women have to be empowered even against views of the mainstream and unification of the women's movement in country must go on. While, political leaders should come out with an action plan to lessen the burden of poverty, women should occupy positions of decision-making power. The right kind of value based intellectuals need to come forward to public life. The women's movement must transcend all barriers of class or race and help support grassroots women to take up leadership with immense solidarity amongst them (elite or grassroots) alongwith concern and initiative.

The women of Ukraine observed that, "We are today prepared to take up any effort that would restore our dignity and give us an opportunity to relocate ourselves as a movement. This courage needs to be channelised either for training towards empowerment, village governing committees, cooperatives or self-management systems."

Crisis of Change – Women in Transition

Any change affects us. The very attempt to such changes leads to a crisis coming as it has in East Europe. The transition from a socialistic pattern to a more open democratic system has neither been easy nor smooth. More importantly, the emotional integration of the people, from the East with their more fortunate counterparts in the West, is proving to be irksome and elusive. While the West European countries in their neighbourhood are doing better, things become more and more difficult in the East. Earlier their links with the West were good, but now when they live as objects of change, women suffer most in this process and have to pay heavily for this change. Few of the courageous women made a crucial move to come together in the OWEN network soon after November 9, 1989. Despite the struggle involved, women are proud to be going through this crisis, came together in a workshop at Guban town, Poland, to exchange experiences and understand each other through a common vision, strengthen the network through common issues and mobilise movements of solidarity. Earlier as workers in the Eastern Block, they could not organise themselves but slowly as they watched their neighbours in a heightened state of development, could now visualise of grassroots/self-help movement, through a learning process. The conference took place from December 2nd to 12th 1993. Women from East European countries like Romania, Lithuania, Yugoslavia, Russia, Albania, Belarus, Guban, people from National Congress of Neighbourhood, women from the US and women from the South Asia, Africa Groots network too attended the conference of OWEN network.

ALBANIA is a country of four million people whose economy is mostly agricultural. 70 per cent are Muslims, 15 per cent are orthodox Christians and the rest are Catholics. Their culture is very much Islamic as they were ruled by Turkish rulers for five centuries. The situation here is the worst among the East European countries. A human rights activist from Albania reported that, women were persecuted if they organised themselves politically or otherwise. She spoke at the conference about the actual conditions prevailing in her country. As the secretary of the Women's Rights Club, she helps women who suffered mental torture due to political persecution in jails to come out of their trauma.

The transition period is marked by heavy unemployment, low salary and deplorable working conditions for women. There is no electricity; water supply is only for about six hours a day, no hospital facilities and the maternity homes run with lantern lights. Abortions are legal, as there are atleast 60 a day. There are only two women's organisations that are a political and are defending women and their rights. Few NGOs are close to Mother Teresa and are quite active in running about 24 old women's homes and organisations for ex-political prisoners. Women are trained in handicrafts but they do not bring in resources and marketing is difficult. The conditions of women in prisons who have their children with them, is another grave human right issue.

Russia : The living condition in Russia worsen as the economic situation deteriorates. Communist Russia was involved in high technical defence industries and there was a lot of hidden unemployment that came to open after the collapse of communism in late 80's. In the communist regime, people were not allowed to attend meetings and it was difficult to organise people under the watchful eyes of the KGB. The word 'Community' did not exist at all after the October Revolution. Now the men and women are contemplating their future in the light of their present dilapidated condition. Families share same bathrooms and two room apartments. There is money with the municipalities to repair even the basic amenities. Men and women work for meagre salary with no employment benefits. There are no social welfare programmes, though the orthodox church has become active after the fall of communism. Abortions is illegal and single mother's problem is serious. A woman from Mother's Club in Moscow highlighted the sufferings of single mothers who face social oppressions. The club gives moral support to come out of economic and other difficulties. Further, the culture seemed to be more patriarchal in Russia, where the women are treated worse than the men. For example, in case of rape it is always the woman who is blamed. But now they are slowly coming out of their shell and speaking out.

Romania : The Romanian representative who set up the OWEN network in her country said that it was equally difficult to organise people in Romania. There is discrimination in the treatment of women in workplace. A local officer in charge of Women's Rights union said, abortions are free, children are abandoned in the maternity homes; they are also facing problems from gypsies – a tribal group who reject any effort to integrate themselves with the local population. They steal a lot and are fast coming into the cities and are disrupting normal life. The problem of orphans is also a distressing one as mothers abandon their children in hospitals. The people do not know whether they belong to the popular government, municipal government or federal government. They find this transition of the political system from collectivism to private ownerships difficult and painful. The churches came forward with some money when they had difficulty with resources. Initially, the women were very suspicious but now they are benefited as they are fighting against unemployment and for women's rights. Another representative from Romania is a teacher and a single woman. She also reported about the social and economic problems which were never discussed during the communist regime. As a writer to many journals, she said, she had created awareness in women about the problems they face and now there was a strong public opinion against the former communist regime.

Guban City : The racial problem in Guban City of East Berlin bordering Poland is a serious one that has arisen due to contrast labour from Angola, Vietnam and other countries. Children of mixed marriages suffer greatly. The collapse of communism has left the people in confusion and chaos. They feel they were better off during communist regime when there was atleast good education for children and health services were free. Now unemployment is as high as 40 per cent while underemployment is 17 per cent. The social conditions are as bad as the economic ones. Young women of 20 go in for tubectomies since they do not want to have the burden of raising children at the present high cost of living. Earlier, for four room apartments they paid just 50 Marks. Now for two room apartments they pay 250 DM. School drop outs are very high since they cannot buy books that cost as high as 100 DM. Out of 1000 children 16 die. 40 per cent of women are unemployed and 45 per cent of women are single. The political changes might integrate the women into political process, but the economic situation is so bad that women are in constant fear of losing their existing jobs.

Belarus : In Belarus of the erstwhile Soviet Union, feminist ideas are not well received as there is a stigma attached to such views. It is only now when the women have had to face economic and other crisis that they are able to accommodate such ideas. There are economic crisis is totally depressing, especially since things were not too bad earlier. Now there is a high rate of inflation, incomes are low and unemployment is rampant. There is no help from the state in this transition period. In the communist regime, women were taught just slogan-mongering and were not organised under any issue. However, they hope that things will change for the better. The only thing that is improving amidst political confusion and economic degradation is human relations. The political participation is better now. They have access to mass media and information sharing. Help is forthcoming from friends abroad.

A participant from East Berlin who was a West German citizen working in East Germany, had gone through the oppressive male dominated mechanism existing there. The women were not given maternity leave but were expected to raise the birth rate to increase the labour force. Those who believed in the patriarchal idealogy were given special treatment. Further, intellectuals were not given due respect.

The view was refuted by another participant who said that the life in GDR was much easier than it is with reference to education, employment and cost of living now.

An African-American from National Congress of Neighbourhood talked about the conditions of the African-Americans and Native American women in the US. She said that laws were passed in the US to systematically oppress certain people and keep them from exercising their rights. Even among jews women are oppressed. The welfare systems of the state perpetuate poverty among the African-American working class. These people are insisting on better work opportunities, following the Civil Rights Movement of Martin Luther King who had followed Mahatma Gandhi in many ways. She was happy to have emerged better after the conference and expressed solidarity for women everywhere.

One should live with an impression that Eastern Block now in this hour of crisis should strengthen their relationship with the developing countries, like Africa, Asia and Latin America rather than being carried away by their West European and American partners. The strategy of power relations of the richer countries would be such that the current romanticism of unification process might initially look very attractive, but soon will vanish and the people of the Eastern Block will be treated as partners in distress and not as first among the equals. The poor must stay together for their own clout.

Despite the unprecedented upsets faced in social, economical and political fronts, it was encouraging to see that women have stood up and withstood these onslaughts and are well on course towards creating solidarity amongst themselves so that they can work for a better future for themselves and their children.

Women and their Role in the Development of Cooperatives*

Introduction

With the ever-increasing population pressure on one side and the sharp decline of natural resources on the other, we in the developing countries are left with only few options as our national plan-priorities. The issues before us are : Is it creation of wealth or distribution of wealth? Is it our-reach process or empowerment process to help option, i.e., develop our human resource material? Then what kind of human material do we have in all developing countries? 40 per cent of them are poor; 60 per cent of them are illiterates, and if we take 100 rural households, 30 out of 40 households are landless. Majority of these poor live and work as unorganised groups in the informal sector and therefore, empowerment of the poor becomes imminent.

Role of NGO's

Who then should take up this work of mobilising and empowering the vast human resources of this country? Is it government or non-government organisations? Successful experiments in the developing countries show that empowering, the powerless has been effectively handled by NGOs being near to the grassroots; their initiatives had been crucial in the promotion of voluntary effort.

The Informal Sector

The concept of this informal sector (where 90 per cent of the working population live and work) is a peculiar phenomena to developing countries alone and there is nothing equivalent to this sector ever found in the developed nations. But paradoxically, even in Indian situations the successive Indian Labour Ministries have been the shadows of colonial past and deal only with the working population of the organised sector. They have failed to recognise the organisations of the rural poor and urban or their occupational unions. The situation worsens for the informal sector where they do not enjoy the solidarity of the organised sector unions. Organised sector unions, on the contrary pressurise the government not to recognise these unions or urban and rural poor.

Informal sector is a growing sector and generates new employment opportunities for the poorest. But non-recognition by the respective governments, results in the invisibility of these workers, making their

---

*Curtsy- Special Commemorative Issue on Sri. Vaikunta Mehta at Vaikunta Mehta National Institute of Cooperative Management, Pune.

work unaccounted in the country's statistics. Most of these groups belonged to any formal or informal unions. Further, lack of access to training, technology or a permanent trading place results in their abysmal working and living conditions. In order to give them a fair deal, a knowledge on the real percentage of India's working population is essential.

Working Population in India

India has 297 million workers - 30 million organised and the rest of 267 million remain in the unorganised sector, i.e., 905 of working population has no formal or informal unions. About 25 million earn about Rs.250 to Rs. 500 per month, rest only earn about Rs.122 to Rs. 300 per month. 150 per cent agricultural workers - 18 millions are construction workers; 17 millions are child labourers; 6 million are beedi rollers, 48 per cent are under-employed and 89 per cent are women. These facts provide the real need to create a better social and physical environment for these workers by a process of unionisation.

Objectives of WWF

Working Women's Forum thus initiated its unionisation process in 1978 to help women in the informal sector with four main objectives.

Cooperative Perspective

(1) (a) Mobilising and empowering the poor women workers; (b) Creating a visibility to their value economic roles; (c) Preparing them for collective action.

(2) Provide an informal structures, easy to make their participation effective at all levels in the organisation;

(3) (a) To be target-oriented, dealing only with women workers. (b) Make women an entry point for development.

(4) The union to address itself to the critical needs of women, such as credit, health and family planning, training, vocational guidance for adolescent girls, child labour rehabilitation centres for child workers and promote inter-caste marriages.

The ideologies of the objectives are (a) To empower the poor women to confront the caste, class and gender situation that weakens their positions. (b) To strengthen leadership, and encourage their total participation at all levels towards a self-management and self-reliant strategy.

In the city of Madras, the Forum works with street vendors, pavement hawkers and service specialists (like washerwomen). It works with landless women in Dindigul, with fisherwomen in the Tanjore coastal area, beedi rollers and match stick workers in the villages around Vellore town and more recently with women weavers in and around Kanchipuram town.

In Karnataka, the Forum mainly works with agarbathi rollers in Bangalore town, beedi and agarbathi rollers around the Chennaptna villages and with landless women in the Bidar district. In Andhra Pradesh, the Forum works mainly with women lace artisans in Narasapur, and the West Godavari district, and with the weavers and rope makers in the villages of East Godavari district. Recently, the WWF has initiated its unionisation work with children embroidery workers in the urban slums of Lucknow city and with children of migrant women labourers in the Kanpur industrial town.

Women form into small groups, at the grassroots, electing their own leader in a given area whether rural or urban. Facilitated by flexible and informal structure, women formed groups after groups and had spread the organisation quickly through mass-mobilisation approach. Their earlier experience made women good and efficient managers of their new groups. Thus, the groups dynamics helped them to built a bottom-up approach and the small group at the grassroots in short had become the real administrative unit for women to learn and share from each other, experiment and expand their leadership and to confront obstacles collectively. In the early days of WWF, poor women joined the union in large numbers and in turn WWF could also reach, the poor in large numbers in short time. Thus, WWF has grown from its small base in Madras City slums and expanded into a multi state union, covering both urban and rural areas. Starting with 800 members, the Forum has grown into a massive union of over 1,60,000 members today.

Formal Systems of Banking in India

To understand the credit needs of poor women, it is necessary to understand the formal credit systems in India. Banking in India still remains a formal system requiring collaterals and securities. As most of these banks depend on the deposits collected from the elites, they have much reflected these in their lending policies too, i.e., preference for high rate of interest. They also have to satisfy their depositors through payment of interests, and above all meet their own high establishments costs. Such a system of banking, as experience proves does not help in the development of the poor. It is nothing, but a reflection of India's colonial banking system. Even the staff and employees of those banks are trained to deal with such formal situations and are very pathetic to poor.

But banks became nationalized in India in 1969 with a purpose only to reach the poor and help them. But then these banks made no serious efforts to help poverty alleviation programmes. Even the differential rate of interest schemes (DRI) introduced to help poor reached only a neglible number of poor women, i.e., about 1 per cent of the total profit of the nationalized banks is earmarked for this purpose. This cannot cover even a small percentage of the poor in the country.

The Moneylender's Role

Therefore, the other indigenous borrowing option of informal credit left to the poor are the moneylenders or the 'loan sharks' - system, disastrous in itself, with exorbitant rates of interest making the poor enmesh into continued indebtness. The poor women thus are even in the vicious circle of poverty. Nonetheless, this disastrous system alone remained easy and accessible vast majority of the poor as the only credit option. The poor pawned their land, house and jewels and finally lost everything in the bargain.

Credit System in WWF

The Working Women's Forum initially carried on their credit assistance through nationalized banks, but as the organisation expanded with more members it had become a problem with the nationalized banks. The banks refused to operate on small loans in large numbers, but women in WWF through their own collective banking system in 1981, both informal and easy to operate. WWF's credit initiatives are called Working Women's Cooperative Societies, and each of them are registered under a separate legal identity under the norms of Government Cooperative Department in state of operation (Tamil Nadu, Andhra Pradesh and Karnataka).

Operational Strategy - WWCS

In the WWCS, the credit organisers are from the slum-neighbourhoods and therefore are to help identify, select, guarantee, and supervise the end use of loans precises. They also take the responsibility for the collection and repayment of monthly instalments. The most admirable quality of these local leaders is that they take even such higher responsibilities, i.e., to provide pressure on default members. This is a phenomenon not found in the nationalized banking system.

A Simple Credit Model to Help the Poor

The WWCS, a simple credit group model promoted by WWF, is an economically system suitable for replication and the Forum has been able to replicate this much faster both in terms of members and the areas covered. Remarkably, the Forum has been able to retain its grassroots character throughout its replication and expansion efforts.

The performance of the WWCS has been uniformly the same in all branches, staff selection efficiency and training, accurate record keeping and a low percentage of bad debts are but the exemplary work of the workers and staff.

Training an Internal Part of Operational Techniques

An integral part of WWF/WWCS is its operational strategy, i.e., the meetings and training programmes efforts give women opportunities to come and share their experience also infuse both social confidence and articulation group leaders, organisers etc. Training efforts are modified to suit local conditions and problems in various branches of WWF.

Further in a year, there are 48 training programmes conducted by these Cooperation society collectively and about 1440 women leaders are trained every year, at the rate of 120 per month or 30 per week in the Madras branch alone. Likewise, in all branches, there are atleast two training programmes every months, i.e., approximately, 720 leaders being trained in each of the branches in a year. Thus, a total of about 6000 to 7000 leaders are trained in all the branches of WWCS. This includes the one-day training the new members receive before their first loan option.

The Client Characteristic in WWCS

Regarding the client characteristics of the WWCS, 35 per cent are urban clientele and 65 per cent are rural, and 100 per cent women intensive. Over 99 per cent of assistance goes to group ventures. About 56 per cent of the members are illiterate, 7 per cent of them studied between classes IX to XI, 15 per cent of them have studied upto class VIII and 22 per cent of them have studied upto class V.

The age group of these women range from 22 to 50 years. About 37 per cent of the members are in 22 to 30 years category, 18 per cent are in the 31 to 40 age group and 34 per cent are between 41 and 50 years of age. Only 11 per cent are about 51 and above.

Regarding the entrepreneurial ventures, 81 per cent of women are retail traders but operating in groups, 16 per cent of them are service specialists and only 3 per cent belong to manufacturing groups. Over 61 per cent of them are sole traders, over 14 per cent of them have their entire family helping their efforts, and 25 per cent of them have two members of the household working in their enterprises.

Cooperative Perspective

Most of the members use their loan both for working capital as well as buying small equipments. 72 per cent of the women invest in their business. 4.5 per cent of them invest in equipment. 17 per cent of them invest in household utensils, mostly by food hawkers, as business infrastructure, 6 per cent of them clear earlier loans. A very negligible number, i.e., 0.5 per cent have used it for education, legal expenses or to attend sickness in the family.

The Loan Process in WWCS

The processing of the loan, in the case of the first loan, is initially a delayed process, i.e., it takes nearly a month. This is so as the banking staff of the society have to find time to make from their routines and schedule, for their field visits and enquiries, for repeated loans the time taken for processing is quick not more than a week or 10 days.

The field officers of the cooperatives always visit the worksite of the loan applicants alongwith the group leader of the respective neighbourhood. After an on-the-spot assessment of the volume of business, the field officers help women to decide the quantum of loan depending on the nature of the trade.

Sometimes, such field visits help to eliminate women who try to duplicate the process of loan, e.g., those women having received loan through other credit groups, such as chit funds or the nationalized banks (which can be found in their family ration card), or use credit for various non-productive purposes. The loans are normally secured by the members on the guarantee of group leaders and the local organisers.

While, the first loan is invariably Rs.200, the second loan is between Rs.400 to Rs.800 depending on the volume of business, their repayment capacity keeping up the schedule. The maximum loan the society offers is Rs.3000 (Rupees three thousand). All the loan between Rs.200 and Rs.1500 are payable by members within 10 months. If the loans are above Rs.1600, members are given 20 months time for repayment.

Interest Rate in WWCS

Regarding the interest rates while it is 15 per cent per annum in WWCS, it works out to be only 8.25 per cent as the interest is computed on the decreasing capital. Prevailing rates of interest elsewhere in the country including in other cooperative per annum but DRI loans are limited to a small amount. About 13.5 per cent to 17 per cent interest is charged for rest of the loans in nationalized banks. The traditional moneylenders charge 3 per cent to 5 per cent per month.

Arrears in WWCS

Regarding the arrears in the WWCS, 30 per cent of the arrears are recovered within a period of three months, 50 per cent of the arrears the recovered in three to six months time and only 17 per cent are repaid over six months time. Regarding the recovery of the loan, the Forum only applied peer pressure through group leaders and does not use any coercive measures.

Default Rate in WWCS

The total percentages of the loan that is written of in the WWCS is very negligible, just 2.61 per cent. In the WWCS, despite the women being the poorest, failures to repay the loan takes place only when they are caught in disastrous situations, like floods or fire in the slums and squatted settlements.

Only 1.25 per cent of the WWCS are default members as they often migrate to other places. Failure to reconstruct themselves from their losses due to natural calamities like floods, fire or family difficulties, such as death, sickness of children or adults or unexpected accidents are other reasons for default.

Recovery Rates in WWCS

In the WWCS, the loan repayment rates are uniform and are as presented below:

Madras	95.7 per cent
Bangalore	95.7 per cent
Dindigul	97.8 per cent
Adiramapattinam	96.5 per cent
Vellore	95 per cent
Narasapur	99.9 per cent
Bidar	94.9 per cent

Savings in WWCS

Mostly clients of the WWCS are expected to participate in the savings programmers, but WWCS never makes savings as a precondition to receive financial assistance, taking into consideration the situation of the poor women who initially struggle to find resources for membership and share, to be admitted to the union and credit society.

Insurance in WWCS

The most innovative efforts of the Forum has been the programme of group insurance. It is said that any such efforts will be difficult to initiate to benefit the works in the unorganised sector. But women workers in WWF, in the age group of 25-55 do have this benefit of insurance through the Life Insurance Corporation of India. The Working Women's Cooperative Society undertakes to collect the premium for these workers. The premium is determined on the basis of the duration of membership of the women in the WWF.

Other Integrated Programme in WWF Health and Family Welfare

There are other examples in the WWF to demonstrate the effective leadership role of these women, such as the implementation of a planned health and family welfare programme both in the urban slums of Madras and rural areas of Tamil Nadu. These health cadres from the slums and rural areas of 90,000 families in the slum and 60,000 families among the rural areas. They have effectively carried out referral services to help women reach MCH facilities and family welfare services both in PHC and government hospitals. These grassroots health care workers, have helped too accomplish a couple protection rate of 70 per cent through group meetings, nutrition demonstration, through educational and motivational methods among the poor slum dwellers.

Inter-caste Weddings

The large scale inter-caste weddings are one of the special features of this union to fight caste and dowry oppression. WWF continuously makes this effort to stand firm to help those who believed in such inter-caste wedlocks, especially among the poor communities.

In Fact of Credit Programme in WWCS

Often, the feasibility studies are conducted in WWF/WWCS from time-to-time to assess both the empowerment process of women and the progress of various programme including credit. The facts emerged have revealed valuable insights as given below. The parameters used, helped us not only to assess the actual tangible changes in the life style and living standards of members but also high level empowerment process these women have reached. The degree of optimism, hope, confidence and courage these women have gained and heightened their awareness of the static situation in which they lived/earned and the desirable changes they perceived to mould their future was evident.

Further such studies indicated some of the direct result of the credit assistance to the poor. Valuable information of women's contribution to family, income and economy become evident from what the women reported. In general, women reported that they were able to pursue many occupations with the help of credit which would not have been possible otherwise.

Women as Contributors to Family Income / Economy

Nearly 84 per cent of the total membership of women in WWF are sole contributors to the family income bearing the economic burden of the families. 92 per cent of women reported that they are able to provide their families two squares meals a day. 75 per cent said they are relieved from the moneylenders. About 40 per cent of the women have diversified their business, some have either initiated new ventures or have additional business now. 98 per cent of respondents reported to own necessaries of the household. 96 per cent of the respondents said to have saved their profits in the forms of investment both movable and immovable, such as livestock. 75 per cent invested their savings on housing and 66 per cent of them have invested in the renewal or extension, of their houses or added civic amenities to their existing households.

There study further proved that women wanted to move from marginal and subsistence level trading to higher options. These are the real indicators in WWF / WWCS of women's desire for an upward mobility from where they are. Women also desire to educate and train female children in their families to make them provide additional incomes to their households. This is a marked change in the attitudes of poor women and a positive step towards postponement of marriage of adolescent girls, preventing their being pushed into early marriage and motherhood. There are further indicators to prove that WWF/WWCS had been able to make women take positive and forward looking steps, and helped them in their decision-making efforts towards a self-reliant economy.

Future Programmes in WWF

In accordance with the desires of poor women themselves, WWF in the second phase of expansion 1992-1996, propose to promote few programmes towards their upward mobility. These are likely to be in the form of higher credit assistance in their present entrepreneurial ventures, technological support to their current trading activities, better housing facilities, add civic amenities to their existing house and drinking water pumps. Also provide smokeless chullah and bio-gas work, to help organising of trade cooperative for collective bargain for better profit margins.

In the previous paragraphs it is evident, that the earlier credit option had relieved women from their day to day struggle of the debt trap of the moneylenders and the consequent continued indebtedness and poverty. Further, WWF's future proposals are to move towards enhanced social development programmes improving the quality of life among the poor women.

Are Poor Bankable?

The details given above prove beyond doubts that banking for the poor is economically viable. Facts further indicate that the poor also can manage their own situations, however, poor and powerless they are if provided the right kind of orientation and empowerment. It is also proved that illiteracy had not been a barrier for the poor to participate in development. Tables enclosed will further prove the accomplishment of WWF in this endeavour.

WWF's Effort to Networking in Sisterhood

Innovative experiments, such as the Working Women's Forum have emerged in response to the global need to have a better world for the poor to live in. In its existence of over a decade, the WWF has collected significant experience to empower poor women towards better working and living conditions. Such experiences have to be effectively transferred to other areas and countries to help create such models.

WWF's recent experiment to transfer its expertise promoted a global network called Grassroots Women Organising Ourselves Together in Sisterhood (GROOTS). In March 1990, in Bangalore GROOTS International and the Working Women's Forum hosted a meeting of nearly 22 women representatives, from 19 countries around the world and 65 of voluntary agencies in South Asia. These women met in a global meeting followed by a Workshop on Leadership Development with an objective to continue this networking process to benefit empower the poor women.

This effort generated lot of enthusiasm among the voluntary agencies in South Asia and each one has pledged to themselves to network within their own region with other small and less known voluntary agencies. The WWF plans a series of such regional networking seminars and workshops among other groups of women in South Asia, South East Asia and Africa and if necessary, in Latin America too.

Compliments to WWF

The following paragraph from the Joint Evaluation Mission, of Government of Netherlands is a compliment to the Forum, "judged by any standard, national or international, the Working Women's Forum (WWF) is a remarkable and successful institution. In terms of numbers, the Forum has more women staff and members than probably any other non-government organisation in India and all but a few non-government organisations in the world. Even more notably, almost all of the staff are from the same social-economic class as the membership, that is, from poor working class households. (Report of the Evaluation Mission, Government of Netherlands).

The prominent development experts in the world feel that Forum is a counter culture aiming at the priorities of the poor women. To quote Dr. Chambers, "Forum works for the poor, promotes leadership from below and exercises clout to get their rights".

Conclusion

The Forum can be perceived as a political process for the economic empowerment of the poor. Such an empowerment process is far superior to keep the women together than any material programmes. Thus, the ideology explains the massive growth and continuity of the Forum.

Table I

Working Women's Cooperative Society Limited
Progress of Credit Programme in Branches in Tamil Nadu and Other States

Place	Year of starting	No. of Members in WWF (I)	No. of Loans	Loan Amount disbursed	Recovered debts		Default Groups	Recoverable Loan Outstanding		Bad debts	
					Amount	per cent		Amount	per cent	Amount	per cent
Madras											
Central Madras	1981	50156	27891	14653776	14018919	95.7	277	396502.69	2.7	2,38,354.3 1	1.6
North Madras											
South Madras											
Rural Tamil Nadu											
Adiramapattinam	1985	17123	15112	5000200	4823268	96.5	149	177877	3.4	5055	0.1
Dindigul	1985	15959	12921	3420900	3344457		79	56690		16753	
Vellore	1984	13906	15035	5061000	4814555	97.8	206	173095	1.7	73350	0.5
Kanchipuram	1990	2561	1943	1996600		95.1			3.4		1.5
Karnataka											
Bangalore	1987	21638	21638	4662800	4450114	95.4	229	113275	2.5	99411	2.1
Bidar	1988	9995	9995	2227600	2113350	94.9	165	110750	5	3500	0.6

Contd.

Place	Year of starting	No. of Members in WWF (I)	No. of Loans	Loan Amount disbursed	Recovered debts	Default Groups	Recoverable Loan Outstanding	Bad debts			
					Amount	per cent	Amount	per cent	Amount	per cent	
Andhra Pradesh											
West Godavari	1984	41480	39382	9314100	930379100	99.9	4	10309	0.1	-	-
East Godavari	1984	6717	6471	1751245	1746245	-	-	5000	-	-	-
Bhimavaram	1988	5158	5570	1601700	1599700	-	-	2000	-	-	-
Total		184690	134283	49689921	46214399	96.4	1109	1045498.69	2.08	436423.31	1.07

Table II

The Position of Progress Report for Health and Family Planning from 1980-1989 Three Projects

Details	*Madras*	*Vellore*	*Adiramapattinam*	*Dindigul*
1	*2*	*3*	*4*	*5*
Total No. of Slums and Villages	319	39	46	64
Total No. of Workers	480	45	45	46
Total No. of Families	1,10,000	10,800	10,200	10,500
Total No. of Population to be covered	5,36,313	53,914	48,406	50,589
Total No. of Eligible couples to be covered	89,548	9,112	8,503	8,496
Total No. of Children under 5 years	79,147	8,307	6,305	7,013
Family Welfare & Child Health				
Total No. of Permanent acceptors	45,446	3,654	2,957	3,757

Contd.

Contd.

1	*2*	*3*	*4*	*5*
Total No. of Temporary acceptors	32,779	3,405	3,437	3,186
Total No. of Family Planning acceptors	78,2 25	7,059	6,394	6,943
Total No. of children immunised	3,353	-	-	-
Total Coverages in Ist Phase (1980-83)	98 per cent	-	-	-
Total Coverages in IInd Phase (1984-85)	88 per cent	90 per cent	87 per cent	94 per cent
Total Coverage in IIIrd Phase (1986-89)	82 per cent	77 per cent	73 per cent	80 per cent

Table III

The Number of Inter-caste Marriage Conducted From 1978 to 1991

Year	*Num-ber of Marriages*	*Marriages where either bride or grooms as a Adi Dravid*	*Inter-caste Hindu*	*Hindu & Christian*	*Hindu & Muslim*	*Christian & Muslim*
1978	63	54	45	8	1	-
1979	91	45	45	1	-	-
1980	106	73	24	5	4	-
1982	59	46	7	4	2	-
1985	101	58	9	30	4	-
1991	51	32	28	-	-	1
Total	**471**	**308**	**113**	**48**	**11**	**1**

Credit Cooperatives Worldwide Answers to Globalisation from the point of view of Developing Nations - Cooperative Vision*

I am privileged to be here at this meeting of the Raiffeisen Union that has been the beckon light of organising the artisans and workmen not only in Germany, but also in other parts of Europe. Further, this innovative cooperative ideology has brought prosperity to small farmers, producers, artisans and micro entrepreneurs in large numbers. Similarly, the cooperative movement in India has been associated with the freedom struggle as its founding fathers such as Sri.Vaikunth Mehtaji were in search of new approaches to economic freedom immediately after the achievement of political freedom in the late 40s of the last millennium. They aimed at the development of a socialistic pattern of society that would enable a balance between individual freedom and state control to serve the Indian masses who until then were exploited subjects of a colonial rule. The promoters of the cooperative movement in India visualised this unique system of a co-operative effort to emerge as a social movement to allow people to play a crucial role at all levels in upholding the principles of democracy and the philosophy of social utility. To quote, the first Prime Minister of India, Sri Jawaharlal Nehru, who stated that the basic principles of democracy rested on "a village school, a village Panchayat and a village cooperative". Cooperatives were thus visualized as effective instruments of social development in the hands of millions of men and women, especially in rural society.

I am particularly happy to participate at this meeting because IRU has been initiated for the same reasons as the Indian Cooperative Network for Women (which I represent here), i.e., to help and support the poor women worker. The approach has not been just to extend only credit per se to the clients but to provide a social platform so that they could commonly find a solution to their problems of poverty and powerlessness. In fact, instead of addressing only the economic interests of the poor, the effort has been to use credit for building a strong socio-political platform where the demands of workers and artisans could have a voice, empowering them to become more self-reliant through self-help process of management. Thus, the Working Women's Forum and Indian Cooperative Network for Women combine with Its unique and innovative experience of over two decades, concentrated on this success formula to

---

*Speech delivered at Raiffeisen, Vienna Austria on 20th Oct 2000.

i.e., integrating the approach so as to build a platform for the poor to carry on their struggles towards their requirements. This dynamic process of ideally combining and integrating credit and other services has been a pragmatic move and a long-term plan to empower the poor for speedier poverty reduction. This prepares the ground for a self-reliant and self-management process that provides collective strength to the mass of the urban and rural communities of the poor. The group process has not only brought divergent groups of people together, but also attended to the diverse needs of the clients including business counseling, health care, social support system and training towards their empowerment. Ultimately this cooperative effort as a training ground has gained clout to solve mutual problems. This innovative methodology not only led to multiplication in large numbers, but also has reached multitudes such as this in short time as a mass movement.

Expectation of Members of IRU

I have an appeal to place at this global meet, i.e., the process of recommendation at this Summit should not only include economic benefits for the poor but also a strategy to address the socio-economic cultural problems that perpetuate poverty and powerlessness in many of the developing countries. An isolated economic process cannot hope to address, social cultural problems but will only end up perpetuating the process of imposing the debt burden on the poor particularly in the developing world. Economic assistance must be only an entry point towards achieving the larger goals of human development process.

ICNW as an experiment has been able to make successful interventions in the lives of thousands of poor women relieving them from the stranglehold of poverty and indebtedness. Poor women workers engaged in varied occupations, such as hawking, vending, beedi (country cigar) rolling, silk weaving, sericulture, agarbathi (incense stick) rolling and lace making are shareholders of the Cooperative Network. The credit system not only styled itself as a grossroots initiative but has rearhedow exclusively to the poorest communities through an innovative delivery mechanism. Such a mechanism has avoided any pilferage of vital resources, eliminating the domination of the educated and the elite, making it a peoples movement managed by the poor themselves.

Poor Women's Banking

In the ICNW, the grassroots women, most of them who are illiterate or semiliterate, are today not only control but are also able to handle sophisticated banking operations with the help of carefully devised field-oriented policies. The lifeline of the credit programme is its unique neighbourhood group concept. Its simplicity being both in formation as well as function. Each group has 10 to 12 members and has proved successful in capitalising the existing neighbourhood relations. The simple credit group concept has been responsible for the rapid growth and multiplication of groups throwing up in ten's and million's of grassroots women leaders in a short span of time.

Accomplishments of the ICNW

The solid grassroots character of the organisation has been maintained in spite of the organisations amazing growth over the years. Women from the poorest neighbourhoods join as members and go on to become leaders, organizers, trainers, managers and programme functionaries in the organisation. The organisers of the credit programme also take up the task of constant monitoring on end use of loans and vigilant follow up action on defaulters. The reason behind ICNW's achievement is its remarkable recovery rate of over 95 per cent uniformly in all the branches of its operation. Thus, reaching out to women from the poorest communities is not only because of its field-oriented policies, but also due to its field monitoring that maximises client participation. Committed grassroots cadres have transcended barriers of caste, literacy and class and have redefined social activism by their active participation in the development process, which has thus far remained the exclusive domain of the elites. Thus the ICNW has proved its effectiveness to serve as an instrument of social change, in utilising the human resource potential and the creativity of poor women, particularly through participatory methodologies leading to maximisation of client participation that is considered in all aspects from design, management, implementation upto the evaluation stage.

The success of ICNW is a testimony to the reality that the poor women are capable of not only surviving but also effecting a change process in their lives even amidst the greatest of odds. Women have proved that they can assume leadership and can be rich human resources too. The fact that the original capital fund of ICNW amounting to Rs. 31 million has grown to Rs. 555 million demonstrates that the enterprises of the poor are bankable, can grow and lead to a dynamic accumulation process too. Through the achievements of ICNW the credibility and the sustainability of the poor women's banking network has been established beyond doubt.

Holistic Approach

Impact studies conducted on ICNW, have shown that, 63 per cent of the women (shareholders) have used the credit exclusively for business purpose (See Figs. 1 and 2) while others have utilised a portion to meet basic survival needs. 60 per cent of the clients who were wage earners are now micro-entrepreneurs (See Figs. 3). The'rest of them demonstrate that micro-credit has generated new employment among those who had no means to ply a trade of their own.

About 62 percent, of these women have saved but 50 per cent of them have invested in drinking water facilities, housing, gold jewellery, electricity, civic amenities and so on (See Fig. 4). These indicators, while demonstrating the level of poverty that these women were originally subjected to also indicates the resilience with which the women have risen from those oppressive conditions.

The Indian Cooperative Network for Women promoted by the Working Women's Forum (India) thus had taken root to serve larger interests as visualised by the founding fathers of this movement in India. It has evolved itself as a network of grassroots women functioning in the three southern states of India.

After expanding its operations to three southern states of India - Tamil Nadu, Andhra Pradesh and Karnataka, WWF in its second phase of its expansion, replicated its efforts in the northern and eastern parts of the country by a process of identification and training of NGOs working among the most disadvantaged communities. These NGOs have been helped to establish credit ventures along the lines of ICNWs credit operations adapted to suit the local cultural context. The sharing of expertise has further been extended across the borders of nationality whereby several development organisations both from the South Asian region as well as from other parts of the world have been able to learn from the experiences of ICNW through an interactive process.

Such a holistic approach that treats poor women as a rich human resource utilising their innate wisdom and creative methodologies through which they have managed to survive for generations in the developing countries can only result in changing the lives of the poor. This alone will lead to the liberation of the powerless, demonstrating that the poor are also rich in human resource and underutilisation of them will lead to perpetuation of poverty and squalor.

Financial Indicators of ICNW

Percentage of women clients	-	100.00%
Percentage of Rural clients	-	74.00%
Percentage of Urban clients	-	26.00%
Percentage of women staff	-	100.00%
Shareholders	-	2,791,618
Working Capital (in Rs.)	-	55 Million
Members Share Capital (in Rs.)	-	23.1 Million
Members Savings Capital (in Rs.)	-	38.4 Million
Loan portfolio (in Rs.)	-	589 Million
Cost of funds	-	11.00%
Interest rate on Savings deposit	-	7.00%
Interest rate on Fixed deposits	-	8-11%
On time repayment rate	-	97.09%
Onlending interest rate	-	18% on declining balance
Average Repayment period	-	10 months
Average portfolio per branch	-	3.46 Million
Average portfolio per staff	-	620,389
Average caseload per field org. (clients)	-	1,182
Average caseload per field org. (groups)	-	147
Average portfolio per group	-	6,724
Portfolio in arrears	-	1.40%
Portfolio at risk	-	0.27%
Loan loss ratio	-	6.10%
Operating Self Sufficiency	-	206.00%
Financial Self Sufficiency	-	125.00%
Percentage of voluntary Savings	-	100.00%

2

Roadblocks to Women's Empowerment*

Women today are at the cross roads and feel that they are in a state of minority even today, despite being one half the human kind in an independent nation, where many social legislations are in favour of them alongwith a constitutional guarantee assuring their equality unlike in many other countries. While democratic process and electoral systems have thrown up a few women leaders at the helm of affairs particularly in this region, such an emergence of individual leaders has had little or no impact on the general status of women. Therefore, one question that looms on every other right-thinking women in this country is, where are the women in the National Agenda today? Is there any gender justice prevalent? Whether such emergence of Women Leaders has had any impact on the status of women?

History bears evidence that how sizable number of women during India's independence struggle participated in the struggle for freedom and fought against the British. Yet after this, when the National Government was formed women have been laid back on the way bereft of their expectations. Therefore, experience shows that in a male dominated system of governance, where men have a traditionally larger say in the day-to-day affairs of the country, women's question received at all time a low priority, even when women were at the helm of affairs. But the country is not left with few exceptions too.

The UN declaration of International Women's Year in the year 1975 has been a provocation for many National Governments. This made the then Prime Minister, Late Smt. Indira Gandhi, enact two important social

*Speech at Parliamentary Standing Committee on Women on March 1st 2003 at Parliament Annex.

legislations in favour of poor rural women workers. Having been the champion of the poor and the downtrodden, Smt. Gandhi took a bold step to challenge the feudals and the rural rich by enacting the two landmark legislations, namely the Minimum Wages Act and Equal Wages for Equal Work. However, at the enforcement level still, it is difficult for the rural women to enjoy its full benefits. The complacency of the bureaucracy and the deep-rooted prevalence of feudal forces are still a great impediment at the grassroots.

Even the question of women's reservation of 33.5 per cent in the local bodies of governance has similar difficulties. While the 73rd and 74th amendments are historic constitutional amendments in favour of women, the implementation remains an arduous job at Panchayat and Nagarpalika levels. It took place because of the exceptionally strong political will demonstrated by the late Shri. Rajivji, the then Prime Minister of the country. In fact, men who cannot tolerate strong teams of women leaders in the tradition bound male bastions and are feeling more secure when the leaderships are in the hands of their own wives and daughters. This is the truth majority of women have to face today in the local body elections.

Therefore, the women's rights movement in the country is facing a major challenge. It has to fight at the outset the perpetuation of inequal social systems. Time to time, it is no exaggeration to quote instances, as a negation to women's progress we find sporadic incidents of such male dominance, in incidents like in the revival of Sati in Rajasthan in late 80's, revival of Devadasis system in the State of Orissa more recently. The caste and class bias are further aggravating gender discrimination in all walks of life. We see today the worst forms of oppression are inflicted on the women of scheduled caste and tribes. For instance, women who are responsible for producing half the food needs of the country, despite prevalence of laws regarding wage question not only are women paid less wages, but also have to work as unpaid workers where the entire family works towards the survival needs in many areas even today. Therefore, women's subordination at home reflects in the workplace too.

In the matter of education and literacy, it is the gender bias that is reflected in the large number of girls being drop outs at school even before their primary schooling ends. Currently, the large prevalence of domestic violence and dowry deaths everywhere, raises a question and doubt in our mind, is marriage the only option for women? Is it a security or an impediment? Nonetheless women are also at fault, being not aware of the fact that when they are even more highly educated than men, why should their families accept to pay a larger amount of dowry for an equal or less educated man as a match? This is where our young women are in a dilemma between the security of tradition and the promise of change.

Women in middle class are largely full-time career persons these days. Many of them are sole earners for the families. Their employment situation in managerial position is based generally on education, professional qualification and personal abilities. It is observed by experience that women largely are potential personnel for managerial positions and are available in large numbers. This fact is not reflected in actual positions. Probably, this is partly due to lack of initiatives on the part of our educated women themselves. They are conditioned by traditional Indian values, lacking effectiveness to integrate their own self to the various roles they have to play. Educated Indian women must become conscious of the demands in their own career-growth and be prepared to redefine their roles and not be conditioned by role conflicts within themselves.

In the matter of health imposition of female sterilisation, towards population reduction efforts, why not men take responsibility? Whose responsibility is it? Is it only women? Why not men? In whatever circumstances women are placed, however poor women are, they not only give birth to children, but are also bearing the double drudgery of home and work? Is she not taking responsibilities to feed her children and family on her own even in case of low male contribution to the family? Instead of more burdens, is she not entitled for a safe motherhood and child survival treating her motherhood as a social role? Instead why impose on her only responsibilities of female sterilisation for population reduction?

Let us take the question of human settlements. Isn't drinking water still a problem in many of the city slums? Why should not people in governance who are at the helm of urban development make an integrated approach to the planning of cities where all the requirements of slum dwellers be taken care off? Daily wage earners, vendors and hawkers do need opportunities for gainful employment and drinking water supply. However, the present multi-storied buildings in many city slums emerging, as concrete slums are not the answer. Women have to carry water to the fourth and fifth floor. Why not people in governance plan satellite towns instead of swelling the existing towns with more people? This will save women from the scarcity of employment, drinking water and safe place for her children to play around. In the rural areas like wise have they ever thought of integration of all irrigation systems with drinking water amenities in rural areas? No, this is because drinking water is women's domain and irrigation schemes are men's domain.

Women suffer more in poverty than men as it is pressured by all that poverty bears the women's face in this country. This is because in our division of social responsibilities in the families, despite constitutional guarantees, the question of women's property rights, wage question are not well-defined in conventions. Therefore, our social legislations are only in paper, women are systematically excluded from all benefits, a reality of micro economic situation at the grassroots. Thus, no well-defined property rights adopted by families till today, as still the male children are the priorities for inheritance. Therefore, even the land reforms process excludes women. Such systematic exclusions of women everywhere are the prime reasons for feminisation of poverty.

The media in the modern times though has a very important role to play in formulating policies and creating public opinion, especially on women's issues for the TV and other visual medias. It seldom realises women's question and needs, rights and entitlement. On the contrary, women are only glorified as objects of lust and enjoyment but not as half of the human kind with creative abilities.

Even among the educated women, the principal impediment that we work towards advancement, whether in education or in employment or other fields, is the problem of exclusion women participants in the process of planning their careers. Non-participation of women, particularly both in the planning and in the implementation process results continuously in the women's deprivation of career advancement in many fields.

To sum up, the analysis take the situation in women's life cycle as it exists today the reality as it follows. She is a victim of foeticide in the mother's womb, a widely prevalent custom in the backward regions of India. If she escapes that she will die of infant mortality, neglected as a girl child in the wake of the male child syndrome. She is a school drop out and has to bear the brunt of the entire household chores, as an unwanted guest in the house pushed into early marriage and early motherhood. Finally, either she has to face a desertion or live in compromise in dowry menace or die as a victim of mother mortality or in bride burning.

Anti-poor policies of the government on the issue of natural resources management further marginalise the poor and women. Poor and tribals particularly in the forested regions have no control over even the minor forest produce. These are often contracted to the private monopolies who device arbitrary, adhoc exploitative policies against the principles of natural justice with a vested interest of establishing their monopolistic powers. State monopoly has given room for private monopoly which is aiding and abetting market imperfections, through corrupt practices at all levels. Also, almost all occupations in the urban informal sector, such as hawking, vending, small manufacturing in residential areas are proclaimed as illegal by municipal authorities in spite of their valuable contribution to the larger economic process. Has the government any better alternative for them?

Besides global economic policies, such as international trade agreements, humanitarian relief efforts, management of balance of payments and structural adjustments all have several implications on women's lives and alter the socio-economic conditions which women have to cope up with. Thus, women are rather not poor but are made poor.

This is evident in the most popular perception of country who glorify the global concepts of "economic reforms" or "market economy" and expect that this would lead us to conditions of prosperity is nothing but an illusion. Handing over everything to the outside forces towards a liberal economy, has not only created wide repercussions among the poor and vulnerable, it further intensifies the unprecedented challenges faced by women. They have to pay more even for basic necessities, and a heavy price during the era of ongoing economic reforms, without adequate increase in their income. This threatens the very survival of women and especially the poorest. Hence, considering the country's economic "growth rate" as more potential to country's progress rather than human resource development raises yet another question. What is the yardstick to the growth rate? Is it growth with the equity and social justice?

The issue of this women's reservation bill requires due attention by the governments and policy makers. Such discrimination and biases relating to human situations has direct relevance to the struggles of women of all sections. Hence this question can neither be overlooked nor be restricted to economic issues alone. This requires a strong political will and a vision to fight the class and patriarchal structure in our society, towards optimistic action. Therefore, the question of women's bill that advocates 33 per cent reservation in all walks of life has not only been a nonstarter so far with the past two governments, but also makes an attempt to divide women on the basis of caste, class, education and dismantling the efforts of the women's hard struggle along the way.

Once again the author's asking a question that how long should women continue to be a silent spectators to all this? Is it not time for women to perceive themselves as agents of social change and fight hard to complete the unfinished National Agenda on women's issues, at least in this millennium? Women today need social activism and self-perception to get over the obstacles towards their progress and empowerment. Sadly, yet another Women Day on March 8th will soon pass through without passing of women's bill.

Women and Development in India – Issues and Challenges*
"Choices before Women"

Introduction

Is it the choice of todays women to be patient or tolerant and be a role model of socio-cultural stereotype or is it the strategy of a tradition bound society to safeguard their outlived tradition to perpetuate gender subordination? Fact remains that majority of women even today live in a mirage brainwashed by the custodians of traditions, customs and patriarchs, sacrificing their honour, dignity, pride and even their identity with no reference in human history whatsoever. Consequently, women's multi-faceted personalities are little or seldom known. Their talents thwarted, they still continue to live as extension of their male counterparts.

Discrimination of Women at All Levels

The tradition bound patriarchal structures have denied women access to resources, capital and power. A prerequisite for any human being is to participate in useful careers, even institutions of marriage and family once again conditioned by customs and religion have limited women's equality and their equal status in society. Discriminatory practices and gender biases prevail on women in all walks of life from time immemorial, whether in education, employment at home, workplace or outside. We are fully aware of the problem of deprivation and discrimination perpetrated on women among the working class and among other classes of women too. Even the conscious changes that occur in the Indian society here and there, cannot be considered as a dominant change but a very vague instability as majority of women in India even today find themselves in a dilemma between the security of traditions and the promise of change.

Women and History

It is a sad reality that history has overlooked half the human existence. Women are invisible in history books. Topics that equally concern women, such as women's suffrage; their roles in country's affairs are given minor importance while they devote pages and pages to describe the adventures of men. Research on women and their accomplishments is a major missing link in all the disciplines as a systematic study. It is disheartening to find that presentation of female experience is totally discouraged in the entire

*At a Workshop held at Birla Institute of Technologies and Science (BITS), Pilani, India January 19th – 20th, 2000.

curriculum. Creation of women's studies department is a must in all the Indian Universities to continue meaningful research on women.

Women and Politics

The political parties not only in India, but also all over the world are in reality male dominated systems institutions and can never tolerate women leaders, who are dynamic in nature, to enter into their political process. When it comes to practice, very little or no effort is taken to integrate women in politics. The number of female parliamentarians as compared to male parliamentarians is not even 10 per cent in the Indian Parliament and State Assemblies. Women's reservation bill being stalled in the Parliament is a reflection of the strong male bastions existent even today.

Why Women alone in Family Planning Programme?

In the matter of family planning, country's statistics show that it is women who have adopted various family planning methods and are engaged in the task of population control and stabilisation. Why not men? As in China, why can't we treat the childbearing role of women as a social role? Absence of social securities and maternity benefits results in the degrading of a female child as a burden and increases the dependence on male child, particularly so among the poorer communities. Parents thus, look forward to the security of having a male child at any cost, even today. Result is that the female infanticide and child mortality among women are on the increase.

Need for Well-defined Property Rights

Well-defined property rights for women, i.e., equal shares for sons and daughters is very seldom practiced. Therefore, social evils like dowry are on the ascendant and continue to oppress women, treating them with such indignity as objects of financial transactions in many families. Dowry is not a one-time burden for women but it continues from birth to death. Dowry is an offshoot of class and caste system. In order to ascend the higher social order, many communities spend lakhs of rupees to find a husband for their daughter from upper class society.

Dowry Menace

Dowry encourages illiteracy as a girl attains the age of 12, she is stopped from going to school and the parents have to at any cost find huge sums of money either by borrowing or by other means to marry off their girls. Dowry encourages gender inequality. There are instances of many families with one or two sons having become very wealthy only by receiving dowries from the families of the girls. In spite of such heavy dowries, women in these households are treated as chattels and liabilities to be precise; they are used as unpaid domestic workers. Practice of dowry encourages illegal mean to acquire wealth. Therefore, one wonders what happens to Dowry Prevention Act, even as the most educated people remain ignorant of this legal provision. Dowry thus, remains as a custom having stronger roots in the communities, contradicts laws, moves in the direction of open violation of legal systems, increases its volume day by day and permeates into societies where it has never been a custom.

In the field of education, we know women are doing better, but still most young women get into jobs to earn their dowries. Parents also invest in women for her education as they invest in consumer goods, so that she can earn even after marriage and contribute to the family. A new education policy should make efforts to restore women their achievements and give them knowledge and methods to re-interpret their life experiences. Non-sexist counselling is a must at every level of education encouraging women to an increased range of options.

Why Social Legislations are Ineffective?

While legislations in favour of women enacted in the Indian Parliament to do away with such discriminations are innumerable, their benefit seem to have very little effect on women. Why? Who enacts the laws? It is the members of Parliament, 80 per cent of whom are men, where women's voice is totally neglected. Who enforces law? It is again the policemen whose total attitude is anti-women as they are cultured in male-dominated traditions. Who does the interpretation of law? It is the judges who are supposed to be the custodians of all the discriminatory religious and personal laws all over the country. Thus, such biases continue against women in the enactment of laws, enforcement of law and in the interpretation of law. In addition, to all these misinterpretations of the religious concepts on the one side, lack of awareness and total illiteracy on the part of women themselves make matters worse for them.

Change of Priorities in Women's Issue

Concerning women's issues in India today, there is a need to change our priorities and involve serious decisions to integrate women in all walks of life. The principal problem that we face in all women's programmes, whether education or employment or other fields, is the problem of exclusion women participants in the process of planning their careers. Non-participation of women, particularly both in the planning and in the implementation process results continuously in the women's deprivation of career advancement in many fields. Non-decision in the passing of women's bill in the Parliament is an impediment towards a decision-making process not only for the present day women also for future women too.

Women in Employment Position and Impact of Economic Polices on Women's Development and Progress

When the attention is drawn to the modern Indian situation, women in middle class are largely full-time career persons these days. Many of them are sole earners for the families. Their employment situation in managerial position is based generally on education, professional qualification and personal abilities. It is observed by experience that women largely are potential personal for managerial positions and are available in large numbers. This fact is not reflected in actual positions. Probably, this is partly due to lack of initiatives on the part of our educated women themselves. This is conditioned by traditional Indian values, lacking effectiveness to integrate their own self to the various roles they have to play. Educated Indian women must become conscious of the demands in their own career-growth and be prepared to redefine their roles and not be conditioned by role conflicts within themselves.

As warned by the Status of Women's Commission, as early as 1974, economic policies tend to further marginalise women's progress. The question before us is, whether poor in the informal sector or educated women have gained any employment prospects due to the economic reforms process. The overall economic liberalisation process depending on the market mechanisms has not been a major gain for any section of women in terms of employment – women's employment opportunities has not increased in public sector undertaking arising out of privatisation, women's position remain the last. The growth in the informal sector has doubled, where women are left to the vagaries and insecurities of the sector. Any power women had has been lost due to technological changes. Men's substitution is on the increase. Price of food articles has gone up and wages in actual terms has not increased. Therefore, fight for living wages, becomes all the more important in the present scenario.

Working Women's Forum – A Social Movement of Economic and Political Dimension

The need of the hour among women is now to take up strong leadership role to awaken the communities on the injustice that is being perpetuated on women for generations. It is also time for them to demonstrate true potential and build up a network of solidarity leading to a strong movement of women. In this connection, author would like to place before you the experiment of Working Women's Forum (India) (WWF), a social movement of very poor women of the urban slums and rural landless initiated in 1978. This action oriented voluntary initiative of the poorest women strategises to integrate all essential services through a convergence process to build a positive base in furtherance of a social change process.

When complicated procedures of government banks made access to credit impossible for poor women, the early members of WWF in the early 80's helped themselves to establish a banking system on their own that is both informal and easy to operate. Registering a cooperative in the name of Indian Cooperative Network for Women (ICNW) women promoted social and financial independence for themselves through micro and small enterprises development. Through a continuous inflow of low interest loans, generated and strengthened the economic roles of poor women, and led to income generation. Today, ICNW is an autonomous financially viable micro finance institution serving 2,54,455 women as shareholders and has effected a disbursement of over 504 million rupees with the recovery of 98 per cent covering 1200 slums and over 3000 villages. About 2,39,075 members have been covered by the social security coverage.

It is worth mentioning about a special project in WWF, which is its large scale of reproductive health care system to serve the poorest women who have been denied even the basic health care. It has been a partnership with United Nations Populations Fund and is a reflection of women's choices to have a holistic approach in the area of health care and not an imposition of crude methods of family planning or female surgeries etc. WWFs selection of women cadre from the poorest neighbourhood communities, to perform marketable skills in the field of health care to the poor, depicts them more as advocates on women's health needs at the grassroots. A human-centred approach of this health care project covers the entire life cycle of women from birth to adolescent, reproductive age group and transcends beyond even to the health care of older group of women. The project of health care covers about 16,00,000 families in 720 slums and 340 villages. In total programme has created employment to 960 health cadres who have been placed in the communities as network of permanent health cadres even beyond the project period, creating health consciousness in the poorer communities. The health care project also focuses on human rights issues, such as child survival, safe motherhood, fight against female infanticide, child mortality, child labour and child prostitution with the particular focus on the welfare and development of female children. Thus, the health care of WWF is a visible demonstration that the enhancement of the quality of life will result in the decrease of fertility rate.

While it is heartening to see that the Panchayat Raj system is picking up at the grassroots, WWF long before has laid emphasis on the decentralisation process toward making the poor women understand that they have to play a major role in their self-development process. They have to take leadership roles in the neighbourhood to educate their neighbourhood communities both to battle for the entitlement of the poor and to take care of their needs. Above all, to build a unit of solidarity, if necessary to organise rallies and demand marches to fight against injustices and atrocities perpetrated on poor, women in particular so as to achieve better visibility of the existence.

WWF success especially in three southern states of the Southern and Western parts of India can be analysed in development terms as growth with equity and distribution and betterment in quality of life resulting in women's visibility, increase in women's consciousness and a strong solidarity at the grassroots. At present, WWF is concentrating on its consolidating process by building up a strong partnership with other NGOs in the other states and is engaged in the effort of transferring its expertise to other organisations particularly in the northern parts of India towards building up a stronger network.

Conclusion

The issue and challenges of the millennium requires multi-focal strategies towards a long battle and continuous struggle process. People who have been monopolising power structures will not give it up easily. Women must therefore, be prepared for a long struggle and an onward march.

Women and Employment*

Introduction

Women workers form nearly 89 per cent of India's working population. Out of which 150 million are agricultural labourers, 18 million are construction workers, less than 6 million are beedi workers, more than 48 per cent of the unorganised workers are either unemployed or under employed. Therefore, women constitute a huge majority and account for 89 per cent ironically and 94 per cent of the world's population. Further, if one has to be conscious about the present India's socio-economic milieu, the realities are disheartening as 44 per cent in India, still live in poverty which means one-third of world's poor are from India. About 30 to 40 per cent of Indian population in major cities still lives in slums, one-third of child population live and work as child labourers and 89 per cent of the women workers work in the informal sector. About 290 million adults are illiterates, 250 million of the population has no access to drinking water, over 64 million live without basic sanitations, about 260 million or more of girl children live in malnutrition, 89 million women suffer from anaemia. Therefore, fighting poverty is a formidable challenge in India equally so in other countries of the subcontinent. Therefore, just simple provision of good services will not reduce poverty.

The above reflections are the outcome of 25 years of experience of the National Union of Working Women, a trade union of women workers in the informal sector. As an informal sector union, it has taken responsibility to bring in its fold over 7,00,000 poor women since 1978, recognising the fact that poor women have little or no control over land, income, other support services to relieve themselves from poverty and powerlessness. National Union of Working Women has predominantly unionised hawkers and vendors, micro entrepreneurs, service specialists, beedi workers, dairy women, fisherwomen, agricultural labourers, lace artisans, agarbathi rollers, silk weavers, landless poor, non-farm workers, handloom weavers and sericulturists, etc., in the three southern states of India, such as Tamil Nadu, Andhra Pradesh and Karnataka.

The Informal Sector – House of Poor

The informal sector in which the Working Women's Forum is focusing its strategies houses the majority of the poor, i.e., about 90 per cent of the working population is faced with unprecedented challenges that is

*The Speech delivered on the event of Gandhi Jayanthi celebration, Congress Party at Mahila Sashaktikaran Adhiveshan Sammelan, Talkatora Stadium on 1st October 2002, New Delhi.

disturbing their very base of survival. Women are forced to work more hours under oppressive working conditions so as to supplement the shortfall in their family income. Even in extreme conditions of poverty and squalor, women have always managed the basic well-being of their families, including nurturing of children, however meagre the resources are at their disposal. In reality, problems faced by these poor women relates to lack of access to market, materials and credit. As a result, are caught in a complex web of exploitative structures, such as middlemen, merchant contractors and moneylenders. Pressures of poverty, patriarchy and powerlessness push women into a closed and isolated world, where they are treated more as a chattels than as human beings.

The Caste and Gender Focus of the Informal Sector

The caste and gender bias is far more distinct among women in the unorganised sector particularly, those who deal with hides and animal skins, leather processing work, etc. This is often confined to women from the scheduled castes and stratified as the lowest in the social hierarchy perpetuating age-old caste bias. The prevalent patriarchal systems further perpetuate women's subordination and subjugation. Lack of clout of these poor women has led to ignoring the fact that they are in need of labour saving needs and technological inputs to reduce their drudgery and sub-human working conditions.

We have seen for over 55 years governments taking up a project-to-project approach regarding poverty alleviation. Ultimately such approaches have failed in our country, as more and more people have been pushed to poverty day-by-day. This is so as the projects were stopped and poor women went back to poverty. Yet another reason why we have to enhance women's employment is the traditional cultural practices of patriarchal system that has always been harsh on women. The under valuation of women's status at home reflects in workplace too, leading to discriminative practices on women's initiatives. Such discriminative practices has not only downgraded the most valuable economic roles of women, but also the kinds of variables she required for her role, besides gender, class or caste ideologies taking upper hand. Even when women are sole income generators or equal contributors to the family's income, her economic role has been considered as an extension of the household work, thus being poor and women disadvantage her. Bankers considered her as a non-bankable person; even access to technology has become very difficult particularly to the most backward scheduled caste women. Such women worked in hides and leather industries and therefore, they had to do it on their own by hands, a drudgery that was never reduced with any labour saving device.

Rural Poverty and its Critical Nature

It is a common scenario in the rural areas and pockets of urban areas wherein home-based work involves the entire family including children. Women working as unpaid labour, face unprecedented anomalies of malpractices in material supply and face severe cuts in their wages, which is largely discriminatory. Such operations continue to impoverish the poor primarily due to the ineffectiveness of implementation of social legislations enacted by the decision-making bodies from time to time. Such legislations are available only in paper, as without recognition of the informal sector unions and these women as workers on par with formal sector by the labour ministries of the respective countries, enforcement of legislations become almost impossible.

The struggle of the rural labour in India, and the aspect of migration of the vast majority of the rural working population to urban slums of the major cities is yet another cause for serious concern. Such migration contributes not only to the population explosion of the ever growing cities in India, resulting in environmental degradation. But it is also a common scenario in all the developing countries. The governments have to think of ways and means to increase employment opportunities in the rural areas to sustain these rural landless workers for atleast five to six months more in a year, to help check the permanent migration to cities as an annual feature. Initiating agro-based industries in rural areas as part of the liberalisation process will definitely help prevent this situation to some extent. This will enable the poor to participate in the reform process. Also, the land reforms have to be speedily implemented not only to create minimum assets for landless in the rural areas, but also make the rural poor to rapidly get out of the vicious circle of rural poverty.

Strategy to Enhance Women's Employment

Need of the hour is a well-planned productive employment process, particularly to women workers engaged in the informal economy as an important strategy is to be adopted. The experience shows undoubtedly poor and particularly women among them are valuable human resource and underutilisation of them leads to only perpetuation of poverty and squalor. Enhancement of women's employment in the informal economy is a relevant strategy. This is a initial step to help the poor women who are already working in many divergent employment options. When strategies to help them acquire new skills, build up their capacities to fight poverty are introduced, poor women are far more committed to their communities and they will take up their own initiatives to help the neighbourhood around and continue to sustain those communities as well.

Smt. Indira Gandhi's Valuable Contribution Towards Poverty Reduction

All of us are aware that how our beloved late Prime Minister Smt. Indira Gandhiji in the year 1969 initiated number of poverty reduction programmes particularly to benefit the poor. She has nationalised the banks, making them accessible to poor particularly to implement the 20 Point Programme, giving a clarion call, *Garibi Hattao* as nationwide strategy. Besides, in the year 1975, when United Nations declared the year as International Year for Women, she enacted important legislations that were landmark steps to fight poverty in rural areas. The Minimum Wages and Equal Remuneration Acts not only benefited women agricultural labourers, which were normally a blow to landlord's authority in rural areas, to make them pay a minimum stipulated wages to the agricultural labourers.

Shri Rajiv Gandhi's Vision and Landmark Initiatives

Later in the year 1984, it was after Shri Rajiv Gandhi became the Prime Minister, women particularly the poor in the nation experienced a real golden era for themselves also in the gender history. Various programmes, ideas and actions were implemented accelerating gender justice in the field of development. He was a missionary who initiated number of technologies to lead the country to 21st century. Particularly to envision that the advanced technological progress and advancement reach the people at the grassroots. Shri Rajivji particularly started providing weightage to women's movement to which many of us belong to, by understanding the positions of both poor women and their vulnerability. He said, "Women shall have the freedom of action for its really at the grassroots the discriminations must be removed as an obstacle to women's development". An ideal combination of a visionary and a man of action, Rajivji initiated a Prospective Plan for women before the country could reach the next millennium addressing all issues on women both in urban centres and rural areas. The Prospective Plan for women was a complete compendium to lead women to 21st century to achieve full progress. Further, he appointed a 28 member committee under his chairmanship to advice the government on implementation of this plan and also on the functioning of the national mechanisms, that were initiated as a follow-up to forward looking strategies of the closing decade of the United Nations conference at Nairobi in 1985. All of us who attended the Beijing Conference appreciated India and the Indian Prime Minister. All the National machineries, such as National Commission for Women, National Credit Fund, transformation of social welfare board by the social welfare ambassador all were setup and which was not so in other countries.

Campaign on the girl child was initiated, declaring the year 1988 as a Year of Girl Child considering them as Future Women. Rajivji realised, that gender discrimination was there even before the birth of girl child. Further, it was when Rajiv Gandhi was the first Prime Minister, to provide 33.5 per cent representation to women through the 73rd and 74th amendment of the constitution. The bill was passed in the Parliament in 1993 during the Congress Government. Again, we are indeed happy following the footsteps of Rajiv Gandhi, Smt. Sonia Gandhi as the Congress Party President and Leader of Opposition Party has reserved 33.5 per cent seats for women. This is yet another landmark decision as women have to make use of it.

Need for Forward and Backward Linkages for Women's Employment

Going back to employment action plan, we have to appreciate and realise that informal options of work prevalent in our country we have majority of women engaged in the informal sector. Therefore, we have to initiate such processes to enhance status of such women who are engaged in such options and assist them to sustain themselves. It requires a careful thinking to provide them a social platform towards a collective leadership leading collective vision towards collective action. Women work as agricultural labourers, fisherwomen, weavers, construction workers and in several occupations as artisans, handicrafts, export and so on. In the urban centres, most of them are hawkers, vendors and service specialists. Some of them are said to be impendent artisans, however they are mostly dependent on middlemen and trade monopolies. None of the social legislation work at the grassroots. Therefore, the most important aspect to strengthen women employment is to provide forward and backward linkages, such as organisation support, credit, skill enhancement training, empowerment training to help them control their resources and markets.

Globalisation and its Impact on the Informal Sector

Currently there is an emerging unprecedented challenge to these informal sector workers and their activities due to the ongoing economic reforms in India that disturbs the very base of their poorer households. Day-by-day the living conditions of these poor women workers are getting worsened, due to steep rise in the prices of essential commodities. Even the small and meagre savings of theirs are getting eroded everywhere. They could see the worst of deterioration in the economic activities. This is mainly so due to the shifting of policies of the governments, especially towards export-oriented industries that favour only the rich and not the poor. Such policies drastically affect the women workers in the handloom and fishing industries, wherein their concentration is very high, and as a result are getting alienated more and more from the reform process.

Therefore, it has become a compulsion for spontaneous workers movements like Working Women's Forum (India) to start lobbying with the Central and State Governments, drawing their attention to the macro socio-economic realities in which these poor workers are placed.

WWF's Holistic Strategy – Towards Poverty Reduction

In a situation, where even the daily survival has become a struggle for the poor, Working Women's Forum (India) has increased the economic returns of the poor through micro credit support, enacted social security measures, such as group insurance and social security schemes that are a means of social safety net to the lives of the poor women and their families. Integrated reproductive and child health services including family planning address the problems of the poor in a holistic manner strengthening their productive roles. Above all, its unionisation efforts has inculcated a worker consciousness and solidarity among women workers to fight for a worker status on par with the workers in the organised sector and ultimately find a place in the class struggle rather than perpetuate a home status on them. Despite being poor, these voiceless millions now have a strong social platform to carry on their struggles to secure their rightful place in the country's mainstream.

Enhanced Plan Outlay for Better Impact

The above mentioned facts on the struggles of the informal sector, endorses the need for a fresh thinking in our development approach to the informal sector as it is done in the agricultural, industrial and other important sectors. Thus, the informal sector needs to have a full chapter in the country's Five Year Plan and larger allocation of funds in our budgets, so as to enable the sector to become more productive and gain visibility, both in the Indian context and in the global context. Thus, it becomes evident that there is not only an immediate need for a database of information on the workers and their conditions of work, but also a comprehensive sectoral approach to the informal sector rather than a segmental one to ameliorate the conditions of these workers.

By way of concluding, the author, don't want to exclude the women in other sectors like management and corporate sector.

Women in Corporate and Management Sector

The case of educated women's employment options is also not much desirable. There are serious deprivations even in their career advancement among educated women. The major lacuna is whether on education, employment, career advancement or marriage market, women are excluded from making decisions on their own. Women themselves are to be heard for it, they who are in a dilemma between security of their life and promise of change.

We are aware that even in corporate sectors where women occupy top positions, they have to undergo tensions everyday. Women suffer from an inherent role conflict whether to satisfy their kith and kin at home or look forward to their career advancement; consequently, in many places men are preferred to women. Therefore, it is now, the educated women must desire to assert and reclaim themselves both to get over the concept of role conflict and the inferiority complex imposed on them for generations by patriarchal culture. Women must strive hard to change the power equations between the sexes and fight for a change to be judged on their own merits, rather on power equations. The discrimination is not due to the biological fact, but it is due to the wide gap between our ideologies and realities in workplaces. Undoubtedly, this new resistance from women may be challenged by the cultural traditions and the orthodoxy, but women must have the conviction to withstand the same. Currently, even in managements, our women executives are making determined efforts to climb career ladder, as management justifies its existence by the economic result it produced and not otherwise. Traditionally, women are born managers. She manages members, materials and resources in her family with competence. A management, which even many men, i.e., even top executives the world, cannot do. Therefore, policy makers, and planners must give 50 per cent of representation to women executives in manufacturing and corporate sectors. With the authority in key positions they will progress so well even without publicity and advertisement. Therefore, as mentioned earlier women managers effectively integrate themselves, into all sectors, get over their complexes and conflicts and redefine their roles towards the much needed change process driven by a desire to go forward. In fact leadership qualities of top executive depend upon 75 per cent of their managerial skills and hence only 25 per cent of technical knowledge, as ultimate perfection in any field is an illusion. Women executives should always keep in mind that success will never be showered on them voluntarily with discipline, determinations and survival skills. Women have to work three times more hard as they should not forget that they have come from a background where they have not been trained to risks. It is not employment alone, but it is an onward journey in pursuit of excellence.

Enhancing Women's Capabilities to Promote Social Transformation – Experiment of Working Women's Forum (India)*

Introduction

Histories of social movements when analysed are always reflections of the struggles of women and men activated by the philosophy of justice and fairness towards those victimised and suppressed. Working Women's Forum's (WWF) initiation too has been a necessity and a turning point at a time when India was going through severe vacuum of political leadership. When there was no physical evidence of any change towards betterment in the lives of the poor in the country, even after three decades of India achieving its independence.

Feminisation of Poverty

Women among poorer families were the most vulnerable (even today), as world's army of illiterates, are found only among women in this country. At the time when this movement was initiated, women have had the shortest life expectancy, something like twice less than that of men. The persistence of dowry, make women victims of abuses, desertion, bigamy and host of others violence against women. Almost 50 per cent (in 1978 which continues even today) of country's masses being poor, their day-to-day sustenance are an abysmal demonstration to sight. Increase of beggars, living as homeless on the platforms, in additions to mass migrations from villages in search of new work opportunities, make the slums of the cities swell and overflow with people. Equally the rural masses were totally at the mercy of the landlords not being able to alter the bonded conditions of employment, hence continue their sustenance on patron - client relationships, low wages that to in cash or kind etc. Women are to work mostly as unpaid labour for a morsel of food. The new political class that had emerged after India's Independence, who had access to wealth and resources etc., had become rigid power structures themselves. It looked as though they had returned back to the feudalistic values and caste networks oppressing women and poor, by adopting outmoded social customs.

There was general resentment among the public particularly among the poor as they felt that this new political class was responsible for shaking up the political system that stood on just and ethical pillars laid

---

*At the Symposium on IFAD's Regional Strategy for Rural Poverty Reduction in Asia and the Pacific on 1st December 2002, Chennai, India.

by the founding fathers of the Constitution and freedom fighters. Around that time, things were also deteriorating in India's counterparts in South Asia too, as all these countries have achieved freedom around the same time.

Everywhere political leaders had their own selfish agendas, moving away from service motive for the people at the grassroots. Further the 60's marked the pauperisation of peasantry by sheer exploitation by the landlords or the new rich. Indifference of bureaucracy, in addition to the corrupt practices of the political class simultaneously yielded to the rise of new civil liberty initiatives.

The failure of the political class and the leadership vacuum compelled many of us to reintroduce the concept of Mass Leadership. In search of leadership and mobilisation strategy, the initiation of WWF was thus a spontaneous initiation and demonstrated to the new political class (after independence), how the socio-economic milieu in India require divergent strategies to generate mass movements and leadership rather than stereotyped leadership that clings on to chairs and mikes in vacuum addressing empty halls. Though non-political, WWF demonstrated more a class based intervention against all vested interests - fight against caste and gender situations had been taken up as and when the need arose.

Objectives of Mobilisation

(a) To demonstrate women's contribution to the family and to the national economy and enhance value of women's economic role vis-à-vis to do away with such an impression that women's role is only an extension of their household duties.

(b) To reach only poorer households so as to reduce poverty among women in the slums and rural neighbourhoods.

Structure

Towards this aim, drastic structural change in the pattern of organisation has been evolved to facilitate the poor women to participate at all levels.

This bottom up structure not only facilitated their participation, but also improved the poor towards their decision-making and leadership roles.

Further, this was a strategy to help them to easily identify other poor, bringing in more and more of them into the fold of the organisation.

Above all, it kept the organisation out of elitist control. They went to the extent of promoting themselves as supervisors, office bearers and staff from their own class.

Group Process

Undoubtedly the neighbourhood group of 10 or 20 women, a small unit at the grassroots was thoughtfully evolved as a manageable outfit, in which women learned all the principles of collective management and action. Though as a credit group, their interest was in trade and business only, gradually these women took up other issues that affected their day-to-day concerns at the grassroots, and started mobilising other women in the neighbourhood for collective action towards achievement of their needs and requirements. Such consciousness raising efforts of women in particular, became an absolute necessity in the existing discriminatory, patriarchal structures towards a new social order with female values, governed by principles of autonomy and solidarity among themselves.

The Need

Therefore, it is with a commitment and urge to deliver atleast some kind of vital services to poor women in poverty that the original idea of providing small or micro loans to women vendors or hawkers were initiated in the slums of Chennai and rural areas. Taking advantage of the nationalization of the Indian banks in 1969, this micro loan service delivery to the poor became possible in 1978.

Conceptual Framework of Class, Caste and Gender

Undoubtedly we at the WWF, have gone through enormous struggles in structuring this movement, particularly in an adverse social and physical environment for women and female children. At a time where everything has been controlled by traditions, patriarchal cultures, where women's equal participation, in the society has been meagre. In this process degeneration, the prevalent socio-economic status only further denying women's access to power, resources and violation of even fundamental privileges and human rights continued unabatedly. This issue of such a widened gender-gap was reflected in education, employment, social or community participation, in fact, in her total existence as a human being.

Thus, women's participation at all levels ran into rough weather due to the fact that the enactment, enforcement, and legal interpretations of all kinds of social legislations in favour of women were in the hands of male dominated institutions and were administered by hard core patriarchal fundamentalists, where women had very little to say.

Therefore at this point of time, the effort to bring total participation of women at all levels needed a drastic, revolutionary approach in all aspects of their living and working conditions. Women's issues and gender questions had to be addressed seriously. The caste and class issues were taken up as and when women had to confront the same. A testing period to WWF.

State of Assetlessness to Accumulation

When it was, an issue of ideology of the Forum to lead the particular target group towards a permanent struggle process, one can't think of a short-lived project-to-project approach. Therefore, we had to think of a permanent strategy that would help them in their day to day life and work, i.e., a strategy to escape moneylenders, negotiate or bargain amidst middleman, with cash in hand, or educate their children, or relieve themselves from the illiteracy they suffer, acquire a technology to reduce their drudgery from their manual labour operations, purchase small piece of land or make small home of their own. In fact, to move away from a state of assetlessness to become asset holders, i.e., a permanent change process towards quality of life. Towards this process, credit thus strengthened their group dynamics, increased their collective consciousness and paved the way not only for collective survival also led to a state of sustainable existence towards their total livelihood security. Studies further showed that women through credit intervention, could move from marginal or subsistence level to trading, servicing to manufacturing or production, steadily towards growth orientation in economic ventures.

Mobilising Poor Women

To think back on what happened in the early days, WWF never went into the drudgery of collecting women from slums and villages for training them in skills, to find some work for them. At that time we in WWF were quite cautions, and only strengthened their traditional, existing occupations and this had its own effect. Instead of searching for the poor, poor started mobilising themselves and reached us on their own in tens and thousands. This contributed to quick outreach to poor women, contributing to Forum's phenomenal growth as a social movement.

Enhancing Women's Social Status

By way of bringing to light the social status of poor women in society not only unmarried women of working class, but also the status of those who do not have the sophistication and resources (in the Indian context) to get into legalised wedlock's and those who lived in common law arrangements are totally unacceptable to elites. Even those who attempted arranged marriages, had to pay heavy dowries and spend lavishly on marriage ceremonies that they can ill afford. Therefore, such of these women, who are in common law wedlock, are abused in derogatory language in the traditional communities even among the poor. Also their relationship as man and wife are equally insecure and women faced desertion in large numbers. WWF was quite concerned about such women mostly, as out of the early 800 initial members two-thirds of them belonged to such category of women. WWF's effort therefore was to legalise these relationships through registration, sometime under Special Marriage Act, if they belonged to different religions celebrating it as a big social event presided over by Governor of States or President or Vice President of India. Such registration of marriages gave women the right to fight for divorce in the court and make compensatory arrangement for her children and herself during times of crisis.

Surprisingly, there were many delightful inter-caste experiments where marriages between high-caste Brahmins and untouchable Harijans, Hindus, Muslims and Christians, also among Christians and Muslims. It was a further evidence and an eye opener that poor can't afford the sophisticated caste feelings nor can they get into costly caste networks and it is a learning process to study their own strategies to escape from those unaffordable networks of caste and religions. WWF made a wide publicity of such wedding events making it as a gender sensitisation effort to fight man's in humanity to women and her children. Women from their subordinate position felt they are in equal status, through such wedlocks.

Combating Female Infanticide, Child Labour and Devadasi Systems

Despite the Hindu code bill and several acts in favour of women, such as Dowry Prevention Act and Bigamy Prevention Act, women's succession to property on a equal basis to men, the messages of these Acts has not reached women in communities, more so in villages and slums, due to illiteracy and ignorance. The traditional preference of a "male child" lead many families to loose their girl children in foeticides and infant mortalities in some case, but in majority of the families it has resulted in large numbers of children who had to work for their livelihoods as child labourers. It was more a common occurrence that adolescent girls were pushed into early marriages and motherhood where their fate became fatal either in mother mortality or in dowry deaths. At the same time, the government sponsored family planning programme in 1977 ran into severe controversy in many villages and slums, by the mishandling of this programme by the bureaucracy. Casualties of death in male and female surgeries have outnumbered the successes in couple protection rates.

The Devadasi systems (Child prostitution), where the girl children have been victims of religious dedication to temples and later falling prey to prostitution was another serious anomally to be tackled effectively. This evoked feministic concerns and needed drastic action to save female children from the victimisation of religion and culture, besides enhancing the status of the girl child treating her as "Future women".

To prevent child labour, female foeticide, infant mortality, Devadasi system and save women from the crude imposition of female surgery in family planning programmes, thus WWF had to look for new forms of programme strategy. Therefore, it was a change from entire character of the state sponsored family planning programme, into a grassroots reproductive health care programme spreading the messages through sound methods of advocacy, and pleasant change from control to life choices for women. This new culture of advocacy in the neighbourhoods of slums and villages created a cadre for every 500 families as an advocate of health consciousness who multiplied in large numbers as "network of advocates" in the course of time and not only took up health issues, but slowly advocated holistic gender or class concerns among the women in poverty.

Through a demonstrative experience, WWF was able to bring to light the fact the under valuation of women at home reflected in the workplaces as well. Unlike in other feministic organisations, in WWF, the conflicts were not the only form of activism but it became a gradual technique or tool adopted as incidents led to that stage. In WWF, we never allowed rightful conflicts to contribute to eternal hostility but it was only on an issue-to-issue basis; where conflicts became a natural phenomenon.

Gender Aware Approach

Thus, at the outset the gender question acquired prime place in the WWF. With this ideology in focus, demand for gender equality had become the prime question. Whether in village Panchayat, or in fighting, caste, religious / traditional barriers or evade customs, also to fight discriminatory wages, i.e., to confront employers, landlords and other power structures like police, municipalities. Therefore, women soon had their way to fight injustice. Everyone had to listen to women. All these women in WWF could do this only with the strength of its cadre-based approach, and the numbers mobilised on the road in long marches or in mass meetings to demonstrate the injustices by creating a public opinion. Therefore, right from its beginning gender question gained predominance at the WWF.

Thereafter the "Class" question became equally important when the above mentioned mobilisation strategy became a way of life among the women workers, particularly where they had to face struggle on wage questions both in their contract labour work or piece rate operations in many of WWF branches in Andhra Pradesh and Tamil Nadu.

Enhancing Women's Capabilities towards Social Transformations: Experiments from the Ground

Being unorganised conglomerations, women workers earnings are so meagre and irregular that they hardly make both ends meet. Further their struggle for housing, water and for civic amenities are enormous in the urban slums. Their landless counterpart in the rural areas suffer equally due to underemployment, low wages, sometimes limited to even 45 to 60 days a year. If they happened to be part of drought prone areas (Bidar, Dindigul) it was even worse. Thus, it is more than an annual feature that 'rural poor' are on their migrating journey to the already overcrowded city slums, in search of new work options and continue to be victims of vicious cycles of poverty.

There women workers work as weavers of cloth, mats and baskets, cigar or agarbathi rollers, food processors, either work alone or collectively. They work as agricultural labourers in farmlands or they work for their kith and kin. They are providers for their families; working in service occupations, i.e., dhobis, cooks, sweepers and water carriers, etc. They are integral part of production process and contribute to the informal economy; unfortunately, they have little or no access to fruits of their own labour, nor that of the government's assistance.

While the Forum is a class structure in terms of its membership, it took up mainly gender and caste issues in its initial days of its organising effort. In the urban situation, the occupations of vending or hawking being micro enterprises, could not relate to class issues since this urban group was the initially organised one. However, gender (violence) caste (most service workers are untouchables) were on its heights due to the high prevalence of alcoholism, in urban centres. Also most service workers belonged to scheduled castes, and hence the character of the group had been more a solidarity or neighbourhood group in a grassroots initiative, and was working towards leadership effort.

The activism of the class nature, came up to forefront when WWF organised, agricultural labourers, export workers, piece rate and contract labourers, such as cigar, agarbathi and handicrafts, lace and weavers of textiles industry. Here the problems particularly for women are low wages, harsh and exploitative working conditions.

As alternate options of cattle assistance, agricultural workers in Dindigul branch of WWF have had, remarkable impact in making a real frontal attack on landlords, who had to make revision in the wage by marginally increasing it. While this marginal increase may be the fruits of their struggle, but this effort in our opinion, had not taken away women workers dependence on landlords.

Similarly, women lace artisans working in Narasapur, rural Andhra Pradesh have been totally neglected by the workers' unions including the Communist Party of India as they are work done by women at home, therefore, branded as leisure time employment.

Similarly, the beedi or agarbathi rolling, fisherwomen's fish marketing activities all have been considered as leisure time activities by male dominated unions. In fact, fish marketing is a more permanent work than fishing.

In the weaving industry, women as their men do weaving, keep out after designing, calling themselves as 'master-weavers'. Similarly, despite major share of work in many occupations as women's responsibility they are only low — wage efforts and branded as leisure timework. Therefore, to strengthen women worker's bargaining position, against vested interests and to expose the class character of the oppression women go through, WWF thus decided to register themselves as a trade union in the year 1982 as "National Union of Working Women" that was a turning point in women workers lives. This indeed is a much-felt need to provide a sharper focus to fight the presence of the antagonistic elements in the production process, wherein women had major thrust. Apart from its original grassroots character, now WWF also had acquired an additional strength by getting into unionisation process that strengthened women's economic roles.

In addition to this, the health programme physically took care of the health aspect of their productive role both as a worker and her role as a mother. More specifically the trade union offered the micro insurance programme with affordable premium covered poor women's lives and that of their families against unexpected disasters, such as deaths, illness and property loss. The health insurance took care of women during her entire life cycle from the stage of girl child to reproductive age group, maternity benefits to old age ailments as well.

Thus it was quite important to break through the vicious nexus between, patriarchy / feudalistic elements, and empower poor women towards leadership, both at home and in the community.

All this were achieved only by relying on the strength of the poor women, both in their numbers, energetic support and could initiate and sustain feministic leadership process. Inadvertently, this effort had strengthened many reform processes towards other women of middle and upper class. (Dowry, male violence, property rights and so on)

To be more precise and truthful to oneself, the strategy adopted in the process of building this movement of Working Women's Forum, has not been a sophisticated one but the same indigenous, sustainable effort followed by Gandhiji years before during the struggle for India's freedom. However, despite the strategies being indigenous it has worked in building up a commitment and solidarity among poor women, facilitating other poor women in small communities and neighbourhoods. This commitment of poor women has been responsible that such a small initiative of 800 women, in 1978 led to a massive social movement of 7,00,000 women today.

With the human potential from the grassroots, comprising of low educational levels, but with high common sense and acumen, a model of a credit union, and a women's union was possible within the parameters of poor women's access. This has assured poor women, food plus economic security but also the much needed social security. Above all, the movement contributed to the over all human security and welfare.

This visible movement of mass upsurge has to be sustained in its future growth. Therefore, conscious strategy of trained and indigenous leaders have been placed in both the urban and rural neighbourhood. Women members in the WWF, despite being the poorest have not been silent spectators to the happenings. Their lives must have been harshly affected by poverty, cultural, physical and social handicaps. Their commitment to the cause of ameliorating the lives of their sisters in the neighbourhood towards empowerment has been a vital force to make this movement of WWF wider and meaningful.

Women Workers at the Grassroots*

Informal Labour Sector—Women Workers

Informal labour sector has long been viewed as a transitory face in the economics of any developing nation. It is mostly viewed as involuntary and caused by high rates of natural demographic increase, placing constraints on occupational structure of the city combined with rural and urban migration. Whatever may be the reasons for the emergence of informal sector of this sector, the reality is it has come to stay as a permanent feature of the economy of the developing countries. Studies have shown the actual worker participants in this sector have always been pushed to "subordinate positions" and have been made "invisible" in the intersectural linkages. Policy option has always overlooked their existence. They have always been considered as a reservoir of cheap labour always available for exploitation. Majority of these workers are unskilled and non-technical workers, but the fact remains they meet the growing needs of the poorer communities and increase the earning opportunity through work in marginal or survival conditions.

When we come to realities of acts, bulk of the third world poor are women workers living in sub-human conditions of starvation and squalor. It is a recurring story of incomplete human existence for the female poor in all developing countries due to powerlessness.

Women Workers in the Informal Sector and their Economic Contribution

Ninety four per cent of the world's working women and 89 per cent of India's working woman belong to this sector. Both in the urban and rural areas, they experience great many difficulties in their daily struggle for survival. They are mostly categorised as hawkers and vendors, piece rate workers, petty producers and those provide consumer services among the class of people who are not be able to pay high services charges for the same.

In the urban centres, most of them are street vendors, pavement hawkers face daily struggle, to ply trades be it procuring goods from wholesale market or in transportation. Besides poor storage facilities, lack of permanent structure and training, long and arduous working hours, sexual harassment, harassment from police and municipal authorities, as well as lack of access to credit are examples of their unfavourable working

---

*At the fourth All India Consultations on Rural Development organised by the ILO at Gandhigram, 8th to 10th January 1987.

conditions. The wholesalers, moneylenders and middlemen provide credit on things, leading to low profits and marginal subsistence for women vendors.

In rural situation, we are aware that rural women constitute 50 per cent of the agricultural labour force in India. They play a major role in the agrarian economy and participate in all stages of crop production. Factually, they are the invisible contributors to the productive process. Lack of organisation and other infrastructure among the peasantry and the landless in India have forced them to a status of low productivity. Their working conditions are harsh, the hours of work are mostly long and the wages are low.

In rural areas, fish trade, livestock rearing, delicate handicraft production, such as lace making, beedi rolling, agarbathi rolling, are mostly handled by women workers. But they are doubly disadvantaged by both harsh working conditions coupled with poor living arrangement reinforced by social disabilities. Caste and gender situation are additional barriers to women workers in India.

Women's Roles

They play a very useful role in the family and community as major contributors to family income both in urban and rural areas. They play a crucial role in the agrarian economy as invisible contributors to production process. During the off season, most of them are engaged in some kind of home-based production or micro business in rural shandies and are victims of harsh working conditions and go through series of economic problems, with no legal protection. The social legislation at the grassroots are totally ineffective. Rampant alcoholism among men results in low male contributions to the family. Thus, women workers go through series of oppressions due to class, castes and gender situations.

Trade Union and Informal Sector

There is a growing feeling among the trade unions that efforts to organise women workers at the grassroots split the working class, which is really not true. ILO stipulates that workers have a right to organise themselves to fight their disadvantaged position. Women as a group of workers handling many single occupations have certainly a right to unionise themselves as a disadvantaged group. Many of the occupations, such as home-based productions and microbusinesses have very oppressive structures in which worker's contribution is under-estimated and undervalued. Therefore, we must have cognisance of such issues affecting women workers and whose status as workers being much challenged in their work environment. How are we going to define a workplace for these home-based workers? What definition is there for a 'worker' in this sector? Is there a proposal of health services and insurance cover for them?

WWF(I)'s Experiment

Working Women's Forum (India), a grassroot organisation of poor working class women, initiated in 1978. The objective of the Forum is to empower the women workers in the informal sector and to strengthen their economic roles. The Forum has achieved this empowerment through credit assistance to strengthen production requirements of women workers, and through intensive family planning programme, which eventually reduced their reproductive roles, to reduce the problem of poverty in working class families.

What are the New Strategies?

We have to narrow down everything mentioned above to a policy formulation options, with following measures, suggested from our experience in the Working Women's Forum (India) working in southern states.

The Category of Workers in the "Informal Sector" Who Need Protection

The category of work in which these women are engaged may differ in its nature, but from the income, the conditions of life and work, all these workers earn more or less the same wages live in same conditions and go through same oppressions. So it is better to bring them under one umbrella called "informal sector".

1. There are home-based workers for whom there are contractors or sub-contractors, who are their well-defined employers.
2. There are vendors and hawkers both in urban and rural areas, who may be called self-employed women or micro-entrepreneurs.
3. There are many handicraft workers and artisans, who work for others on piece-rate wages. These are workers who are subjected to vary large-scale exploitation by exporters and merchants.
4. There are construction workers who work in jobs of high risks.
5. Above all, there are category of workers to whom even protective legislation, does not prove effective due to weak enforcement machinery of state government, at the worker's level and awareness for empowerment is a rare effort at the grassroot.

Five Year Plans and Plan Measures for the Poor in India

Agriculture and industry have a full-fledged chapter in the country's Five Year Plans. Likewise, we must have a sectoral approach to these workers and must be brought under informal sector and find a chapter in the Five Year Plan.

There is a large-scale elite consumer need with reference to agriculture and industry, but with reference to informal sector, there is very little that consumers can benefit out of it. Therefore, in the government plans, it is the consumer-oriented agriculture and industry get great priority and are allocated large amount of resources. Thus, informal sector, bereft of consumer-oriented benefits, becomes a neglected sector.

All that we can expect from this informal sector is that the work role of poor labour should become more productive through provision of more facilities, infrastructure, such as credit, family planning, insurance and other services and help them to reach a stage where they could achieve the basic needs of food, shelter and clothing. This is more or less an attempt which is being tried in modern China.

State of Anti-poverty Programme and its Implementation in the Country

At present, all the programmes with reference to this sector are completely jumbled up in one Chapter of the Five Year Plan as Anti-poverty programmes. These programmes are totally entrusted to bureaucrats and various departments of Central and State Governments for effective implementation whose accountability on enforcement of the programmes are unquestionable. Such implementation and effectiveness are totally dependent, at present, on the personal initiative of the local officers.

Chapter in the Country's Plan

Therefore, when it goes as a chapter in the Five Year Plan to help workers in this sector, it will certainly empower the workers with a legal clout to demand the implementation or enforcement, that will eventually lead to the questioning of the accountability of the officers on the enforcement and implementation issues. Unless this is done, the resources allotted to anti-poverty programmes remain a wastage, will not reach the poor for whom it is meant.

Role of Banks

Yet another difficulty in the anti-poverty programme, is the failure and non-cooperation of banks, who are expected to supplement the resources on whom the programmes depend heavily.

Policy Option

Thus, a policy has to be evolved for the total benefit of the workers in the unorganised informal sector through a planned approach. As these are not only self-employed workers and as many of them well-defined employers they may be either called "the workers in the informal sector or un-organised sector" which can include as many schedules of workers as are spread throughout the length and breadth of this country.

Database for Women Workers

The most immediate and important concern for everyone as India's 89 per cent of women workers work in this sector, there is a real need for a database or information details with reference to women workers in India. The details of their work are so complicated and are multifarious in nature. Some are over-employed in some activities; therefore, low returns. Some are under-employed in some activities and receive discriminative wages. The multiplicity of female employment is so complicated that even in some cases, it depends upon patron-clients relations. In many cases, women and children are given a meal and are asked to work for hours. Thus, to prepare a profile of female workers, there should be a commission on women workers with clear-cut terms and references.

Commission on Women Workers

Recently, Government of India is trying to appoint a panel for self-employed women. It will be more appropriate to name such a panel as a "Panel or Commission on Women Workers" rather than self employed. The commission can go round the country and visit the piece rate women workers in a large number of industries, or unit women workers who work as home-based producers, study many such occupations in which they are micro-entrepreneurs their own right, alongwith the conditions of life and work of rural based women artisans and prepare a profile of women workers state-wise. This would give enough details to formulate a policy and programme for women workers through country's Five Year Plans and social legislations. In case, if there is a need to discuss these matters, a national workshop can be organised to discuss the matter to draw the attention of national governments.

The author write this with her experience in the union of women workers, i.e., the Working Women's Forum, where over 50,000 in three southern states are so far unionised.

Social Activism – A Strategy to Face The Challenges of India In Transition*

We are all aware that India is in transition facing the crisis of change, therefore, to meet this new situation of challenges we have to redefine social work as social activism. Such an activism requires new class of social activists, promoting leadership from the poor and deprived classes to take up social development not as welfare measures but as a serious business. In an era systems, negative environmental effects on this planet, what with the new economic policy encouraging market oriented economies and structural adjustments that burden the poor the most. These are some of the real challenges our country is facing today.

The challenges of poverty and the deteriorating powerless status of poor both in rural and urban areas require a new form of social activism to combat the problem at the grassroots. While situations were totally different until late 80s, changes have certainly occurred in early 90s. Thus, empowerment of poor and women with a new thrust and enthusiasm among the grassroots communities over the world has manifested into mass movements in many developing countries, where the poor and women have not only been able to take up extraordinary leadership roles, but also made their presence felt at the U.N. Status of Women's Commission. This was particularly possible in women's groups as these grassroots women were able to build up a strong network for themselves and pressurise the U.N. Commission on the status of women to accredit as many of them to facilitate their presence at the 5 or 6 global conferences as equal partners making them to become aware of the challenges of poverty and its adverse effects on poor and women in particular.

Yet another challenge is that of the imposition of social hardships on the poor due to high level of unemployment leading to extreme conditions of poverty. It is in fact that vast majority of the working population both in India and other developing countries look forward to informal opportunities of employment. But as informal sector occupation are characterised by low levels of wages and low standards of living, it does not provide the much required full employment but it further marginalises the poor and enmeshes them in poverty. Therefore, this sector of work option needs protection from government through implementation of social legislation alongwith other benefits, such as insurance, maternity benefits and social safety net progammes including due partnership between the

*At this Institution of Management, Trivandrum – January 4th, 1998.

workers and employers emphasising investment in their human resource potential.

Poverty affects women much more than men and the women in the extreme poverty have to bear several burdens. They are living with indignity and humiliation in established social hierarchies they face exclusion from all benefits which is a vicious circle in itself. The working children are yet another objects of social exclusion. At a fairly young age, in many poor families poverty pushes children prematurely into the labour market resulting in their exclusion from not only opportunities for education, but even of their right to a normal childhood. Social exclusions, such as this, was the focus of discussion at the World Summit for Social Development in 1995, where approximately 90 heads of state came together discussing to find solutions.

Female child is yet another neglected resource facing systematic subjugation being provided less food at home, educated less, given lesser attention and care, yet given the major burden of household chores and childcare. She works for longer hours paid less or even unpaid at times. Sometimes, a victim of patron-client relationship, she is often discriminated from very birth or even before birth extending to adolescence as well where the girl is at the threshold of womanhood. In her own home, she is treated only as a guest. In many places, especially in Karnataka, dedication of girl children of the age group of 7 to 8 to female deity is a common occurrence. A system such as this known as Devadasi system, is not only a hardship on the child, but also inflicts the worst form of oppression on the girl child.

Structural adjustments programme in this transition period of economic programme of reforms in India undermines the very livelihood of poor and destroys all people initiatives and civil society. This is yet another challenge to the social activists. The de-stabilisation of national currencies and collapse of the internal purchasing power are the major devastating economic and social consequences of this globalisation process. The country's unfavourable macro economic balance threatens even the process of empowerments which the poor have achieved so far and they have to pay high price in all walks of life, unaware of any strategy to balance the market economy and their social demands.

Anti-poor policies of the government on the issue of natural resources management further marginalises the poor. Poor and tribal, in particular, in the forested regions have no control over even the minor forest produce. These are often contracted to the private monopolies who device arbitrary, adhoc exploitative policies against the principles of natural justice with a vested interest of establishing their monopolistic powers. State monopoly has given room for private monopoly and is aiding and abetting market imperfections, besides pouring bribe into the coffers of bribe takers at all levels. As is evident, almost all occupations in the urban informal sector, such as hawking, vending, small manufacturing in residential areas are proclaimed as illegal by municipal authorities. Inspite of their valuable contribution to the larger economic process.

Working Women's Forum (I), a spontaneous women initiative in the slums of Madras has organised this most neglected and vulnerable segment of the workforce. WWF today has a membership of 4,50,000 poor women workers facing constraints and oppressions both in their occupation front and home front. This segment has been mobilised through credit co-operatives and collective spirit of unionism has made a sea change in their lives.

Poor women in the urban context have graduated from petty trading to becoming micro-entrepreneurs in their own right. In the rural context, women have pursued gainful economic activity instead of being totally dependent on the uncertain agricultural work options. In the absence of resources or any form of productive assets, WWFs strategies has let to a holistic human development for the very assetless poor.

Women at the WWF empowered that they are realised that they are equal contributors to the economic process of the family and communities nation. This empowerment has also elicited increased male participation as well as contribution to the family, and given women a social standing in the community. Socially and politically aware women are today members of the Panchayats (Local Self Governing Bodies in several villages) and Municipal Wards. Increase in their socio-economic status has let to increase self-perception and social security that has in turn provided opportunities to train the next generation, i.e., their sons and daughters in vocational skills and technology. As mentioned earlier, in the light of all the programmes of WWF, the recent economic programmes of reforms has imposed a severe burden on the lives of the poor. While on the one hand, WWF is engaged in the delivery of credit and health services. It is also lobbying with the government to initiate pro-poor measures to sustain the lives of the poor during the process of economic restructuring.

The experiments like WWF brings to light the visual realities at the grassroots where there is a phenomenal growth of independent social movement as more and more people are losing faith in the country's political systems. These social movements have been successful as they harnessed the leadership of the poor so as to create a social platform for the poor to voice their rights and concerns independently even if the elites withdraw from the scene completely. WWF's experience shows that the poor are excellent resources, if reinforced with training inputs to become strong leaders in the community. Such experiments of course challenge the conservative forms of welfare efforts, yet it is much more political in nature. The trade union strategy empowers the poor on their rights and responsibilities and the strategy of the cooperatives provide them the scope to come out of their daily oppressions. WWF believes that a strong regional networking of these movements will induce a new momentum to the NGO movements.

Part I

A Social Movement and Platform for the Poor -Working Women's Forum (India) At a Glance

Dr. Jaya Arunachalam, President, WWF (I)*

1. Looking into the history of Working Women's Forum as a social movement of the poorest women and its struggle process, the historical context was to do justice to the most oppressed group of women in all fairness. Such a movement of the poor and the vulnerable had to be an alternate political process (apolitical of course) to combat the complacent attitude of the then ruling class, who actually were ignoring the needs and requirements of the poor. Way back in 1978, i.e., even after almost 30 years of completion of India's independence from colonial rule, the conditions of poor were not only abysmal, but also moving from bad to worse. Neither did the elected representatives pursue the agenda, of the poor in the Assemblies and Parliaments nor did their manifestos contain the agenda of the poor. At that time, as much as 50 per cent of India was poor, the beggars and homelessness among the destitute had increased and mass migration from rural to urban areas was then the order of the day. The rural poor worked in bonded conditions under the landlords and there was no employer-employee relationship but only the patron-client relationship. The exploitation of the working class was to the core. Mostly, it was the women who were affected very much; they were working as unpaid labourers and getting even a morsel of food was very difficult for them. So, one had to imagine that the days of colonisation (colonial rule) were returning back.
2. The new political class that was emerging after the independence was found to be returning back to feudalistic values with the caste-networks hindering the political processes, oppressing the women and poor, especially as the righteous and honest never found them. The discrimination was unabated as demand for dowry and vulgar display of wealth on every occasion had become a common occurrence. Therefore as people resented, there was resurgence (in the early 70's) of other social movements like the WWF, which were anti-caste and anti-party politics. All this had to happen because the

*Presented at Global Marshall Plan Conference Musgrove, St. Simons Island, Georgia, US June 6th to 8th, 2003.

earlier reformist movements that existed in the Gandhian days, transformed themselves into mere relief and/or welfare organisations, often institutional issuing themselves and using their past reputation as a trump card (of their founders) for not taking up any new Presented at Global Marshall Plan Conference Musgrove, St. Simons Island, Georgia, US July 6th to 8th 2003 and the much needed reforms. The rural areas witnessed the total pauperization of the peasantry. Administratively, the bureaucracy continued to be indifferent and inefficient.

3. The cooperatives that were visualized by the founding fathers of the freedom struggle, crumbled into a hot bed of corruption. So all this and more had yielded to many new civil liberty initiatives in the 70's.
4. Such failures, by both the political and the administrative class in the country compelled many of us to reintroduce social mobilisation, focusing on poverty and economic freedom, as it was one of the agendas during the struggle for India's independence. One had to leave active politics at the time to visualise a better future for the women and the poor, and to demonstrate to the country the need for a mass leadership approach to eradicate poverty. The strategy at the outset was mass mobilisation and a search for such leadership.
5. Therefore, Working Women's Forum was a spontaneous initiative and a demonstration to the new political class that the socio-economic milieu of the country, as prevalent at that time, required divergent strategies. A generation of new mass movements with leadership role models had become an absolute necessity rather than the stereotyped political leadership that clung to the chair and mikes addressing empty halls backed by no action whatsoever for their people including the poorest.
6. At the outset, gender based interventions became necessary to confront the personal interest of women. The caste and class problems were taken up later. Women organized themselves on trade lines to demonstrate to those concerned that the contribution of women's economic role is a valuable income generation role, contributing to the family income and it is not an extension of the household.
7. The objective of women was only to reach the poorest households aiming at poverty reduction, concentrating on employment of women, particularly in the slums and rural neighbourhoods where the poor lived and worked.
8. The drastic structural change had to be planned not only to reach the poor in large numbers, but also to facilitate those poor to participate at all levels in equal terms. It was not an easy task as it

warranted more decision-making on the part of the poor, taking leadership roles for themselves, their families, their neighbourhood and their communities. The poor had to improve their overall skills to identify and help the other poor, facilitating in bringing more and more of their class into the fold of this massive union. Later, it was a remarkable episode that not only the movement had. Thrown up more and more leaders enthusiastically from their own class who mobilised the poor enmass, but also promoted the staff, supervisors and majority of the office bearers from their own class. Soon, women promoted the neighbourhood solidarity groups in 10's and 20's, a small unit where they could learn the principles of organisation, collective management and collective vision. There are more than 1,12,000 groups today. Besides, in the Working Women's Forum, unlike in other organisations, we never made it a project-to-project approach, as that is a short lived one. The organisation concentrated more on the empowerment process (rather than on mere material benefit) in its struggle towards a social change process of empowerment, solidarity and collective action.

9. The relief from hunger and starvation was possible by facilitating sustainable livelihood promotion and employment generation of a large scale effort to escape from moneylenders. To sideline the middlemen and merchant exporters, cooperatives were established in which women participated at all levels. Such cooperative experiences helped women to negotiate and bargain for resources, relieve themselves from illiteracy and ignorance, take on responsibility for themselves and the like. The assetless poor thus gained access to land, housing, productive assets and technology.
10. Strategic attention to health issues, both as mother and workers, really strengthened the productive roles of women.
11. The women themselves promoted a cadre-based reproductive health care advocacy programme, building up a network of advocates in their own rural and urban communities. These cadres hailed from their own class and were able to remarkably strengthen health consciousness of women and children both in the villages and in the squatter settlements of the cities and chanty towns, to utilize the government's health care facilities. A further learning from this programme was that, female surgery was not the only means to population stabilization, but it was a crucial decision on life's choices for women based on selective methods of contraceptive practices.
12. Women in the Forum established, through their reproductive rights, the process that the child bearing role of women be perceived as a

social role and therefore, they have a right to safe motherhood, to take care of their children and also make the decisions regarding number of children to have as well as the contraceptive practices to use, as a matter of their basic life choice. The programme impacted about 16 lakhs (1.5million) families in Tamil Nadu alone.

13. Reaching 460,000 women through the social security process became a household event. The insurance products are for life, disability and health care aspects.
14. The institutional building for the poor on various aspects became possible through the Working Women's Forum (India), Indian Cooperative Network for Women and National Union of Working Women. While the mobilisation and social platform was through Working Women's Forum, sustainable and affordable need based on financial services could be accessed easily from the Indian Cooperative Network for Women. Finally, unionisation, collective action, training, insurance, lobbying in the public and with the governments drawing the attention of everyone on issues impacting the poor became possible through the National Union of Working Women.
15. Taking up leadership through a political process in their own villages and city municipal wards, women fought for their representation as guaranteed by the 73rd and 74th amendment of the Constitution of India in the village Panchayat and urban local bodies of small towns. They never shirked or failed to go on long marches to draw public attention or create public awareness, against atrocities and injustices against women or for their demands, rights or entitlements for better roads, electricity, water, sanitation, schools for their children. Hospital facilities and other public utility services and most importantly sustainable livelihoods.
16. By way of building partnership efforts, WWF not only within India but also, in South and East Asia, in few African Countries, regularly engages itself in a consciousness raising process as an ongoing programme with other NGO's. Many U.S. University's including Pittsburgh, and Lunenburg from West Germany came and took part in the WWF's programme, thereby this helped them to learn more about the poor women's successes and empowerment.

Part II

Issues Presented before the Marshall Plan for Discussion - Innovation and Entrepreneurship for Development Visions, Challenges and Enabling Conditions*

Dr Jaya Arunachalam, President, WWF (I)

1. After about 24 years of working Women's Forum's experience we realise how urgent the need is at the outset to fight poverty around the globe, particularly in the developing countries. Therefore, an overall dialogue towards a New Economic order depends much, on how we get into pragmatic innovations and implementation strategies for an overall reduction of poverty, both in the developing and developed world. In reality, the overall human security dimension is an invaluable and inalienable right of every human being. What has been achieved through our own experience so far is miniscule when compared to a billion people in the developing world -, i.e., 20 per cent of the world's population who are still not able to satisfy their very basic needs on a regular basis. Therefore, access to micro credit and employment cannot be a solution by itself. Nonetheless, the continuous micro-credit campaign of Mr. Sam Daley Harris (who leaves no stone unturned to reach 100 million households through women) is a very laudable effort indeed.
2. However, we need to integrate other basic requirements like housing, land, education, health care, productive assets/technology and sustainable livelihoods. We also need to examine the intensity of social exclusions imposed on the poor for generations. To mention a few, the class, caste and gender exploitation in the developing countries, particularly in South Asia, are some of the glaring examples that women are fighting in the recent times. India's caste problems have manifested into gigantic dimensions and -therefore, the Dalit movements are at the fore today.
3. We cannot ignore the interlinkages between uncontrolled growth of population, which is a very significant factor in the destruction of our eco systems. Even more important is the fact that 90 per cent of the current growth of the population is taking place only in the developing countries where the poor live and work. Such interlinkages result in high incidences of child labour, child prostitution and many

---

*Presented at Global Marshall Plan Conference Musgrove, St. Simons Island, Georgia, US June 6th to 8th 2003.

more disastrous consequences on female children. Therefore, under development and population growth are thus two sides of the same coin.

4. The problem of rapid deforestation and exploitation of groundwater resources pose a great threat to the rural population in the developing countries. Despite reaching the 21st century, we still find our rural womenfolk walking several miles to collect water and fuel. Such exploitative ventures always ignore the needs and requirements of the poor, and marginalise them into further subordination, bypassing their roles and responsibilities and thereby aggravating the concept of feminisation of poverty and assetslessness.
5. Currently, the irreversible globalisation process, taking place (everywhere) in all countries of the world, not only affects all aspects of human activity, but also poses a serious threat to the overall human security. The free market economy imposes restriction on the freedom of capital, leading to resource insecurity, land insecurity and livelihood insecurity. Above all, it is a massive roadblock to any new developmental ventures. So the advocates of globalisation have to be reminded that they must have new vision and a real concern of the consequences of economic liberalisation by understanding the realities of the poorest and most vulnerable. Hence, the new ventures should visualise new forms of partnership.
6. The objective of globalisation must therefore include such laudable efforts, as providing opportunities to even the poorest and vulnerable, enabling them participate in the globalisation process, as equal partners. Without preparing and enabling large numbers of poor in the world (India, South and East Asia, Africa) to participate in economic liberalisation, a mere imposition of this process will only push the poor into dark corners of hunger and starvation. The thrust of the globalisation process in the developing world will divide the world into two, i.e., one for the poor and one for the rich.
7. The end of cold war does not mean that the world has consolidated its social change and democratisation process. The real fact is that while different social movements are still fighting against poverty and terrorism, the people are still being marginalised by the globalisation agenda. Thus, the world community should understand the human security angle correctly and in its true perspective – not just as a temporary rehabilitation and relief measure. Undoubtedly, human security is more a permanent resettlement of human aspirations and entitlements.

8. The health aspects have to be extended to working population, as an occupational facilitation. In developing nations, the need of any developmental programme requires an integrated approach of the overall human welfare and security aspects instead of single aspects of housing, credit, employment, water or deforestation. Particularly, the population stabilization measures, as they are closely interlinked with under-development and poverty.
9. From our experience in understanding the causes of poverty, we strongly feel that the generations of social exclusion imposed on women and men, i.e., exploitation of class and gender cannot and should not be ignored. Therefore, our Global Marshall Plan should initiate a dialogue process with National, International, United Nations and Bilateral Agencies and emphasize the fact that building of a New Economic Order depends entirely on how such social exclusions can be got rid off, especially with facilitation by local governments through various measures including land reforms, water access and irrigation programmes, women's succession to private property and housing rights, prevention of child labour, child prostitution and caste discrimination and the like.
10. The new economic order should therefore advocate the transfer of resources from the north to areas where globalisation has disastrously affected the human security. And this would have to be done on internationally accepted norms. Further, the irreversible globalisation phenomena must now provide a way to involve poorer communities as equal partners in the economic liberalisation process by finding markets for the products of the poor, spending resources on orientation and training to enhance their capacity to produce products of excellence for the world markets and above all to facilitate with the best labour standards, not as one for the South and another for the North.
11. For instance, globalisation and economic liberalisation worldwide, has resulted in the price rise, non-availability of raw material, deprivation of income among the unskilled workers in the countries where people neither have land nor productive assets. Such a consequence pushes many families into extreme poverty. Similarly during war, military spending increases, depriving the people of all basic needs and impoverishes a country's resources, not only among the connected nations but also their neighbours and friendly nations.
12. The experiments that we have gone through and the lessons we have learnt so far remind us that there is an urgent need for a new security paradigm not only for the developing countries but also for

the developed world. This must be a global obligatory agenda manifesting itself as a Global Marshall Plan binding the International Communities the world over. There must be a definite correlation between human security and individual welfare. If the concept of human security is equated with basic human needs and welfare, then both globally and nationally, the current anti-people policies not only need to be reviewed but also prevented from implementation, lest they generate disastrous consequences, impoverishing the poor even further of their basic needs. If such checks and balances are not adopted, the result will be that whatever has been achieved by collective vision and collective action of the people themselves, will be a counter-productive move, pushing back poor peoples economies' several years backward.

13. We are happy that the recent war on Iraq has come to an end but the shadow of such costly episodes remain in peoples' memory for a long time as they live in fear and insecurity. The war might be a global war against terrorism, yet we cannot deny here its consequences on the world's poor and the vulnerable, leading to displacement of poorer communities and also affecting large numbers of innocent civilians. Undoubtedly, poverty will assume gigantic proportions as a Consequence of the war. Therefore, the concept of human security should not remain as a one-nation security but rather become a collective responsibility of many nations.
14. War pushes the world's economy particularly in the developing world several steps behind and its people into persistent poverty. It infringes on the human rights of peaceful communities and is a threat to human security displacing more innocents from their safe habitat to refugee camps. It contributes to the vicious cycle of poverty as well. Consequently, millions of such poor unemployed youth engage themselves in cross border terrorism, and arms trade. If the vision of the global plan is to provide a global human security and have the people's welfare at heart, then it will oppose the military action and political conflicts, thereby paving a way to a harmonious and peaceful world.

3

Issues before the World Summit*

The World Summit for social development meets at Copenhagen between March 6th and 12th, at a time, when the world is in the grip of a range of social, economic and environmental problems. Approximately, 90 heads of States will come together at this Summit after 15 years, to take stock and decide on wide ranging social and economic development issues concerning the world. Little wonder that the Summit's major agenda items are: Enhancing social integration, alleviating poverty and expanding productive employment. The theme of sustainable development that is key to the Summit's concern is more than a global issue; it is the right of the majority of people in developing countries to sustain themselves given the resource transfers from their economies that sustain the richer minority. The Summit is also indication of the fact, that neither have the countries of North found solutions to their problems nor have their strategies in the South reduced poverty, but have in fact further marginalised the poor in these countries. A major part in this context is the onslaught of the economic policy reform and structural adjustment policies being carried on in the South at the behest of the North.

The three issues at the Summit – poverty, unemployment and social integration are mutually reinforcing. Poverty leads to unemployment due to low investment in human resource development; unemployment leads to poverty due to low income; and together, they lead to social disintegration and erosion of family values. As any other developing country in Africa, Latin America, and Asia, India too, is currently passing through the real burden of stabilisation and structural adjustment of

*Appeared in the 'GROOTS' as Editorial, February – March 1995.

economic reform programmes. Innumerable examples can be given. The social hardships imposed on the poor due to high level of unemployment and lesser attention towards the social sector have wide ranging implications on the poor. Lowering of wages leading to a lower standard of living is the consequence of negligence of social sectors by the respective governments. Further, cut in subsidies of the basic needs, i.e., food and free trade policies continue to marginalise the poor enmeshing them in extreme poverty.

The largest chunk of the poverty sector, whether in India, South Asia or elsewhere in the developing countries, falls within the informal sector. Both in the rural and urban situations in all these countries feminisation of poverty is an evident reality as women work for reduced wages, apart from housework and childcare. The Human Development Report 1993, observes that one-third of India's rural poor people are paying a high price for the ongoing economic reforms, but are yet to see any benefit. The curse of poverty, which is reinforced and heightened by structural adjustment policies is both urban and rural. A pro-poor strategy is essential and critical with an efficient use of food and human resource surplus to reduce the growing poverty.

While searching for alternatives, the World Summit must look into the growing network of private and non-governmental initiatives, both at the national and international levels. This will be a crucial option to the centralised government options, that threaten the decision-making power and thereby livelihoods of the people both in rich and poor countries today. The community development initiatives that democratise the systems and sensitise the communities to be self reliant; encourage local production for local use; experiment with various forms of ownership patterns capable of serving different social and economical purposes; explore possibilities to orient people towards capacity building and self-development; form new trading relationships and generate income for asset creation among the assetless poor at the grassroots are some of the practical solutions. The World Summit should focus on strengthening the network of non-governmental efforts and institutions for support, and sustainable livelihood of the poor around the globe, within a set time frame.

Eliminating cultural and economic biases, the summit should further strive to effect atleast 0.75 per cent resource transfer of the developed countries to the developing world. The integration, orientation of macro economic adjustments, environment action plans, national development plans to the comprehensive objective of sustainable development of the vulnerable sections in order to eliminate poverty, promote productive employment and social integration are issues to be addressed. This issue of the South Asian newsletter of GROOTS attempts to highlight the plight of women workers of the informal sector, primarily during the period of EPR and SARP. It mirrors the sense of social desperation, hopelessness, and feminisation of poverty by the predominant interplay of market forces.

The outcome of the Summit must be to encourage poor women to have better access to productive resources, stabilise small microscale eco-friendly workers-employers emphasising investment in human resource development, fair trading practices and critical linkages between economic expansion and sustainable development. The trade policies must address issues of equity, community integrity and attend to development, structural change and unemployment. Governments must provide more attention to social sectors accelerating direct participation of women ensuring their equitable access to productive resources and decision-making. A pro-poor strategy with a gender focus is absolutely imperative.

The measures adopted towards reduction of unemployment must be policy directions to balance labour market efficiency and human resource development. It must become aware of the economic and social realities that need a new framework of policy measures towards sustainable development. It must be an effort to promote cultural integrity across the barriers of race and ethnicity, avoiding sectarian and national prejudice. The Summit must provide directions to respective governments to include pro-poor measures. It must echo the reciprocity of practices between various actors (World Bank, IMF, bilateral agencies, governments, civil society) in the process of development on agreed relations and facilitate them to work with relative autonomy and interdependence.

The World Summit for Social Development meets at a time, when the planet is threatened by a host of social and economic challenges. Our endeavour is that the Summit should strive to become a vehicle to mobilise efforts for a transitional path between market responses and social demands, towards sustainable development.

After Beijing What Next?*

The challenges of poverty in imposing innumerable social hardships on women has been the major concern of all four UN conferences on women. The first two conferences held in 1975, Mexico and 1980 as a mid-decade conference at Copenhagen have made an in depth analysis of these concerns which laid the ground towards the formulation of Forward Looking Strategies at the 1985 UN conference on women at Nairobi, declaring the next 10 years after 1985 as a Decade for Women. They called upon the national governments to create suitable national machineries not only to implement the forward-looking strategies so as to enhance the economic, social and political status of women, but also to include substantial assistance to facilitate NGOs as well. At the end of the decade, the UN authorities still found very inadequate action being taken towards the implementation of the forward-looking strategies by respective national governments barring a few. Therefore, they wanted to create a Platform of Action declaring 12 areas as Critical Areas of Concern. To name the same, they were poverty, education, health, violence, armed and other conflicts, economic participation, power sharing and decision-making, national and international machineries, human rights, mass media, environment and development and the girl child.

With reference to India, if we have to objectively evaluate the action that has been taken after the Beijing Conference, as one who belongs to one women's movement heading the largest grassroot organisation, such as the Working Women's Forum, which has a membership of over 4,50,000 women, it is felt that the government has neither been very serious in the implementation of the critical areas of concern nor have they assisted the NGOs.

The Prospective Plan prepared in 1988 by the Government of India was released with much fanfare everywhere. But now, it is almost shelved in the various government departments for want of resources for its implementation. While the New Economic Reforms is an ongoing process. There is no pro-poor strategy being implemented as a simultaneous process by an increase in the allocation to the social sector to help the poor in the country. With steep rise in prices due to inflation and a scarcity of even essential commodities coupled with an enormous increase in the cost of living, the poor are paying a very heavy price to make the reform process a success. Adequate measures to safeguard the interests of the

*At the Platinum Jubilee Conference of Guild of Service, Chennai – 20th & 21st March 1998.

poor by a provision of space to allow them to move forward should become the primary agenda for national and state governments alongside the reform process.

In the area of poverty alleviation which includes access to land, credit and other productive resources for women, there are several Yojanas, Mahila Samithi Yajana, Indira Rozgar Yojana and so on. To implement all these programmes the poor women at the grassroots everywhere are deprived of even their small earnings as they part with it by entering various savings progammes that are cropping up everywhere in the expectation of achieving big returns. Not much has happened in this line.

India has been a party to the CED resolution (Convention on the Elimination on all forms of Discrimination against Women) but has not been very committed in implementing the clauses of the resolution within the country. Even when the question of informing UN bodies on the implementation of the resolution and its impact on women's issues came up, it is only India that has not given the facts and figures.

In the matter of equal wages for equal work, though ILO is aware at what is happening within the country through their own Trade Union sources. The government has been very slow in taking remedial steps, particularly in the case of informal sector workers who still form 90 per cent of the working population in India.

Religion takes the upper hand in all matters today in the country alongside with that of casteism. With the blend of caste and religious forces in a tradition bound Indian society, women face oppressions at all levels and more so at the grassroots. Atrocities on scheduled castes, scheduled tribes and tribal women continues unabated. The recent happening in Uttarakhand region of Uttar Pradesh and Jahana Bagh in Bihar are glaring examples of this reality and the protection of vulnerable groups is more of a myth than reality in the Indian situation. Barring a few daring decisions of certain judges, the system has been very weak in protecting the human rights and the very survival of women and the safety to their honour and dignity is still a distant dream.

The government talks of access to land, productive assets, technology for trading, etc., for poor women for which implementation of land reforms should be topmost in the agenda of the government programmes meant for the poor. This has been a very slow process in many states and even where it is being done the surplus land is not even distributed to landless poor men. So, where do women stand? When it comes to the question of distributive justice, it is again a case of collusion of the rural rich with the local government authorities in most rural parts of India.

In the matter of education and health, there are still many fields in which women do not have access to training in significant numbers so much so that even the percentage of their representation cannot be worked out in many areas of human resource development. The girl child is a major casualty everywhere and the oppression perpetrated against these girl children continues through the entire cycle of their life. The discrimination starts even before birth or immediately after birth when sex determination of the child is followed by female foeticide or female infanticide. The higher rate of infant mortality among girl babies is due to the selective discrimination of the girl children in their own homes with respect to providing good food and health care. This kind of neglect is also the reason for a higher level of girl children dropping out of school right at the primary levels after which they are imposed with the burden of taking care of all the household chores as well as the younger siblings. Left with no other option, the girl child is pushed into early marriage and motherhood. She could either become a small wage earner in order to contribute to the survival of the family or could end up a victim of maternal mortality after a series of early pregnancies and deliveries.

In addition to all this, there are many instances wherein girl children are victimised in the name of tradition and superstitious beliefs. A case in point is the dedication of the girl child as a Devadasi in the temple of the goddess in some parts of Karnataka at a very early age of seven and her subsequent exploitation (sexually). Another instance is the killing of the girl child immediately after the birth in certain parts of Salem and Dharmapuri districts of Tamil Nadu. These are nothing but blatant violations of the human rights of the girl child.

India has created a number of national machineries even before the Beijing conference for the implementation of all programmes for women as mentioned in the Nairobi's Forward Looking Strategies. It has a National Commission, a National Credit Fund, and Social Welfare and Advisory Boards all for women. Unfortunately, most of the work in these institutions remain superficial and especially, in the case of the National Credit Fund for women which has affiliated more male-dominated organisations which run women's groups. It will be no surprise when the general body of (RMK) National Credit Fund elects a male member, as its chairman in a few years. The National Commission on Women operates without a task force at the grassoots in the Panchayat and Nagar Palika levels. Not only creations of such grassroot functionaries are essential, but they should also have to be empowered with the requisite power to take action against atrocities of women. Thereby making it a cognizable offence, to make the effectiveness of these commissions felt at the grassroots.

Illiteracy is a disadvantage for women in India and many a times even the social and legislative measures that are favouring them are not known to the most women in the country. Women are ignorant of their legal rights, which proves to be a major handicap for them both at work as well as within the family. Day after day newspapers bring in shocking information about the frightful incidences of rape or atrocities on women. The victims are either girl children or women, who have been violated either by a stranger or by a known relative.

While the media can without fail play a very positive role in promoting better awareness amongst women, the past few decades has seen drastic dwindling of media standards that has completely shifted its priority to sensationalized its news items. Media needs to focus on women's issues with a gender perspective and a special inclination to provide information rather than making it media savy. There needs a better and sharper focus on women's concerns and taking on the role of gender sensitising the common public.

Talking about the gender equality in political participation and the decision-making process one wonders as to where the political process of the country is heading towards today? The parliaments still remain male dominated and no measures are in sight to alter this scenario. This has been demonstrated very evidently by the treatment, which was recently accorded to the women's bill in parliament for 33 per cent reservation for women in all walks of life. Not only is it a non-starter in making an attempt to increasing political participation of women in the decision-making process, but has succeeded in dividing women's issues by narrow barriers of caste, class, education and ethnicity. This undermines the efforts of the global communities who by virtue of their long struggle had successfully build a global network of conscientisation of women and women's issues cutting across barriers of language and ethnicity. This can happen only in India as a yeomen disservice to women's cause.

While before the Beijing conference, women's organisations world over through their concerted effort had provided the way for women's emancipation, the question is who in our country will provide the will for it? This is before the August body.

Why Women's Movements?*

Women Need Movements to Challenge Evils of Traditions and Customs that Offend Against Human Dignity and Cause Infringements on Human Rights

Due to time-honoured traditions there had been discrimination among men and women, mainly imposed on women and partly accepted by women themselves that had been the cause of the backwardness of our women. Man and nature have probably conspired to make the women weak and passive. But she has been protesting against this in some way or the other. The present Women's Liberation Movement in the West, mainly focuses to fight this discrimination, refusing a system that pins them to restrictive role of time-honoured traditions. Their argument is in the present circumstances that women have many new roles to play and therefore, being a wife and mother alone is not the duty of a woman. In the modern times, in many areas she is full-time career person and sole earner for the family. Therefore, she protests and feels that marriage thus will be one of her many options. She will accept marriage only if it doesn't come in the way of the development of her many-sided personality as a human being. Also, in India there is a greater need to make people understand the woman's role and the economic contribution which she makes to the community and country.

The growing conditions of the backwardness among women in this country make us also feel that there is a very urgent need for such a movement in India too. Such movements alone eventually will make it possible to raise the status and dignity of the large number of women who are subjected to all kinds of exploitations and oppression economically and socially. It is time now in India, to make our men and women understand themselves better and accept their diversified roles without one restricting the other. An equality based on human considerations alone will bring about the required completeness in day-to-day life of men and women.

For instance, women of the poorer sections in India are treated merely as chattels and are prone to large scale exploitation in their work roles (class exploitation). Things are no better in lower and upper middle classes of Indian society, where they are secondary entities and an object of financial transaction in the marriage market (social gender exploitation). The struggle therefore, is not between individual man and woman but to fight a retrograde system prevalent over generations and safeguard human dignity. When this is said, one should not misunderstand that women are

*Convocation Address, Lady Doak College Madurai, 4th April, 1987.

interested in such movements to disturb the sweet variety, nature has offered to humanity and to fill up the whole world with one sex. It would be sensible to understand that discrimination against women is an offence against human dignity and infringement of human rights, as men and women are born with equal dignity and effective complementarity.

Dowry, Women as Objects of Financial Transaction

Traditions and customs have imposed on women such indignities where they are treated as objects of financial transactions. Dowry is not a one time bargain in the lifetime of women, but it is a bargain that starts with marriage and continues throughout her life until her daughters grow up to leave the home with dowry and the sons of receive dowry. Dowry is given not only at the time of marriage, but costly gifts are also given even after the birth of the first, second and third children. In many Brahmin families, the author have seen, for thread ceremonies, 60th marriage anniversary, etc., lots of gifts have to be brought from women's parents home; they fix up a quota for such things.

Dowry is of a very recent practice, and does not form part of our ancient traditions. In many of the tribal families and scheduled caste groups, there is no dowry practice. Dowry is also an offshoot of the caste system as untouchability.

Dowry : An Offshoot of Caste System

Dowry is a phenomenon, initiated by the middle class group to buy a good boy from the upper class families to buy their way to higher social order in communities. Similar precedents date back to the 18th century in East European countries, where rich merchants and bankers paid heavy groom price as dowry to purchase a boy for their girls into the families of bankrupt aristocrats. This was mainly to go up on the social ladder in traditional communities. In late medieval times, similar things must have happened in India too. Therefore, it is the practice among the rich and well-to-do to achieve a higher social status through vulgar display of wealth, and at the later stage the evil slowly had spread from middle class to other communities using women as an object of financial transaction. As a result, this not only lowered the status of women but also involved many families into debts for generations together. Though Zamindari System has been abolished, still the heritage of feudalism hangs on heavily us through the rural rich and rural elites. Is it not clear that it is merely the attitude of people to acquire social ascendancy using their sons and daughters as tools and how do we bring in a change in their social attitude?

Mass Education Campaigns

Is it not time for us to see that the 'Haves' do not impose such wrong values on common people? Should we not tell in mass campaigns, the recurring stories of hundreds of young women in dowry deaths? Should we not narrate the stories of those women left in distress shame whose marriages being stopped as dowry options are not obliged? Should we not mobilise the affected mothers, who have gone through the drains of economy in their respective families who will tell the country their continuous indebtedness they face all through their lives?

Dowry Encourages Illiteracy

The practice of dowry in many areas have resulted in an mass illiteracy among women. Rural parents strongly felt that women should not go in for higher education as they have to go in for a more educated grooms, resulting in higher financial commitment. Therefore, women in rural areas adopted illiteracy as an asset and ornament.

Ineffective Social Legislation

What have social legislations achieved in this country? We have Child Marriage Act, Widow Re-marriage Act, Polygamy Prevention and Dowry Prevention Act. Except in Rajasthan and a few other states in North India, the author is sure, child marriages, are discouraged in other states. In a way, in progressive states, widow re-marriages are also taking place. But in the Polygamy Prevention Act, as the custom has stronger roots and in as much as the action has to be taken only by the wife in such cases of polygamy, implementation becomes very difficult. Many wives accept it and suffer indignity in silence, as it is a stigma attached to term if she does not live with her husband. As long as woman is compromising in nature, in addition, to lack of awareness about her own rights and situations, things will remain unchanged and will get worse in rural areas. For the sake of property and assets, polygamy is still practiced on a large scale in rural areas. But the worst can be said of what is happening in Dowry Prevention Act. Most people including highly educated people remain ignorant with reference to this Act. Therefore, dowry as a custom with stronger roots in communities contradicts law and moves in the direction of open violation, increases in volume, and permeates into distant communities, where it has never been in custom. Studies of anthropologists show how many families, which had the custom of paying bride's price in early days from the boy's side, have stopped and changed over to dowry. Such families have become prosperous and have educated their sons to increase their value in the marriage-market and on contrary in many ordinary rural families; daughters and wives have stopped working.

Dowry Encourages the Gender Inequality

To acquire social status in the society, women have sacrificed their economic stability. The economic justification for this, is that they have educated their sons who, in turn will have to take care of the girls at home (who cease to be economic assets for those families) will pay heavy compensations to the other families who will agree to shift on themselves the economic liability of these women where these women can be perpetual child producing machines. Many families just having four sons alone have made them richer and live in lavish styles that their family can afford. Women in these families are not only treated as chattels and liabilities, are being treated worse, as unpaid domestic workers.

Dowry Encourages Illegal Means to Acquire Wealth

Practice of dowry encourages black money. The dowry system is one way to dispose of unaccounted money, but bring with it a new status to the family.

Coming to the point of a dialogue with you young women, that author feels it is disheartening to find that the most of the young women compromise on this, most of you suffer in silence. It is only very few sensitive rebels protest, and few are still those who take drastic action on this but majority accept this indignity.

Need for Changing of Attitudes at all Levels

Most young women get into jobs to earn their dowries. It is found that how young men who oppose their parents and defy them for many silly reasons, become slippery on the question of dowry. Why should they become so obedient only on the question of dowry? A house, a car, fridge, replacing the clothes and jewels of earlier days is worth this golden silence and obedience to their parents.

Indian Parliament has passed innumerable laws to eradicate oppression on women in this country which no other country has done in the world. But laws can do nothing in this country without a strong public opinion.

What then must we do? Can we go back to the days of Mahatma Gandhi who fought colonial imperialism, and Martin Luther King fought for the emancipation of blacks in the US. The world knows that their mass movement sensitised the countries to wake up against discriminations of the worst order. Mahatma Gandhi brought political freedom to this country and Martin Luther King's peace movement brought the blacks nearer to few higher positions in the US amidst rampant racial discrimination.

Can there be similar movements to prove that the issues affecting women are human rights issues, challenging the very existence of human beings with dignity and honour?

With reference to education and employment of women, one must remember what "Partricia Palmier" a student in Harvard University, mentioned a few years ago. She says, "History has overlooked half of the human existence". Therefore, there should be a definite direction in which we have to move, to see that such discrimination of women at all levels of educations be removed.

Integration into the curriculum of programme of study should be to restore to women their history and achievements and give them the knowledge and methods to re-interpret their life experiences. Non-sexist counselling is a must at every level of education, encouraging women to increase range of options. Such choices should include both non-traditional alongwith the present traditional occupations. In addition, to all these creating social awareness among women on women's rights and status in various occupations, is equally important and must be a continuous process.

Women in Teaching Profession

It has been traditionally imposed on women, that they are most suited to the task of teaching and therefore, women become teachers in overwhelming numbers, and teaching became essentially a women's job. This is nothing but professionalising the work that women do at home, therefore, the effects of such an educational system resulted in discrimination against women, that ultimately damaged even teaching as a profession, having a devastating effect on the status of women in general. Because any system that is run by men has the capacity to deny women the opportunity to develop their talents and abilities.

In text books and rooms women have been taught to undervalue themselves by offering them more limited options than men. Women have been denied the training that would enable them to enter a more accomplishing, more rewarding field of work. Women in educational profession continue to lag behind men in many respects. Women students are still being prevented from making full use of their capabilities due to limited options.

With very few women in leadership positions, it is not surprising that women students often are inadequately prepared for the world of work. Vocational education does not prepare them for gainful employment. Women have been discouraged from learning the skills that would prepare them for highly paid technical work. Women have been conditioned to believe that they do not have the skills for these jobs. Thus, women are under represented in technical and scientific fields.

The message of many textbooks and story books is that girls and women always take an inferior place to men and must accept only certain roles. In the textbook contents, women occupy very few roles as compared to innumérable male roles. Sometimes, textbooks still depict women occupying more traditional female role, like housewife, teacher, and secretary and so on. Even in the primary school materials, boys are pictured as active and outdoor persons whereas girls are pictured as indoor and passive. Boys perform adventures and skillful tasks whereas girls groom themselves and had to keep their homes. Girls are affectionate and nurture dolls and pets; boys are brave and fierce. These stereotypes are still the limiting factor to the equality of boys and girls. Such stereotypes do not stop at the primary level alone, but continue in the high schools and further more in the entire curriculum as a whole.

Women are invisible in history books, topics that equally concern with women such as women's suffrage, their roles in country's affairs are given minor importance, while it devotes pages and pages describing the adventures of men. Research on women and her accomplishments is a major missing link in all disciplines as systematic study and accurate presentation of female experience is totally discouraged on the entire curriculum.

An ILO report mentions : "A world profile on women, using selected economic and social indicators, reveals that women constitute one-half of the world population and one-third of the official labour force; perform nearly two-thirds of work hours; but according to some estimates receive only one-tenth of the world income and possess less than one-hundredth of world property". That is our position today. Let us then think over a concrete plan as to what then must we do?

Integrated Approach to Human Settlements*

Case Study of Working Women's Forum (India)

Introduction

A large number of households in developing countries survive in conditions of abject poverty and squalor, where even basic needs of poor are denied or not attended to. The real 'shelter or habitat' to the millions of citizens in the developing world still means a thatched or a tin roof, or a piece of cloth stretched over bamboo on four sides. Women are more involved with the problems of habitat than men, in and around their neighbourhoods of the poorer settlements.

Invisible Needs of Women in Human Settlements

United Nations Conference on Human Settlement covers a wide spectrum of policies with reference to programme strategies to combine 'Shelter, Infrastructure and Services'. However, nowhere in the report one finds a mention on the special needs of women and children. Even while planning programmes strategies, neigbourhood approaches and plans could have taken care to improve the quality of these vulnerable groups. The report while referring to the need for the 'relief of urban man from intolerable and psychological tensions due to over-crowding and chaos in human settlements', and crowded human settlements, its women more than men, suffer in tensions at water taps, at washing points, at polluted drainage canals and children playing in dangerous environment. Though the report advocates the need to conserve energy 'as human settlements consume more energy' has not taken into cognisance the hard task of women carrying fuel and water from long distances, and their labour intensive methods of cooking and washing. There is little or no mention whatsoever about the much needed day care centres for children or the ownership of house sites, other assets or other needs around the neighbourhood.

Need for a Campaign for Housing Rights

The growing concern among the poor and shelterless warrants the need for a campaign for housing rights in their respective countries to fight for the basic needs of 'Shelter, Infrastructure and Services'. The campaign should focus on the following aspects:

(a) Requirement of a basic minimum area of land or buildup space to live.

---

*As a chief guest of the Ministry of Foreign Affairs, Netherlands – October 5th 1987, U.N. Habitat Day.

(b) Legal and social security of tenure
(c) Right to the due process of law
(d) Knowledge about availability of all housing resources
(e) Right to participation in local planning and in allocation of housing resources (land, water, building materials, etc.)
(f) Freedom of choice in location, community and special organisation
(g) Freedom from discrimination of any kind
(h) Access to low-cost building materials
(i) Access to basic services: potable water, road, sanitation, drainage, postal services, etc.
(j) Right to vote (franchise).
(k) Effective distribution of food articles and rations
(l) Access to fuel or energy for cooking, heating and lighting
(m) Access to open space, natural and a safe environment
(n) Availability of local public transport
(o) Access to health and educational facilities
(p) Right to employment, training and access to production resources.

Working Women's Forum (India) in the Context of Habitat

Within the context of providing access to such basic right to have a permanent shelter, healthcare, means of production, there are few initiatives here and there and one such grassroot initiative is Working Women's Forum (India).

Over 1.38 million people live in the city slums of Madras, constituting roughly one-third of the city's population. Most of them live in squatter settlements in thatched houses with disputed ownership. A few live in the multi-storeyed colonies of Slums Clearance Board of Tamil Nadu Government. Women in these slums are in the grip of extreme poverty and indebtedness. An earlier survey of members of the WWF reveals, the existence of 83 occupations in the informal sector in Madras city, and throws light on the conditions of these members before joining WWF:

(a) 25 per cent of the total women in the slums were heads of household and over 60 per cent equal contributors in income of the family.
(b) The average income of the women trader lay in the bracket of Rs.50 to Rs. 250 per month.
(c) 85 per cent of the informal workforce are scheduled caste, i.e., Harijans and other backward castes.
(d) The average family size was 4 - 8 members.

(e) Indebtedness to moneylenders was as high as 90 per cent. All the surveyed claimed to have gone atleast once or twice a month to the 'moneylenders' houses.

(f) High incidence of drunkenness and wife beating is concomitant with low male contribution of income to household.

(g) 93 per cent did not have a permanent structure on the streets and hawked carrying headloads in baskets, gunny bags or sold on pavements of under trees.

(h) Long and arduous working hours for vegetable sellers (6 hours), fruit sellers (14 hours), green sellers (13 hours), idli or rice cake sellers (14 hours) etc., was a common feature.

(i) Child labour was widespread in at least 70 per cent of the families.

(j) A combination of low productivity, low income and perpetual debt, little credit, training or support of any kind was evident among the majority of members.

(k) Source of light for over 61 per cent of the population was the kerosene lamps. Only 25 per cent had electricity in their house.

(l) Source of drinking water for 61 per cent of the population was situated quite far from the house.

(m) 72 per cent sewage facilities were community owned.

(n) 69 per cent fire-wood, coal, cowdung cakes etc., as sources of energy as opposed to cheaper or easier kerosene stoves.

Forum created collective consciousness among these poor women, to look for basic necessities for their survival and seek access to better living and work environment. As a mass-based union of women workers, Forum has in the last nine years worked to provide relief to poor working women both in the urban and rural areas. In many cases, in spite of the government being the major disburser of services it has never failed to act as a catalyst or a pressure group to pressurise the government in providing housing, roads, electricity, water as basic needs for human survival. Further, the Forum has widened the concept of human settlement to the social environment of women workers. An ideal human settlement, according to WWF, is one that provides human dignity, combining employment, training, health with access to credit, in other words, decent housing with better sanitation and environmental conditions. Thus, WWF started to create a social environment to their members, recognising the women as their basic human resources rather than the economic power of plan outlays, focussed its attention only to develop such human resources potential so that its impact will be on the total improvement of their living and working conditions.

Forum's major intervention is in the area of employment and income generation, through its own innovative banking system provided through a series of women's co-operative societies in all its branches. The Forum has thus provided opportunities to these poor women to become productive members of the workforce in the informal sector through employment and micro-enterprise efforts. These women are first organised as neighbourhood groups around issues or employment and credit to come together and build up solidarity among themselves through their grassroots initiatives and self-management process. Using their local leadership potential, women now empowered themselves to defend their right for equal opportunities. The WWF becomes a pioneering effort to provide all basic services like credit facilities, family planning services, child labour centres, non-formal education centres right in the heart of squatter settlements.

Survey – Findings on Housings, Assets and Savings

A recent survey of WWF programmes and their beneficial impact on

(a) Housing, assets and savings

(b) General standard of living for its members reveal the following facts:

With reference to housing conditions, Twenty-five per cent of the Forum members have moved from rental houses to their own houses. Eight per cent of members of the Forum have got the ownership of house sites, Fourty-one per cent of the people have moved on to their own pucca houses. Thirty-one per cent had access to better flooring facilities. Thirty-three per cent have access to wells. Twenty-four per cent of people have constructed bathroom facilities. Twenty-two per cent have access to lavatories. Eighteen per cent have access to water taps in their own houses. Eighteen per cent alone have access to electricity. Ten per cent of members have moved on to houses of higher rent. With reference to assets, Eight per cent of members have been able to acquire assets like fan, vessels, chairs, clocks, radios and stoves. Fourty-six per cent of the members have access to assets like cupboards, cattle, sheep, cots and cycles. Fourty-eight per cent have access to gas stove, television and jewels. Six per cent had access to land (small holdings).

In the matter of savings, Fourty-seven per cent of the members have had Rs. 50 to Rs. 150 savings. Twenty-one per cent of the members have had savings of Rs.151 to Rs. 300. Six per cent of the members have saved Rs. 301 to Rs. 450. Six per cent saved Rs. 451 to Rs. 600. Twelve per cent of the members have saved Rs. 600 and more.

Food, Clothing, Education and Health

Ninety-three per cent of the members of the Forum have access to healthy food. Seventy-three per cent have access to decent clothing. Twenty-four per cent have access to more clothing. Sixty-six per cent the members have adopted family planning methods. Twenty-nine per cent of the members said that their children had access to immunisation. Thirty-eight per cent of the members were aware of and practiced environmental sanitation. Fourty-four per cent of the members had access to the healthcare programmes of Working Women's Forum. The percentage of members whose capacity to buy books and educate their children has been Fourty-two per cent. Fourty-one per cent of the members have taken decision to educate their girls. Twenty-nine per cent of the members could afford to send their children to good schools. Eighty-three per cent of the Forum's members have had access to employment and micro-business ventures.

Reasons for Failure of Government Housing Plans

In Madras and other cities, failure to involve the community in planning and decision-making has resulted in the unpopularity of multi-storeyed tenements in slums. Women were never consulted even with reference to maintenance of surroundings and neighbourhood facilities. The quality of drainage pipes and other materials are so sub-standard that they often go out of order, creating stagnant pools of drain and sewage water, mixed up with cowdung and garbage, resulting in the breeding of mosquitoes everywhere. This poses a big health risk among its residents.

Besides, there is a lack of coordination among the several institutions that are responsible for human settlements. The government, slum-clearance board, municipal corporations and metropolitan authorities, rarely come together for planning and implementation, as each has its own policy and set of rules. Thus, from the point of view of residents of slum and especially women, it is always better to live in a hut with traditional means. According to her, it has access to drinking water nearby, without the drudgery of carrying it to the fourth floor of a multi-storeyed building, children can play outside the hut before her, without the worry of them falling down from the multi-storeyed flats. A micro-business, like selling vegetables or a snack shop outside her thatched house is a possible and on an economic activity. Lack of employment potential and access to market place in the multi-storeyed tenements poses a major problem for a slum resident. With reference to toilet facilities in the multi-storeyed buildings, women feel that toilets without water are meaningless.

WWF's Programme for the Shelter and Homeless

Forum plans a Housing Bank, sometimes this year which will facilitate long-term loans to the homeless to buy house sites, contract houses and civic amenities. In the rural areas, the Bank will facilitate the poor to invest in small landed assets and houses and retain what they already have, preventing them from pawning the same to landlords and moneylenders.

Forum's Integrated Approach

The WWF with its grassroot initiative and innovative delivery mechanism made an immediate impact on the lives of poor women. It was initiated with 800 members in the city of Madras but slowly spread to other rural areas and to the neighbouring states as well. It is now a union of over 60,000 women workers in the poorest of human settlements of Southern States in India. WWF achieved this through a process of training poor women in group initiatives and self-management.

The WWF experiment shows that the programmes of ameliorating the conditions of the majority of the people who live below poverty line. These people must have a processual approach and not a blueprint approach imposing pogramme strategies from above. The programmes should recognise the full economic role played by very poor women, who are mostly the residents of the slums and squatter settlement. Their needs have to be integrated in all the programmes planned for them, since many occupations are handled largely by women themselves. Therefore, it is not merely a question of the provision of shelter or employment or other services alone, but one of integrating the various facilities to create better working and living conditions for the poor.

Conclusion

Within the context of what is mentioned above, Forum's experiment can be a model for the other developing countries and the Habitat Commission to take up intensive studies on such innovative experiment and disseminate information to other parts of the developing world (if necessary, in the local languages, so that information can reach the grassroots). The Commission can bring people together from the developing countries, especially the representatives of the shelter and homeless to share and learn from each other through sharing and learning workshops. It can also facilitate the exchange of experts within the developing countries to share their expertise through consultancy services, and give visibility and recognition to successful experiments.

The author takes this opportunity to record her deep sense of gratitude to the United Nations and the National Habitat Commission of Netherlands for conferring this unique honour on the WWF and herself to the Dutch Development Authorities for having offered financial assistance to WWF for the next 5 years starting from the Year of Shelter and Homeless.

The author also express her desire to UN and the Netherlands Habitat Commission to extend their helping hand to more NGOs around the world to help people's initiatives, among tens of millions of the poorest in the third world. Success of our pogrammes will ultimately lie in forging new links amongst the poor in the world.

Let the poor be awakened to a new consciousness, to a new environment which offers them unlimited opportunities for self-employment.

References

Arunachalam Jaya - Credit Needs of Women Workers in the Informal Sector, Case Study of Working Women's Forum (India) submitted by Appropriate Technology International, USA, September, 87.

Azad Nandini - Focus on Women Workers at the Grassroots. Strategies of Working Women's Forum (India). A Report to the U.N. Closing Decade Conference of Women. NGO Forum, Nairobi '85.

- National Union of Working Women – A New Replicable India Development Alternative.

- Empowering Women Workers – The WWF Experiment in Indian Cities, published by UNICEF '85.

Chambers Robert - The Working Women's Forum – A Counter Culture by poor women, Institute of Development Studies, published by UNICEF '85.

Jaffers Hilde - Organising Women Petty Traders & Producers : A Case Study of Working Women's Forum, Madras, MA Thesis submitted to Department of City and Regional Planning, University of California, Berkeley, November '81.

Neponen Helzi - Organising Women Petty Traders, paper presented at the Asian Regional Conference on "Women and the Household" New Delhi, January '85.

Rounaq Jahan - Women in South Asian Politics published by Third World Foundation, New Zealand House, London '87.

Proceedings of the National Campaign for Housing Rights, National Campaign Committee '87.

Proceedings of World Conference of the United Nations Decade for Women Equality, Development & Peace, Copenhagen, Denmark, July '80.

Social Platform through Social Innovations A Coalition with Women in the Informal Sector*

Working Women's Forum (WWF) was born out of an activist's commitment that the poor are entitled to their rights, in terms of organised social platform, access to credit, education, health care and all the other basic services. The suffering of the poor, especially women in extreme poverty and squalor led to the initiation of WWF in the year 1978, taking responsibility to relieve them from hunger, indebtedness and invisibility. Forum's several initiatives not only strive to address the economic and social problems that confront poor women, but soon manifested into an alternate development model. As an initial step, it began organising women around their households, markets and communities. Emphasising a strong field base, Forum encourages group structures, transcending barriers of caste, gender, and religion crystallising the social integration process among the poorest of several divergent groups on a social platform towards a common cause. This, Forum has been able to achieve through its innovative structure that facilitated a bottom up approach in its organisational efforts.

Innovatively, the Forum entrusts key responsibilities of the organisation and its administration to poor women, by selecting and training cadres from neighbourhood communities. Besides this a major chunk of organisational business takes place in the slums, markets, village courtyards and places of worships. Such strong field base encouraged the women in WWF to manifest themselves into a mass movement of over 5,91,000 women, though they were only 800 in number at the time of its initiation.

The Forum's greatest success lies in its innovative approach to integrate the poor at all levels in its institutional framework as well as towards better delivery systems to reach large numbers of poor. Be it an informal banking system of a Co-operative or United Nations partnership project framework of Reproductive Health Care or Trade Union initiative to organise the unorganised. Forum demonstrated a conscious attempt to integrate the concerns of the poor at all levels.

As a credit network, WWF branches off into Indian Cooperative Network for Women (ICNW) promoting social and financial independence of women through micro or small enterprise development for women providing them low interest loans generating employment

---

*Executive Summary of the Book *Social Platform through Social Innovations Expo 2000*, 1999.

and strengthening all forms of economic roles of poor women. The ICNW as a legally registered and autonomous Micro Finance Institution has over 2,30,000 working poor women as shareholders and has effected a disbursement of over 440 million rupees with a recovery of 96 per cent covering 1003 slums and over 2700 villages.

In its special projects of Reproductive Health Care for women in partnership with United Nations Population Fund, it echoes the voices of poor women that such a healthcare effort is nothing, but a reflection of their choices as holistic approach and not imposition of crude methods of family planning, female surgeries etc. The health project, selects and trains women cadres from the poorer neighbourhood communities to perform marketable skills in the field of healthcare to the poor as advocated at the grassroots. WWF's healthcare programme conceptualises the dimension of human-centred approach covering a wide spectrum of women from birth to adolescence, reproductive age groups and even beyond reproductive stage among the older age group of women as well. The healthcare system of WWF has impacted a population of about 1 million covering 16,00,000 families in 720 slums and 340 villages through 960 health cadres from the grassroots.

Considering women's reproductive role as a social role – WWFs projects focus on human rights issues. Apart from child survival and safe motherhood, it fights the complicated issues of heinous practices of female infanticide, child labour and child prostitution. Above all, a firm emphasis on the welfare and development of female children, the most neglected resource in all the developing countries. Forum healthcare effort is a visible demonstration that the enhancement of quality of life ultimately results in the reduction of fertility rates.

WWF branches off as National Union of Working Women (NUWW) when it lays emphasis on a concept that poor themselves have a major role in their self-development process, by taking up conscious leadership roles and advocates within every neighbourhood. Remaining in the community these network of advocates continuously strive to educate the members of the community in the matters of entitlement of the poor and health consciousness. Be it the problem of unfair trade practices, better occupational safety measures, better wages according to stipulated legislative provisions and legal norms, child labour, child bondedness or exploitative working conditions, Forum helps women fight for their rights and entitlements. Women 'Unite in Solidarity' on a common platform through NUWW, on various other issues that affects the larger interests of the poor, by organising rallies and demand marches in order to achieve better visibility and better deal for themselves. The micro insurance scheme offering social security to women workers has referred over 1,18,000 policyholders to the insurance company giving them access to the much needed social safety net.

Amidst the challenges of the millennium like persistent poverty, environmental degradation and excessive population growth that continue to threaten human survival world over, more significantly in India and other developing countries, it becomes imminent that besides governmental efforts people's voluntary initiatives have to step-in to defuse the crisis. Initiative of the Working Women's Forum (India), is a future-oriented effort of multi-pronged initiative that will be found in the following pages of this book. In fact in its consolidation phase, WWF proposes to establish a training orientation module to benefit the most backward districts of Bihar and Orissa in India and the other Asian countries like Laos, Sri Lanka and Nepal etc. Currently, large numbers of training teams from these countries do visit WWF for an orientation on a short-term basis. Therefore, the future would be devoted more to effective sharing of experiences both within and outside the country reaching the growing network of civil society initiatives. In fact, the training teams from Government of Nepal and Madhya Pradesh have already visited WWF for short-term orientation of government functionaries. Surprisingly, some of the groups from the political parties are also taking initiative to visit WWF and to learn from its experiences on social mobilisation process. Thus, a concept of transferring this 'Pro-poor Strategy' will be a continuous process in WWF locally, nationally, regionally and globally.

The current process of liberalisation and economic restructuring demonstrates neither perceptible gain nor tangible benefit to the people of India, where still about Fourty-one per cent of its population live below the poverty line. The economic restructuring needs to be brought into an environment of building up growth with equity. The reform policies need alternative alliances which can be sought into the growing network of private and non-governmental institutions, both at the national and international level as against the current option of centralised government partnerships. WWF has built up one such coalition in partnership with the poor, experimenting/expanding their leadership roles in helping them to build up their capacity for self-development and towards generating income, asset creation and establishing right consciousness at the grassroots. Unless such new coalitions are formulated between the actors of various sectors nationally and globally, it will not be possible to achieve a sustainable livelihood for the poor around the globe within a set time frame to fight poverty. WWF believes in moving in a transitional path between market responses and social demands towards a sound pro-poor strategy with an imperative gender focus.

Strategies for the IVth U.N. Conference on Women and Social Development*

In the late 19th century, there was a general awakening in the Indian subcontinent against the colonial rule. Every section of the community in India were vying with each other to organise themselves and consequently the history of women's movement in India could also be linked to the same. Women's Movement in India had been more a social movement initiated by a group of gender sensitive men in India, such as Raja Ram Mohan Roy and Sri Kesavchandra Sen as a prerequisite to freedom struggle. They had a compulsion to bring every section of the weaker links, especially in the undivided Bengal, there had been great movements through the provocations of powerful writers like Sarat Chandra and Bhakim Chandra. Such publications became the focal points social revolutionary measures to correct the values of community or society that posed obstacles to women's progress. Manu, the Indian law giver, said that "Sthree Swatantriya Arhathi", which means women shall not have freedom. Later, Gandhiji arrived on the scene of India's freedom struggle, who not only gave a new momentum to the India's Independent struggle but also gave a clarion call to all sections of the people like women, scheduled caste, minorities, to participate in the struggle from bandage to freedom. Nowhere else in the history of the world, women had such privilege of participating in the liberation struggle of the country as early as that.

After, India had attained Independence during the late 40's, the Gandhian vision of women's liberation's cause had been enshrined in the constitution. However, this could help only a few elites like Rajkumari Amrit Kaur and Sarojini Naidu who then were the Ministers of Central Governments and Governors of Provinces. This is how Madame Bandaranayake in Sri Lanka rose to power and the families of Humayun, Kabir and Tagore came up in Bangladesh, Bhotoos' family in Pakistan could hold the top high positions in the subcontinent. So, while all this had only benefited the elite class, the spirit of the constitution has not percolated to the grassroots reaching the illiterate masses either by education or by mass media programmes. As any social change programme, media has an effective role to play. Now that we have doubled our population there is a further deterioration in the standards of public

*"Strategies for the IVth U.N. Conference on Women and Social Development" Presented at the Grassroots' NGO Centre, Beijing, China - 1995.

or private life; dowry, child marriages and discrimination dominate still the educated or middle class families. In Rajasthan, in early 80's we had watched the practice of 'Sati'. The girl child continues to be an object of discrimination and treated as a guest in her own house. Many parents are refused to beat girl children as a human resource and are always in a hurry to push her into early marriage and motherhood.

Women continue to be discriminated as mothers, especially among the poorer sections. Even as wage earners, women have not been covered by maternity benefits. The poor woman not only loses her working opportunities in her late pregnancy and lactation period but also is not eligible to get maternity benefits. In the case of family planning, the large-scale tubectomy surgery performed on women demonstrate, women alone becomes the target of family planning, their counterparts do not take things seriously. Also, looking after the large number of children in majority of the families in the Asian context is a female concern. Therefore, poor women is in a dilemma and what are her options? Is she to look after the large number of children or to become a victim of family planning target?

Besides gender bias, women of the working class in the Indian subcontinent, also face caste and the class biases. In the case of class oppression, her dispossession of asset is taken for guaranted. To quote an example of caste bias, in leather industries, the work is mostly handled by various sections of the scheduled castes especially women, as it is related to hides and skins. If you watch progress of Indian leather industries, technology has discriminated them as many of the leather work is done mostly by scheduled caste women and handled by their own hands with outmoded equipment, with no support of labour saving devices. However, the mass awakening among all shades of women, which came up in late 1975 after the First International Women's Year, still has to reach in large measures our women in the subcontinent. It is very slowly percolating in the subcontinent.

The Structural Adjustments of World Bank and IMF and the New Economic Reforms

The structural adjustment policies of the World Bank and IMF often lead to slashing of the budgets in the critical areas, such as nutrition, rural employment and other urban basic services, education, literacy. This adversely affects the welfare services for the poor women. In most cases, poor women can't spend on their own for such programmes. Also, as we have depended on many of the demi-gods, like the great revolutions and so on. We are now depending upon the economic reforms and restructuring of the economy. However, with the ongoing new economic reforms, there will be greater encouragement to market economy, and nowhere in the world the market economy helped people to come out of the poverty traps. The author doesn't know how far can we wait on the results of the open economy to get out of poverty traps? Living examples of Latin American and some African countries show that such encouragement to market economy have made the rich become richer, the poor are getting deteriorated to more and more to poverty. There will be more free-trade zones created in all our countries. The women and the workers will have no freedom to organise themselves and thus during the initial stages of this open economy, there will be a further deterioration of situation, especially for women working in export and manufacturing industries.

Unless pro-protection measures for the poor and women are taken care of, results are going to be more disastrous. Leaders of the women's movements have to keep awake. There is a greater compulsion for the poor and the weak to stay together and expand their networking because the message we carry home is to strengthen our networks and the sharing experiences of critical issues.

Women's Agenda for 21st Century Take up Unfinished Task*

Despite decades of hard struggle and even after four UN Conferences on Women and Development issues, discrimination on women continues unabated at all levels. Yet another Women's Day, 8th March, 1997 will pass through ending up in many more meetings, rallies and camps. But for many urban and rural poor women in the slums and rural areas, dignity and equality is still a distant dream.

Is it possible to remove the undervaluation of women's contribution to production process and her economic role, which is but the result of her subordinate position in the family/communities and further intensified by the cultural traditions that define their roles in the family and in the workplaces.

Why should women alone go through such oppressive situation? She has been systematically excluded from the control and the means of production. Due to the time-honoured sexual division of labour women are assigned the responsibility of only childcare and home maintenance as of prime importance gradually excluding her from the work process. Such stereotypes situations make the man to take over the control of production and resources and women the sole reproductive responsibility.

In a country like India, poverty has much more severe consequences on women than on men because of their exclusion from the various benefits and privileges, with no well-defined property rights, unpaid work, discriminative wage structure, that ultimately leads to a feminisation of poverty.

The caste and class bias, in addition, to above mentioned gender bias are some of the issues where enormous amount of awareness has been created by the emergence of women's movement all over the world, including India. Yet, there is an unfinished agenda of women's problems and feministic concerns that should form the major tasks for women and women's group before the turn of the century itself, even before one reaches the 21st century.

In the wake of the dowry problem and other atrocities on women, despite being equally educated, middle class young women live in a constant dilemma of a choice between security of tradition and promise of change, which warrants us to think whether marriage is a security or an impediment or is it the only option for women? The oppressions inflicted

---

*International Women's Day - Message on 8th March 1997.

and perpetuated against the poorest of women most often assumes violent and inhuman overtones, be it female infanticide, bride burning or sexual harassment. The large numbers of infant mortality and school dropouts of our girl children are proofs in themselves that such bias is inflicted on the girl child in her own home, by her own parents. It is not a common occurrence that she is treated as a guest in her own home? Strategy to do her away from home is to push her into early marriage and early motherhood. Are we aware that 65 per cent of these adolescent mothers are victims of mother mortality in this country? If they survive by any chance, it is still a surprise, but they live only to compromise their survival in their married homes, by the continuous provision of dowry for all occasions.

In the area of health, in all government programmes, women are victims of imposition of female sterilisation, HIV and AIDS. Why should it be only the responsibility of women towards population reduction? Why not men?

Media in these modern times, has a very important role to play in formulating policies and creating public opinion, especially on women's issues. But the TV and other visual medias seldom realise this, on the contrary, women are glorified in the visual media as objects of lust and enjoyment and not portrayed as human beings with creative abilities.

The question that looms around us today is how long can women continue to be silent spectators to all this? Its time for women to perceive themselves as agents for social change and fight hard to complete the unfinished agenda on women's issues atleast in the coming century.

Social Movements and the Social Economy*

Social movements are the outcome of the political struggle by the people against exploitation with a view to achieve economic freedom and guarantee basic human survival. South Asia in general, and India, in particular, has given birth to innumerable such movements from time to time - all of which have broken new ground, undermining anarchic, oppressive structures to empower people and communities.

The earliest of such a refinish movement was initiated by Late Raja Ram Mohan Ray of Bengal. He was a nationalist and he could gather a handful of individuals and kindle their spirit of social awakening on matters relating to the freedom of the press and liberation of women (Sati) on constitutional lines.

Later, around 1936, peasant movements were designed in India to bring about a strong agrarian revolution in the states of Bengal and Bihar by mobilizing particularly poor peasants, Thus, movements known as Tebhaga, Tanka struggles in Bengal and Bakhast movements in Bihar brought to the forefront, the issues of the oppressive working and living conditions of poor peasants across barriers of caste, religion and ethnicity (Hindu, Muslims and Tribal peasants) ensuring the very active participation of the poor or peasants in organized unions as a primary move.

The most prominent example of a strong revolt in India is the freedom movement of the country. This national struggle of India proved to be an event of worldwide significance, resulting in its transformation into a political party of national governance. Further, the movement had opened the floodgates for similar movements in most of the Asian and African countries, breaking the chains of slavery and leading to freedom from centuries of bondage for the masses.

One remarkable feature in all the Indian social movements is that, they are strongly guided by the Gandhian Philosophy in thought and practical wisdom. Coming from the land of Mahatma Gandhi, one feels proud to say that he always pursued the path of non-violence, tolerance, benevolence and responsiveness to higher values even with his adversaries. Thus, all movements, while concentrating on their achievement of unity and independence as immediate objectives, also tried for the economic and social upliftment of the target groups involved in these movements.

---

*Presented at the International Congress on Social Economy (North and the South) on 7-8 March at Oostende, Belguim - 1997.

Working Women's Forum (India) is one such spontaneous social movement of poor wómen in the informal sector, who form a critical component of the workforce in India. WWF, though registered itself as a Trade Union, also functions as a Co-operative. Apart from these two identities, it is a movement marked by voluntarism of its membership, motivated to act on specific class objectives. The Forum, therefore, is more a process of empowerment, that binds its members together, rather than just a non-profit organisation providing material benefits such as employment or credit. While addressing the economic interests of the poor, WWF felt it is equally important to build up a strong socio-political platform to reflect the voice of these poor women and to carry on their struggles and confrontation towards sustainable livelihoods on a permanent basis.

The neighbourhood approach and the group dynamics adopted at WWF, deals with diverse needs of the clients such as business counselling, social support systems, solidarity and so forth. The credit process served as a training ground to gain clout and share and solve mutual problems, as an alternate strategy for their survival. This innovative concept, eventually, not only led to its multiplication in large numbers, but also has reached multitudes of the poor in a short span of time as a mass movement.

It is a challenge, both to social activists and unions to innovate new strategies towards expansion and sustainability of peoples' initiatives. Beyond simple wage bargaining, for casualties workers, there are other important aspects that need to be addressed by Trade Unions, such as training, education and micro-enterprises for, which the process of economic and social empower rent becomes more appropriate. When unions link up with economic activities, it makes it an advantage to make the informal sector worker not to be able to perceive herself as a "worker" in addition to having access to credit and achieving a dignified livelihood.

"A novel system of group borrowing, initiated successfully by the Working Women's Forum (WWF) in India, and described in the case study by Claire L. Bangasser (Chapter 13), thus points to, yet another way of establishing the unions' relevance among poor self-employed women."[1]

"The Cooperative Movement in India has been closely associated with the freedom struggle of the country described earlier. When the founding fathers of India's Independence were in search of new

1. "Women in Trade Unions, Organizing the Unorganized: Claire L. Bangasser".

approaches to economic freedom, after they had achieved political freedom through non-violent means, they turned their attention to the critical role of cooperatives, expecting this movement to become an inevitable instrument of economic development and social change, especially when the country and its people were passing through difficult times, due to ages of colonial rule and exploitation. They visualised this cooperative venture as an enabling strategy and step towards extensive social development, making it more a vehicle of change process in the hands of millions of men and women. They expected this venture further to interact with the public, promoting a sense of social cohesion and mutual obligation, especially in rural societies.[2]

The scenario is different today. The Cooperative Movement in India has currently been identified more and more as an effort with a lot of state control and intervention. For visionaries it was meant in the early days, that such a social control was essential as a method of approach aiming at a socialistic pattern of society, ensuring a balance of individual freedom and state control, especially when it was meant to deal with greater degree of illiterate masses. Such state control and intervention have later become impediments to community participation. Hence, the cooperative system which was evolved by pioneers as an ideal vehicle for the reconstruction of our rural societies to build a sound agrarian economy in rural India, has almost turned itself into a bureaucratic venture negating the spirit of co-operation by its members.

Despite all this, a few innovative ventures of cooperatives have routed such state control and interventions. Such initiatives started seeking new ways to move forward to maintain democratic standards in the struggles of people, fought the governmental bureaucracy, and tried to relieve the co-operatives from the domination of urban elites and rural rich, making it a vehicle to serve the less fortunate clientele, i.e., women, poor peasants and artisans. These ventures tried to move forward to help non-farm ventures of rural and urban poor in villages and slums, facilitating even the march of the poorest towards better employment.

As the normal and commercial bankers always considered the poor and their ventures as non-bankable, it has become all the more necessary to initiate a non-formal credit system, since in the cases of poor men and women, it was the insecurity of production credit that had been a major constraint creating a vicious cycle of poverty. It is in this context that the

---

2. "Co-operative Perspective" Vaikunthbhai Metha Centenary year, Commemorative Volume.

Working Women's Forum (India) promoted the Indian Cooperative Network for Women - a successful cooperative initiative of very poor women workers to work in three southern states of Tamil Nadu, Andhra Pradesh and Karnataka, both to help the assetless and disadvantaged poor women and to improve the quality of their lives. Initiating itself from below, unique in structure, maintaining grassroots character, the WWF/ ICNW combine innovatively structured itself to reach large number of poor women workers. As this small venture started spreading itself, far and wide, benefiting large numbers, it became a movement of about 450,000 women workers at the grassroots in three southern states of India. Further, it promotes friendship societies in the northern states of Orissa and Uttar Pradesh, encouraging other NGOs to take up such ventures.

Initiating in 1978, with 800 members, within a period of 18 years, both WWF and ICNW have grown into a voluntary action process culminating into a massive cooperative venture making the concept as a way of life. Further, WWF and ICNW, through the innovative structure, both informal and easy to function, facilitated the participation of the poor members and borrowers at all level of its operations.

Members of the cooperative were mostly working class women, such as fisherwomen, beedi (country cigars) rollers, landless group of women, handicraft producers, women weavers/rope makers, street vendors/ pavement hawkers and service specialists each having organized to confront oppressive situation of their living and working conditions.

The role of these women from poorer neighbourhoods in keeping up the standards of cooperative banking system has been extremely remarkable. They helped the banking staff to select, guarantee and supervise the end use of loans. Some of them took up even higher responsibilities to provide pressure on default members for effective repayment. This effort of organizers and area leaders enabled WW and ICNW to reach a recovery rate of over 95 per cent uniformly in all the branches. The initial capital of 18.2 million rupees in the ICNW has been rotated to 140 million, which amply shows the tremendous potential for capital growth towards long-term financial sustainability even within the network of the poorest women.

The recent study of internal assessment of WWF and ICNW among its members on its socio-economic aspects reveal the following details. Over 550 women involved in 25 different occupations, responded, both on the utilization programme benefits relating to business, consumer need, relief from indebtedness and investing the profits towards better standards of living conditions, such as civic amenities and housing needs. The degree of economic empowerment, among the most deprived communities leading to a social change process, has been rated very high, indicating their children being sent to school, better contraceptive practices, small family norm, better nutritional standards and the like.

Thus, WWF and ICNW laid the foundation for economic empowerment leading to better democratic standards especially in a non-profit organisation of peoples own initiatives, reducing the domination of bureaucracy at all levels. An ideal cooperative venture, ICNW, stood up to the objectives of the founding fathers of India's freedom movement, upholding the human dignity and basic challenges in the economic and social structure.

4

Human Rights Violation or Dignified Co-Existence?*

Man's inhumanity to man has been the most condemnable black chapter in the history of mankind. History has innumerable examples of human rights violations pushing people to the worst of consequences, such as hunger strikes, land encroachments and even armed struggle. In such situations, even judicial interventions have failed to protect the innocent. Many activists have sought solutions only through popular resistance movements that gained momentum to protect the rights of their citizens.

Unfortunately, violence and terrorism have become the order of the day. It is very difficult to protect the rights of the poor who continue to remain powerless, as all solutions including that of judiciary mostly favour the privileged rather than the poor.

One of the glaring example is the judgment of the Rajasthan High Court in late 80's, in the case of practice of 'Sati', where Roop Kanwar, was burnt alive alongwith her deceased husband. No doubt, the culprits had been immediately arrested as an eyewash, but ultimately all of them were acquitted on the grounds that "there had been no eye witness" despite the gruesome and cold-blooded murder taking place openly in the public. The subsequent judgment that favoured the culprits stated that, "There must be respect for people's sentiments", i.e., the sentiments of those who believed in their religious rights. This was one of the worst precedent for even cold-blooded murder being justified in the name of religion and culture, denying a woman even her fundamental right to survive in this world.

---

*Appeared as Editorial in *GROOTS* in December 1998 to commemorate U.N. Human Rights day – December 10th.

Often when it come to the question of human rights, legal solutions are mellowed and softened as justice is denied to many victims by addressing their grievances only marginally. Such actions of justice, instead of offering appropriate legal solutions often instil fear in the minds of victims, was witnessed in the case of the Bhopal gas victims. Invariably, it is more often, on matters of protection of the rights of working class, that the victims are not only treated as inconsequential but, also their rightful demands are dismissed as unconstitutional. Is there a possibility to empower legal systems in this country in favour of the poor? Can there be positive action to protect the rights of the poor so as to assure equality and dignity to their lives?

Yet another example of inhumanity against women, in many parts of the country is that she is considered as a drain on the family's resources. The female child is seldom given a fair status in the household, being treated as an unwelcome guest in her own home, discriminated right from birth and sometimes even before birth. The evidences are the rampant occurrence of female infanticide in Salem, Dharmapuri and many parts of Bihar.

The worst forms of human right violations do not come from elsewhere but are practiced by the vested interests that are within the country. They thrive on inciting and inducing the innocent emotionally through religious fundamentalism, terrorism and casteism. These are, in fact, the worst enemies of a growing nation and a cancerous growth that eats away the healthy trends in our society.

Recent information provided in the Parliament by the Honourable Home Minister in the month of June 1998, is a testimony to gross violation of human rights, especially on women, despite CEDAW declaration proclaiming women's rights as human rights. He informed the House that in the past one year more than 14,000 women were raped, around 27,000 women were defamed, out of whom 1000 women belong to scheduled caste and over 300 of them are tribals. While Madhya Pradesh tops the list with over 3,000 women being victims, the union territory of Delhi has over 600 women victims. Does anyone need more evidence to say that our enemies who violate fundamental human rights are not from outside but are only from within this country.

Man's dearest possession is a piece of land of his own that assures him his fundamental right to a decent, secure and safe livelihood and even that is denied to many. As at times, whatever little that is left with him is also sold to pay off debts, when even this becomes impossible mass suicides result in an effort to escape debt burden (the recent occurrences in many parts of the country). The denial of a piece of land or a state of landlessness is the most blatant denial of fundamental means to productive resources. This pushes people into chronic poverty or they sustain themselves through marginal wage labour.

Landlessness is the single largest agrarian problem in India, driving every individual in the country into abject poverty. This landlessness includes even those who do not own a small piece of land to construct their house, as even today we have nomadic tribes practicing shifting cultivation. Despite occupying a piece of land for generations tribals in many places are denied access to land in the name of so called "conservation". On the other hand, it is a common occurrence in many places that large scale deforestation is the result of exploitative practices of the government supported contractors. While the trees are cut for commercial purposes, the traditional inhabitants (tribals) in those places are refused access even to minor forest produce.

Sometimes, land tenure is discriminatory because the poor have no land. If and when they have access to a piece of land, either it has no water or is too small or of poor quality where nothing can be grown, not even meagre food products. Under these circumstances, where do the poor and landless stand in the midst of powerful landed gentry? In many parts of India, such as Bihar and Orissa, the colonial land holding patterns such as permanent settlement that were assigned by the British still prevail, assuring land holdings to rich farmers, that nobody can touch despite land reform legislations.

Denial of land rights in rural India, leads to mass migration of rural people to urban centres. In their unending pursuit of a decent livelihood, these rural landless jump "from the frying pan of rural poverty into the pyre of urban squalor". It is a devastating state of deprivation wherein the rural areas are deprived of its rich human resources. The conditions of people in the urban slums is a different story altogether with prevalent demolition sprees. These are glaring evidences of demonstration of a denial of the right to a decent livelihood, access to food and shelter to the poor in our major cities.

Cross border migration are but by-products of unemployment and landlessness that result in the worst form of racism ending up in ethnic conflicts and the victims are classified as economic migrants. In several countries, such conflicts often lead to the outburst of terrorism, creating a climate of insecurity in the country. All these are but common occurrences in the nook and corner of the country. India has never been so badly divided, as it is today full of divisive movements and armed conflicts, resulting in insecurity to life and personal property. It's a historical irony that India, a country that has been so much committed to Ahimsa, non-violence is the one that is the worst affected by terrorism and conflicts of all kinds making it an unsafe place to live in.

The practice of untouchability was considered as the worst form of discrimination and a practice condemned, by the framers of the Constitution, as it is opposed to the very fundamental principle of human dignity. Human dignity being the birth right of every woman and man, no one can ever be regarded as an untouchable. Besides, all the Indian religious scriptures also preach only brings down human status absolutely but provides no framework to bring about a change, such a practice disregards the very social structure of India. This restrictive, reactionary practice provides no freedom for the exploited section of the people to move even a step forward.

Despite the declaration of the rights of the child stating that the working children have a right to protect themselves from physical and mental exploitation, unabated child abuse and indiscreet use of child labour and bondedness are the order of the day. Hundreds of children often face exploitation at workplace and are engaged in hazardous occupations. Female children are the worst victims and face even sexual abuse at the workplace.

The father of the nation, Mahatma Gandhi, said on the concluding day of his famous Dandi March, "I want the world's sympathy in the battle of right against the might". But even after 50 years, the battle to fight for justice continues with freedom from colonial rule having little or no meaning for many. A nation that has completed 50 years of democratic rule has to remember that it has to infuse self discipline, responsibility and compassion in the minds of its citizens. Only then their personal and collective freedom will survive to shape the human destinies to higher echelons. Therefore, the need of the hour is a human-centred action to fight and conquer the citadels of self-interest and irresponsibility that lead to conflicting and divisive ideologies. The day when human relations dominate the thinking of a nation will be the day when this country will learn new lessons for the survival of the human race by pursuing reconciliation of ideologies guided by the principles of co-existence.

Are Child Rights not Human Rights?

"My father always quarrels with my mother, one day he slashed a knife on my mother and lot of blood came out and my mother fell down. My father later drank poison and died. After my mother was treated and brought home, police came to my house and my father was cremated", says 12 year old Anandhi.

Being mute witnesses to such violence at home, umpteen number of children in this country enter directly into adulthood at very young ages, shouldering the conomic and social burden of their families.

"We are four girls in our family, my father left my mother because all of us are girls, she works in the fields and I go with her for work to earn. We eat if anything is left over of the previous night, most days we starve. I get 2 padi (measure) rice and my mother gets 4 padi rice for a week's work. We pound it to make porridge and fill our stomachs".

The above words are ample evidence to the fact that persistent poverty forces children to work, and creates in them a strong desire to earn money at the expense of foregoing their valuable childhood, despite their earnings being meagre as it is crucial for the very survival of the family.

Vicious traps of economic backwardness and dispossession of assets not only leads to perpetual indebtedness among the parents of these children, but also makes them blind to the realisation of a child's right to recreation, education and physical and mental upliftment. Thus, the acute problem of assetlessness in many poor families leads to a practice of child mortgage and bondedness (among beedi workers in Vellore and silk weavers in Kanchipuram) thus, relegating a valuable human resource into mere economic assets.

"When my mother gets Rs.3000, she will give it to my employer and release me from their loom. But it is very difficult, as my father has mortgaged all the silk zari to the pawn broker to drink alcohol and it has to be redeemed first. So, I should continue to work and earn Rs.5 everyday to help my mother", says Kanchana, a child worker in the silk looms of Kanchipuram, who is bonded to an employer (i.e., an affluent weaver).

Unless there is a strong attempt to prevent the involvement of children in family trades or to take the load of household chores off the female child and simultaneously strengthen adult employment, especially that of the women in the family, it will be impossible to prevent the incidence of child bondedness or child labour particularly due to the fact that these families are heavily indebted due to low male contribution to the family.

"I can easily lift sugarcane bundles on my head atleast 50 times in a day. When I go to reap groundnuts, I get groundnuts in return for my work", says Kumudha of Navampatti village, who is paid for her work not in cash but in kind.

Roughly 150 million child workers are engaged in a variety of occupations. Child workers are, as is evident, dominant in the informal sector working as agricultural workers, housemaids, helpers, rag-pickers service industry etc. In the view of the employer, the earnings of the child are very negligible as he has formulated it to subsidise the cost of production and thus consciously keeps the adult wages at minimum levels. Ultimately, such labour practices in the long run has only led to depression in adult wages in that section of economy.

It is equally important to note that many children are allowed to work in hazardous occupations. Exposing children to such hazardous jobs is not only physically taxing, but also impairs their mental and physical growth permanently. The cramped sheds in many slums with poor lighting, house several women and children working in sub-human conditions amidst dust and smog. Children inhale this everyday with no healthcare as the shed does not strictly qualify to be called a factory.

Industries, such as agarbathi and beedi rolling, matchstick making, cracker and chemical manufacturing units are but few examples of innumerable number of industries that employ children who have to work for long and hard hours in extremely hazardous conditions.

"My brother studied upto college, he could never get any steady job. He is now working in the loom, therefore, my father did not educate me after IV class. I now know how to weave a sari," says Murugan of Pillaiyar Palayam.

While it is meaningless to presume that the introduction of compulsory education becomes an automatic prelude to abolition of child labour, it is equally impractical to think that legal solutions alone can dislodge children working in traditional units. Therefore, such attempts by governmental authorities have only resulted in children being thrown out of working units and who have, as a result, taken to loitering, vagrancy or beggary.

The judicial directions or sensitive legislations have little or no meaning if they are not followed up with strong political will and stringent enforcement measures. How to make this possible is anybody's guess, as most often the enforcement machineries support only the employer rather than the victim due to the feudal setups prevalent in rural and urban areas.

Non-formal educational systems imparting functional literacy is most crucial, although it may be only a short-term solution to this complex problem. Special provisions, like the conscious attempt to promote vocational and employment-oriented courses can become a bridging effort to facilitate children to enter into the mainstream educational system. To draw these children to schools, the educational system must be made more innovative and schooling more interesting. Strengthening adult employment and increasing budgetary allocation for the social sector in this era of globalisation is a dire need to save these children.

It is a shame that despite 50 years of independence, the economic balance of a country of this size should desperately be dependent on its child labour, which is just a guise for slave labour. How long can a democratic country hide behind excuses?

Violence Against Women Thriving Symbol of a Disgraceful Culture*

If women had a choice or say, they would never adopt 'patience' as their strategy to safeguard the tradition-ridden heritage in all our developing world. Despite such women's continued sacrifice of their dignity for the sake of a male dominated society, chapters in human history have little or no reference of any concern for womanhood. The need of the hour is to work towards a conducive social environment to establish a healthy concept of equality between the sexes making it a reality, rather than pushing the burden on women and their proverbial patience.

Currently, a situation analysis of the day demands that it is no more a virtue for women to be "tolerant", but it certainly could be worse than suicidal for them. Nor is it sensible to believe that women are endowed with these qualities by birth. Brainwashed by the custodians of patriarchal values and dogmas for centuries, unfortunately women themselves perceive that their virtue lies in being subservient, as ideal wife and a role model of socio-cultural stereotypes of gender subordination. Thus, women lost their identity, consequently their multi-faceted personalities were eroded, talents thwarted, capabilities ignored and initiatives suppressed and they continued as extensions of their male counterparts without a voice of their own.

The story of this dependence of womanhood is as ancient as the days of 'Manu', the great law giver, who had laid down the Hindu social order. This great personality, in addition, to his codification of the unwritten law of ancient Hindu customs has forewarned the society that women should never be given freedom. Unfortunately, these laws cannot be ignored as mere fiction of a bygone era, but remain alive as horrors that continue to haunt the lives of many women making them inferior, dependent and lesser equals.

Violence against women is the most disregarding example of treating women as inferior beings. Such violence manifests as rape, dowry deaths and many forms of domestic violence. Most of them are planned atrocities on women too. Such atrocities affects women's dignity, keep women in perpetual subordination, wantonly confining her within the four walls of house or make her remain closed to the world. Further, such atrocities when condoned or ignored by the States or society as unimportant domestic incidents, further instils only insecurity in the minds of women, creating permanent stumbling blocks to their progress.

---

*Appeared in *GROOTS* as Editorial, April 1999.

To trace its origin, violence against women is but part of the cultural pattern, throughout their life cycle yielding no dignified place of respect for women. Women according to religious and racial values are incapable of possessing any intellectual, rational powers and are worthy of being treated only as mere objects of pleasure or lust. Thus from time immemorial, such prejudices promoted the sexual subjugation and paved the way for the exploitation of women.

With changing times, the atrocities took different forms and shapes but continued to persist and torment women. The female foeticide and child prostitution are all but the other side of the same coin. The increasing number of sex determination centres mushrooming even in many far corners of the country are ample proof of the atrocities and discrimination perpetuated on girl babies even before they are born in this world, due to tradition bound "Male Child syndrome" of the parents.

This obsession creates a sense of hatred and repugnance against a girl child and is prevalent among all caste and classes of Indian society. It does not end with attempts to kill the unborn girl child right in the womb or soon after her birth, but continues right through her life, as she is condemned and thought of as a drain in the family at every stage for being born a woman. Thus, she is denied proper nutrition, medical care, equal opportunities or even an honoured existence. The irony of it all is that the perpetrators of all these crimes are not strangers but her own family and friends.

Child marriage is yet another atrocity practiced on very young children denying them even their normal basic childhood. It is still a practice in some of the semi-tribal families in states like Rajasthan that when these married children grow up, the couple lose track of each other, the parents arrange for a second marriage for the girls called 'Nutra' where huge bride price is collected from the bridegroom. This is a practice that exploits the girl children, as sometimes the same girl is offered to several bridegrooms for huge sums as bride prices.

The burden of dowry in modern India has made many parents transact their daughters, as business objects under the guise of marriage, where they in turn are sold away to beggary or prostitution. Currently, hundreds of stories of brides having been burnt alive are carried in the news, for not being able to comply with repeated demands of dowry. Dowry in India is not a one time practice but is carried throughout the life time of the bride. It is well known fact, that the number of women going down statistically in the sex ratio are nothing, but the result of atrocities on women and yet dowry deaths and crimes against women continue unabated. Even the 1980's witnessed the occurrence of 'Sati' in Rajasthan.

The Devadasi system, which is a sheer exploitative practice of dedicating girl children in the service of God, who later end up as prostitutes is common phenomenon in many parts of the country. This practice is highly prevalent even today in Andhra Pradesh and Karnataka despite legal ban. The fact that degenerated, oppressive and exploitative customs continues to flourish in the name of culture and tradition even in a democratic country condemning hundreds of young girls and women to a life of poverty, sexual exploitation and misery, is reflective of the incompetence of the legal systems, law and order mechanisms and the lack of political will. With the indifference of society at large, a revolution seems distant and remote.

The worst forms of violence against women is that which manifests in forms of rape, molestation and sexual harassment. Such violations cause both mental and physical torture leaving the victims permanently scared. To make matters worse, even for the very few victims, who are courageous enough to resort to legal recourse, the prolonged legal process only aggravates the pain and suffering of these victims, as the onus of proving that she had indeed been raped is on her, while the offender is free to wait and watch. With an appalling rate of actual convictions, i.e., even on the small percentage of reported cases, victims are discouraged to opt for legal redemption, as they would only be stigmatised socially.

Despite the four UN conferences, fighting to improve the status of women, the oppressive social orders are so strong that women in many developing countries continue to suffer inferiority, dependence and are yet to find ways to improve their own situation just because they happen to be women. They are overtaken by problems of daily struggle of poverty and are burdened with the responsibility of providing for the family.

While media has stepped up its coverage on women, it does not depict such everyday struggle of women as experienced both inside and outside their homes. The focus is mainly on sensationalism and dramatisation of repulsive and unpleasant events, rather than gender sensitive and objective presentation of hard hitting realities. The miseries of widowed wives and daughters who are sold due to poverty and deprivation do not figure much in the media. The images in the media on violence against women, particularly portrayal of rape or sexual slavery using women and girls as objects of lust, further contributes to the enhancement of such crimes inculcating wrong values in the minds of the younger generations.

The constitution of independent India has proclaimed a new social order guaranteeing equal opportunities for all. However, with over 40 per cent of the population in the country being illiterate and poor, unaware of their legal rights, vulnerable and exploited, such proclamations continue to remain meaningless rhetoric. Even the periodical judicial activism practiced by our judicial system in the recent times has not succeeded in reaching the grassroots to provide justice to the aggrieved millions. The feminists struggle not only in India and South Asia but also in the entire regions of developing countries, such as Africa and Latin America, continue to focus on such atrocities against women, and bring to the fore, the glaring realities.

For instance, experiences are presented by less fortunate women in International meetings and conferences about the practice of Female Circumcision in Africa, a grave human tragedy, an evidence revealing the perpetuation of barbaric practices on female children. These are but inhuman practices that deny women the right to control or regulate their own sexuality and reproductive behaviour. This brutal practice inflicts on young women untold miseries, pain, trauma, severe physical complications, infections and even death. It affects the very self-esteem of women through psychological fear. In these African communities, the girl children who go through female genital mutilation are between 4 and 8 years of age, which according to those communities is the age for their children to know their social roles as women. This practice unfortunately not only propagates the existing myths and mindsets in these countries but also over the centuries, has become an accepted social behaviour. Far from being perceived as a mere superstition, it is a local custom and a recognised health practice as well. A radical change of attitude is required to get rid of such crimes against women and to improve the status of women in these countries.

Yet worst are situation in Asia and Latin America where women are denied even the basic right to live as normal human beings. The systematic and organised trafficking of girls and women (who struggle for their daily survival due to poverty) in flesh trade and forced prostitution, make them dependent and inferior beings. The girls and women from the rural areas who are struggling for livelihoods are lured by anti-social elements with a promise for a better life and are brought into major cities for such lucrative flesh trade, even though

FEEDBACK FROM NATIONAL HUMAN RIGHTS COMMISSION....

"The Commission would like to express its deep appreciation to Ms. Arunachalam for the contented range of the articles contained in the newsletter, the subjects covered being of considerable and continuing interest to the Commission. The Commission noted in particular the article on 'The Devadasis of Kudithini Village' which is of special relevance to the Commission, at the Commission is, at present, engaged in a programme to deal with the problem of child prostitution in that area".

prostitution is deemed as illegal in many of these countries. The legal recourses are often pitted against the victims, as they are the ones who are often apprehended and punished, while the offenders go scot-free. Very often these girls and women after involving themselves in such forced prostitution for several years end up being swindled of even the meagre resources that they manage to earn out of this profession by those who introduced them to this trade. While such trades and industry thrive well with the owners becoming rich and affiuent, the women who are instrumental in making these traders wealthy, find themselves mostly in abysmal conditions trapped in the vicious cycle of poverty. Women are the worst sufferers in ethnic conflicts, violence and very little is heard of the sexual abuse that women suffer at the hands of the soldiers.

It is no exaggeration to say that incidences of violence against women not only in India but all over these contemporary societies in the developing world are on the increase. They have become rampant and gruesome threatening the very basic right of women to lead a life of dignity and self-respect. Therefore, as mentioned in the beginning of this editorial, over glorification of virtues of "patience and endurance" among women will only lead to perpetuation of injustice and inequality against women. The need of the hour is "intolerance / impatience against such social discriminations to accelerate the pace of social change, instilling a new social order promoting genuine fraternity between both the sexes.

Participation – Case Study of National Union of Working Women – Indian Experiment

Human Resource and Development Issues in the Third World

Deplorable conditions of poverty and misery combined with a host of oppressions are heaped on the rural and urban poor, in all the third world countries. They raise a number of queries as to what does development mean to achieve? Is it the development of people, things or places? What does development imply? Why do the poor alone suffer in oppressive situations of hunger and poverty? Who exactly are the targeted poor? Of them, about half are women, 60 per cent are under 20, 400 million are illiterate, 60 per cent live below the bread line and 80 per cent are rural. Out of the 100 million rural households, 30 to 40 million households are without land or possess only marginal holdings. Thus, it is the poor who are unorganised, undernourished and form the long suffering mass of humanity.

What is the calibre of this human resource (both young and old men and women) available in rural areas? Often very poor, living much below the subsistence level, illiterate, unemployed and underemployed, invariably highly indebted, ill fed, vulnerable to disease, they suffer from a lack of confidence and are an easy prey to exploitation. They also suffer from malnutrition, lack of sanitation and lack of maternal and child care.

Answers to the above mentioned questions are simple. While the rural poor are landless or marginally landed, the heritage of feudalism and colonialism bear upon them. The urban poor on the other hand, though smaller in number are equally unorganised as compared to the rural poor in all developing countries.

It is evident, therefore that development is not merely reinforcement of natural enterprising attitudes in people, but also the most important process by which, human dignity should be contented, assuring a quality of life for every individual.

Thus, human resource development and equitable benefit distribution are two important criteria for any successful development system (as against the prevalent system of denial of equal opportunities) that continues the perpetuation and promotion of islands of prosperity amidst the vast ocean of human poverty.

People's Participation a Pre-condition for Development

What then is the strategy for successful development? It is a strategy that requires people's participation at all levels. Nonetheless, such a participation is a long drawnout process to be awakened among the masses through mobilisation, education, extension, organisation, action consolidation, and growth towards fulfilment.

Participation of the people sometimes means the organisation of movements of magnitude in which the poor have to learn to decide, control and empower themselves at the grassroots. They have to train themselves to new responsibilities of leadership, self-participation, management orientation through a process conscientisation.

Obstacles for People's Participation

Despite widespread calls and concerns for increased people's participation in development, many obstacles remain hindering the emergence of genuine participatory efforts. Scattered distribution of productive assets, local power hierarchies, elite domination and conflicts among the poor themselves are some evident obstacles that still impede this progress.

Women and Development

When we come to realities of facts, women from 50 per cent of the third world poor, living in sub-human conditions of starvation and squalor. It is a recurring story of incomplete human existence for the female poor in all developing countries.

In particular, the problems of women workers in rural areas and in urban slums are but additional barriers and constraints to smooth development. The most disheartening feature is that women workers contribution to the community and country is totally invisible. A recognition in their own right for such a contribution is often denied. Women's work is under-valued and under-estimated even if they are widowed and deserted; their work is always considered cheap, flexible and disposable labour as workers they have no bargaining power. Undoubtedly development in rural areas demands a great from women, both in production and family care, yet women do not have access to resources and a fair share in decision-making. Therefore, access to political and economic power is a precondition to perform these roles effectively.

People's Initiatives

However here and there, there are small initiatives where the poor rural and urban women have effectively organised themselves to defend their rights for equal opportunities and treatment, to raise income and employment levels and to enhance their access to basic development resources. Onc such initiative is the National Union of Working Women (NUWW) reflecting an innovative approach, demonstrating that women though poor can organise themselves and participate in rural and urban development efforts and work to combat poverty, enhance their status, raise income and employment levels. The efforts of NUWW clearly demonstrate that social awareness can be raised, provided women show their collective determination to participate in development and be treated as full members of the community. Such an initiative as the NUWW raises a variety of issues concerning the opportunities and conditions under which poor women can effectively organise themselves, the approaches and methods adopted to stimulate their determination to collectively overcome the barriers and obstacles that limit their total participation in development.

The Objectives of this Paper are four-fold :

1. To discuss and analyse the experience of poor women's participation in programmes of development (i.e., the experience of the NUWW).
2. To describe the obstacles encountered by these poor women while organising themselves.
3. To describe the strategies that were employed to overcome these obstacles.
4. To provide policy guidelines for community work even in difficult areas such as family planning and rural development.

National Union of Working Women

The National Union of Working Women, a grassroot organisation of poor working class women, has branches in six centres – Madras, Dindigul (Anna district), Adiramapattinam (Tanjore district), Vellore (North Arcot district), Bangalore (Karnataka State) and Narasapur (Andhra Pradesh). Initiated in 1978, as a women intensive organisation, it has recorded a growth of over 52,899 members and is operational in three southern states of India; i.e., Tamil Nadu, Andhra Pradesh and Karnataka.

Objectives of NUWW

The aims and objectives of the National Union of Working Women which was started in 1978 as a political women intensive unit are as follow:

- To provide organisational support to women workers on trade lines to improve their living and working conditions.
- To device the organisational structure to be grassroot in nature, in order to reach women workers in large numbers.
- To be women intensive in nature so as to address itself against caste, class and gender oppressions of women workers in India.
- To adopt a programme strategy that addressed women workers' critical needs in the informal sector / (Credit and Employment) to carry on an intensive health and family planning programme among women

workers to strengthen their productive and restrict their reproductive roles.

Several studies on NUWW show that while the urban poor women are major contributors to family income, the rural poor women play a very crucial role in the agrarian economy. These women who are actively involved in farm operations are socially and economically disadvantaged and are victims of harsh working conditions, unemployment and lack of legal protection.

Schedules of Women Workers in NUWW

The descriptions of the schedules of work of women workers whom the NUWW has unionised are of wide varieties. In the urban areas, they are mostly vendors, hawkers, petty producers, construction workers etc. They sell most of their goods and services to other clientele, who are also below the poverty line living in the city slums with very little purchasing power. Sometimes, they are also piece-rate wage labourers, contract labourers or home-based occupations that are very exploitative in nature, in which there are no stipulated working hours nor fixed wages. The workers in this system live in isolation and therefore, their knowledge on working hours and wages are almost nil. Most of the consumer items like beedis, cigars and cigarettes, are produced in India by these workers either under the home-based production system or contract system of labour.

In rural areas, during the non-agricultural season most of the women are engaged in some kind of micro-business, either home-based or in mobile markets. Some of them are rural artisans, and are engaged in production of beautiful handicrafts that bring in abundant foreign exchange to this country.

Nature of Organisation on Tradelines

Ineffective social legislations and male alcoholism (which results in family neglect and low male income contributions to family income) increase the drudgery on these women workers. In the case of agricultural wage labourers, landlessness (amidst sizable land ownership by a handful of powerful people) the irregular nature of agricultural work and the prevalent powerlessness augment the oppressions of the rural women workers. The other category involves traditional handicraft workers who are caught in the complex web of contractors and merchant exporters – each interested in a larger margin for themselves. The category of women workers working as home-based contract labourers under an exploitative system makes the efforts of these women workers totally unproductive. Thus, the oppressive situations mentioned above clearly demonstrated to the women the class character of the society in which they live and work.

Therefore, to sharpen their focus and to combat such a class character, the NUWW realised that its original grassroot character had to be supplemented by the character of a trade union in order to protect the rights of its members. With that end in view, the NUWW registered itself as a Trade Union under the Trade Union Act, with an aim to unionise women workers and to be national in character.

Besides economic oppressions of class character, these women workers go through a series of social oppressions, such as caste and gender situations.

Case Examples I: Women Workers in Madras City Slums

1.38 million people of city of Madras in Tamil Nadu state in southern part of Indian subcontinent live in slums settlements. They constitute one-third of the city's population. The range of employment that generates income varies in such informal sector occupations. Socio-economic surveys of Madras city indicate that women in this sector are employed in various activities, such as hawking, vending, service occupations, but such studies show that these workers are invisible totally in statistical terms and there is a general pattern of under-reporting of their work and productivity as elsewhere in all developing countries.

Social Conditions of City Slum Women

The social conditions at home in terms of divorce, desertion, flexible unions, wife beating and alcoholism are very common. Large family (i.e., a large number of children) sizes and very active reproductive roles for women workers are common features of these households. An investigation of the spending patterns in such households reveal a lack of access to even basic amenities of the family. But at the same time, our studies have also confirmed the full economic roles of these women and indicate that many of them are equal income contributions, supplementary income earners and sole providers in terms of physical material contribution to the family.

Case Example II: Women Lace Artisans of Narasapur

The next case examples of the women lace artisans in the agriculturally prosperous Narasapur town in West Godavari district in Andhra Pradesh is a glaring example of years of class exploitation. These women artisans produce lace articles for the world market, but the major profit of such an excellent production goes only to the exporters. These women artisans receive marginal wages and are objects of sheer exploitation. In the monopolised lace industry, exporters have introduced a hierarchy of middlemen. Thus, the women artisans are victims of low wages, long hours of work, poor technology and eye, hip and neck ailments. To break the vicious hold of the exporters, NUWW organised these women art into groups. Credit was provided to strengthen their own business potential. In four years, the NUWW has been able to organise over 10,895 artisans in East and West Godavari districts. 4000 artisans have been provided DRI loans. A lace-producers' cooperative consisting of 4660 shareholders has also been initiated. ILO's technical collaboration division has helped the NUWW set up a production unit for trial to export through producer cooperative effort. The Government of India's Ministries of Labour and Commerce have provided these lace artisans cooperatives with lace orders. Exports to international markets are also being dealt with by the unit in a small way.

Exporters have been pressurised by the existence of the Forum and by the option the female labour force have for engaging themselves in their own micro lace business. Exporters have now increased the wages from Rs. 5 per reel to Rs. 7 or Rs. 8 per reel for lace artisans.

It was found recently, in these areas that women workers, who are engaged in lace handicraft, are increasingly adopting rope-making and weaving as occupations as they have better income potential. Equipment and credit facilities for these two occupations (as a process of diversification from the low income lace handicraft to other lucrative options) are very essential to increase income potential.

Case Example III: Women Beedi Rollers of Vellore

A large number of women and children are engaged in beedi rolling work in Vellore town and the surrounding villages in North Arcot district. Also, men work in this industry, but mostly in factories. Women and children, are largely involved in this occupation and work for (both during the day and night) long hours to provide for their families. NUWW has so far organised 3643 women beedi workers in Vellore, North Arcot district. A study team of NUWW has given enormous facts on the conditions of these women workers and issues that confront them.

The material distribution system in the beedi rolling industry involves a highly exploitative method using series of contractors and subcontractors. The deficit aspect in the raw material distribution system owing to bad quality of materials and fraudulent measures of distribution to workers in their homes confirms the exploitative piece rate character of the work.

While the employers in this industry maintain many workers as permanent on their records. In reality, only a few of the above are treated as permanent workers in terms of facilities. Also, the employers account for the distribution of materials for all the 7 days in their registers while in reality the materials are distributed only for 4 days in a week.

The beedi rollers like all other categories of micro-business women are enmeshed in a web of indebtedness. Jewels and vessels are also mortgaged at 10 per cent monthly rate of interest (120 per cent per annum). This system of compensation for the deficit of materials puts a family in debt for years together and is the main reason for the indebtedness of beedi workers.

Children, mostly drop outs from primary schools in this area, are involved in beedi rolling work vigorously. It is interesting to note that mortgage of children to employer middlemen is a common phenomena here for a small loan of even Rs. 200 or Rs. 500. In fact, these children have a capacity of rolling about 4000 beedies and they work whole day for their employers. Their total wages in reality values much more, but the employer pays only a reduced amount. Also even half out of this low wages is cut as interest towards the loan given to the parent. When women don't have anything, such as jewels or vessels to pledge, they mortgage their working children.

The children are often beaten up by the employers when they refuse to work. Many women workers through the wages of their children have paid up more than the actual loan to employers. Still when they ask the employer to release their children to work for better wages outside, the employer would demand the principal loan in each case. Thus, the employer purposely keeps no account for the work done by these children.

The NUWW has had a hard time trying to unionise women workers of these categories for collective action and to fight local power structures.

Case Example IV : Women Agarbathi Rollers of Bangalore

In Karnataka state, in the suburban slums around Bangalore city (i.e., in the case of agarbathi workers), the character of the oppression turns still more antagonistic; women agarbathi workers face sharp exploitation at the hands of the contractors and subcontractors who distribute raw materials to these workers at several interventions. Poverty and powerlessness among the women workers make them agree to work in such a piece-rate system, a system undoubtedly exploitative in nature. A worker's effort in such a system becomes totally unproductive. Thus, the two above mentioned examples provide typical cases of sheer exploitation of women workers in the informal sector.

The objective being that it is ideal for a National Union to work on both sides of the border, a few oganisers from Madras went over to Bangalore and met these workers casually. As elsewhere in India, the majority of children and women were engaged in agarbathi work in the slums of Bangalore and its suburbs. Since their social background being one of migrant nature, National Union proposed a study to collect important details on the conditions of migrant workers besides organising women agarbathi workers into the union's fold.

As mentioned earlier, this work was predominantly being done by the migrant women who had migrated from rural Tamil Nadu several years before. Later the local communities also started getting involved in agarbathi rolling. The system of work is best explained as home-based contract labour or piece rate work. More than 6198 workers have been unionised by NUWW in 30 different localities. At present no minimum wages has been fixed for agarbathi work. In almost all the localities, the members who joined initially were Tamil migrants, and after seeing them getting credit assistance for their work the Kannadigas came along slowly. It needed tremendous skills to organise Tamil migrant women among poor Kannadigas as it involved a problem of ethnic nature.

When the Kannadigas realised that it was indeed a genuine organisation empowering them for collective action against employers and moneylenders, they too joined in large numbers without reservation. Besides, Bangalore being a traditionally alcoholic area, women have suffered in poverty primarily due to low male contribution to family income. To quote Dr. U. Kalpagam, "The Forum on its part has realised the importance of recruiting Kannada women and had taken efforts to employ them as 4 out of 11 organisers whom I interviewed".

Agarbathi rolling requires a place of work to dry the wet products. As many of these women workers live in vulnerable living conditions, they don't have this drying space. The option they have is to go back to the employers to work in a put out system. Women workers made it clear to the organisers, that if credit was made available to them they could buy materials at cheaper cost which would in turn increase their income. Nationalized banks have been approached and the women have been provided with credit assistance.

Case Example V: Women Workers of Rural Moving Markets

NUWW has already an intensive programme for rural women workers who are engaged in business in rural weekly markets. This has to be expanded to other rural areas in other branches.

The programme details are to organise and assist these rural women vendors (shandies as they are called in India) by providing credit, training and family planning services. NUWW made a feasibility study of these women petty traders in shandy towns and found that these women are not at all reached by banks or other credit institutions and are subjected to all kinds of oppressive situations. They carry on their trade in weekly moving markets (shandies) and suffer from a lack of access to credit, storage facilities, transportation etc. Travelling many miles, sleeping on pavements, carrying heavy headloads and paying a high cost for transportation, these vendors barely earn subsistence income. A major share of this subsistence income is further reduced due to the exploitative role of the middlemen. The need to provide organisation and credit for rural vendors therefore had become imminent. NUWW has initiated this in Dindigul (Anna district) and in Adirampattinam (Thanjavur district) recently, and is proposing to take it up in other rural areas where NUWW has branches.

The Innovative Structure - A Unique Delivery Mechanism

The most effective instrument for women workers participation in the NUWW is its innovative organisation structure which was devised for preserving its grassroot nature as well a reaching as large number of beneficiaries quickly. Promotion of small groups through neighbourhood ties became a unique effective device that helped in gaining widespread participation of women workers at the bottom level. This group system which strengthened the purposeful approach of learning from the poor, has also helped to formulate suitable programmes through a learning process, based on user needs and requirements. The system has also helped in successfully implementing the programmes with the help of the beneficiaries themselves.

Solidarity

Such strong neighbourhood ties instilled a strong feeling of solidarity and cooperative spirit among the poor women. Specific problems faced by women at the local level are brought out at local group meetings; it also became easy to identify the local needs and problems, the facts regarding the details of employment or petty trades and the constraints. Above all, this concept of group consciousness preserved the grassroot character of the organisation.

Organising Skills

In the neighbourhood concept, poor women were able to acquire leadership skills, learn the process of organisation building, gain effective control through cooperative power, receive benefits of their hard work directly and formulate a plan to serve the larger community. For the

NUWW, it is an ideological commitment to integrate different castes and religious communities through this group concept and bring them to work collectively for their economic and social development.

Training in Communication Skills

NUWW continuously moves forward as a movement with continuous addition of members and groups. Every leader of an organised group automatically becomes a member of the governing body. Every month, atleast 4 to 5 groups, i.e., a minimum of 200 members are newly admitted. While there is no fear of stagnation anywhere, such a fast growing organisation has to take many precautions to check its efficiency when it becomes unwieldy due to expansion. There are ongoing leadership training programmes in NUWW to train women in the organisational techniques to take over the management of the organisation at various levels. Training methodology is both by formal as well as informal means. Training and education are mostly provided to group leaders in the community primarily through group discussions and classes held at the Forum's various centres (i.e., in the slums as well as in other places). Sometimes, they are trained in field activities as apprentices (i.e., on the job training). The most important aspect of the training is to train the women to speak out, i.e., in communication skills.

Training for Consciousness and Awareness

The basic objectives of raising community consciousness by awareness, skill dissemination and exposure through analytic, creative and very little academic methodology makes the training programme unique. It represents a significant deviation from the formal or simple rabble rousing / techniques. The existing harsh realities of the third world such as inequitable distribution and administrative ineffectiveness are cited as reasons for 'more awareness / exposure' in the training programmes. Leadership skills in this context relate not merely to pressure, mobilising, planning, community and group dynamics and organising skills, but also to removing of ignorance and disseminating skills on Income Generation, Family Planning, Nutrition etc. (i.e., issues directly related to the causes of non-participation of women in the development programmes taking up leadership at the grassroots).

Leadership of the Non-elite

Further, within a period of 8 years, the NUWW has been able to demonstrate an alternative leadership pattern by training and conscientising women to harness their power and thereby learn to control their destinies. In the final analysis, it has become a proven fact that success has been due to withdrawal of elite participation at various levels allowing local leadership to tackle all the situations. This has proved that leaders are not born, but are creations of encouragement, opportunities, and such leaders can also be multiplied.

Training for Employment

The most important aspect of NUWW's training programme is that women workers in the informal sector do not have many of the skills required to find employment. Therefore, development programmes like health and family welfare with a little enforcement of training skills and education, are excellent avenues of employment.

Thus, NUWW tries to bring back the type of leadership that Gandhiji evolved during the freedom struggle in India or even the pattern followed by Martin Luther King in the Civil Rights Movements in the United States, who closely adopted the operational techniques of Mahatma Gandhi.

Having promoted an organisational structure to reach women in large numbers, the next rational strategy of NUWW was to device a programme option addressing women's most critical needs (i.e., the supply of credit and employment and health and family planning). These are the two main instruments through which NUWW has reached women workers in large numbers in these 8 years.

Credit Instrument of Social Change

Credit assistance became the vital programme and strengthened the economic roles of women, who until then were largely dependent on the availability of credit from local moneylenders. Moneylenders charged exorbitant rates of interest for a very small amount of working capital. Consequently, women's income was reduced to marginal low returns earned through real hard work. Through their collective wisdom, women workers could realise and perceive the fact that the most critical need for survival was access to cheap working capital. They joined the NUWW to relieve themselves from the exploitation of the local moneylenders. NUWW's first effort thus, has borne result in enhancing women's access to credit and production resources and has thus, ensured them better profit margin in their business and work. Women participated at all levels in the project. Decision-making in every women's life became crucial to her own effort and benefit. The credit intervention could ensure improvement in the working conditions of women workers and enhanced the quality of their life.

The large scale benefits of credit assistance can be summarised as follows. The emergence of the group leaders as the sole guarantor of the credit group has assured women workers increased income, its custody, as well as access to credit. This has reduced the drudgery of professional moneylenders, to a considerable degree.

Many a dependent home-based worker's working under a subcontractor had become an independent micro-entrepreneur in her own right and had helped many others engaged in unproductive work by persuading them to change over to productive work (Narasapur experiment). Credit experiment has reduced the pawning of the household articles to the moneylender considerably.

Material Impact of Credit Programme

Above all, creation of such small credit groups certainly has provided an opportunity for women to come together, to gain courage and self-confidence. To many poor women, it has been an extra household linkage bringing about remarkable social change in their attitude. The large scale advantages of the loan programme are :

- Employment of the individual
- Material impact
- Promotion of collective consciousness
- In numerical terms, there has been a very large area of coverage (in numbers) in the credit programme.
- It has been assessed that it is the most assetless women (engaged either in micro-enterprise, home-based production, cattle breeding or fish trading) who have become owners of assets.

Family Planning

An evaluation conducted two years after initiation of the credit programme of NUWW discovered that increased income could not by itself bear the desired results in many poor families. The major factor that limited the improvement of the living and working conditions of women workers was the presence of a number of children in each slum family. A large number of them were "working children" in abysmal conditions. Thus NUWW's health project was evolved out of a need to provide supportive services to workers, integrating the same into their economic programmes (1980 November).

This particular programme of Family Welfare of NUWW does not have any blueprint approach but adopt a processual approach, involving the participants at all levels of the project from planning to implementation through a process of collective control and evaluation. Attention is given to effective implementation of the programme among the poor clientele, and this has resulted in significant success yielding a high percentage of couple protection.

Equal emphasis is given to the choice of the cadre from among the poor clientele (i.e., from the slums or from among the landless women workers). Such a process narrows down the communication gap between the cadre and the clientele as both belong to the same class.

The delivery mechanism is an innovative neighbourhood concept which retains the grassroot character as in other programmes. Every health worker (cadre) is trained for 45 days, and is allowed to select certain number of families in her neighbourhood and work among them. Being acceptable to the community, she is able to effectively communicate with her clientele through an interpersonal communication method, and is able to create confidence, remove misconceptions and fears about the Family Welfare Programme.

There cannot be a better mechanism than this to popularize programmes of IEC and female literacy. The cadre is trained as an agent of social change, and it is a leadership of the poor and the non-elite. If the poor are to benefit through development programmes, then the leadership must come only from the poor.

Yet another aspect of this programme is that workers in the informal sector do not have much skills, training and education to find employment. Therefore, programmes like Health & Family Welfare, with a little enforcement of training skills and education, in combination with other programmes of social action and social change, are excellent avenues of employment. Details of population and targets of eligible couples and number of families adopted by NUWW are enclosed for reference.

Productive Roles Vs Reproductive Roles

NUWW's experiment among women clientele is yet another innovative process, i.e., a process of voluntary action among women themselves aiming to get over the debility of frequent pregnancies and reproductive roles giving birth to several children, year after year by providing them an opportunity to utilise their time, energy and human resource potential to build up their productive roles and use it towards their social and economic development.

Other Service Provisions

The NUWW runs tailoring classes, several night schools (to help school programmes of poor children) in the city slums, it runs child labour centres for adolescent youth who are mostly "working children". These services have to be started in other states and other rural areas.

Accomplishment Replicable Value

Though started as an urban based movement, NUWW has now

replicated its experiment in three southern states and to many remote rural areas. Its current membership is over 52,899 women workers who mostly belong to city slums, in rural Tamil Nadu and in two other states of South India. Apart from replicability, it has also introduced programmes, such as credit and healthcare in all the new branches.

The Forum is a unique model due to its innovative low cost delivery system that has been able to provide 1,20,28,802 loans to 52,899 members within a time span of 8 years. The repayment rate has been 89.4 per cent according to a commercial bank study and 95 per cent according to NUWW's Working Women's Cooperative Society study.

The process of conscientisation exposure to extra household sources has led to the need for limiting the family size and improved health care. Semi-literate slum women were trained for six weeks in Mother and Child Health, Family Planning Methods, Nutrition, Sanitation etc., and provided with the responsibility of a sizeable number of families in their neighbourhood. Hailing from the same locality and belonging to the same class as their clients, the health leaders have been able to provide 94.5 per cent coverage in family planning services to 30,000 people in the first phase of the programme within a time span of the targeted three years. Immunisation goals have been achieved within half the targeted time (3 years). Further, the organisation has been able to generate employment for semi-literate women through the provision of basic services.

Assessment and Suggestions

The NUWW initiated as a well defined group in April 1978, has built up a membership of 26,746 urban and 26,153 rural women, belonging to the lowest of social groups in less than eight years. Few organisation with such a short history have as many achievements to their credit. Women workers now feel that grassroot organisations such as this alone, will make women potent powerful agents of social change.

Need for People's Own Organisation

An analysis of the experiments of the NUWW reveal the extraordinary leadership roles played by urban poor and illiterate landless women have to a large extent contributed to the success of the organisation in achieving the desired results. The initiation of the organisation has been in many places by the group leaders themselves and in some places even members have been responsible for setting up the local units.

Processual Approach in Programme Planning

Programmes to ameliorate the conditions of the vast majority of the rural urban people who live below the poverty line must have a processual approach and not a blueprint approach imposing programmes from above. We always presume that there is lack of employment opportunities and therefore, visualised a need to create and find more jobs for the poor. Case studies of NUWW explain that the grassroot experience however, is totally different and a point to the contrary. These facts are based on the issues that confront women workers and the lessons we have learned are those learned in our trials.

Recognition of Women's Economic Roles – Need for Better Working / Living Conditions

Time has come for us now to recognise the conscious and full economic roles played by women and the fact that many occupations are handled by rural women workers on their own single-handedly. Trades, such as fish-trading, livestock rearing, and handicraft production are mainly occupations in which majority of women workers are engaged. What they need is therefore not merely occupations or employment but measures to strengthen those efforts to be more productive with improved working and better living conditions leading to higher income and wages.

The most immediate and important concern for everyone is that in India, 89 per cent of women workers work in this sector. There is no real database or information details with reference to women workers in India. The details of their work are so complicated and are multifarious in nature.

Need for Database International Commission for Women Workers

Some are over-employed in some activities with low returns. Some are under-employed in some activities receive discriminative wages. The multiplicity of female employment is so complicated that even in some cases it depends upon patron-clients relations. In many cases, women and children are given a meal and are asked to work for hours. Thus, it will be appropriate to prepare a profile of female workers. A suggestion therefore, is that there can be an International Commission on Women Workers with clear cut terms and references for this purpose for collection of data on women workers in third world countries.

Policy Option to Involve them in the Country's Planning Process

While agriculture and other industries with their heavy consumer demand have large allocation of funds on a priority basis, the informal sector benefit of consumer-oriented benefit becomes a neglected sector. All that we can expect from this informal sector beneficiary is that the work role of poor clientele in the developing countries should become more productive through provision of more facilities, infrastructure, such as credit, family planning, insurance and other services and help them to reach a stage in which the basic needs of food, shelter and clothing could be achieved. This is more or less an attempt which is being tried in Modern China.

At present, all the programmes with reference to this sector in the National Planning Commission of India are completely jumbled up in one chapter of the Country's Five Year Plans, as anti-poverty programmes. These programmes are totally entrusted to bureaucrats and various government departments for implementation whose accountability on such implementation is unquestionable, as implementation and effectiveness of these programmes now are totally dependent on the personal initiative of the local officers and implementing authorities. Also, the major difficulty that impedes the enforcement of anti-poverty programmes is the non-cooperation of banks, who are expected to supplement the resources and on whom the programmes depend heavily.

Therefore, the informal sector needs a chapter in the countries Five Year Plans and this will eventually empower these poor workers with a legal clout of social legislations, inducing them to demand the implementation or enforcement, that will eventually lead to interrogation of the accountability of the officers by the beneficiaries on enforcement issues.

Unless this is done, the resources allotted in anti-poverty prorammes will remain a wastage in all developing countries and will not reach the poor for whom it is meant.

Family Planning Project (Project of 3 Years, 1986 – 1988)

1.	Total No. of Slums (Urban)	-	200
	Total No. of Villages (Rural)	-	81
2.	Total No. of Workers (Urban)	-	300
	Total No. of Workers (Rural)	-	96
3.	Total No. of families per worker (Urban)	-	300
	Total No. of families per worker (Rural)	-	300
4.	Total No. of families (Urban)	-	90,000
	Total No. of families (Rural)	-	28,800
5.	Total No. of Population (Urban)	-	4,50,000
	Total No. of Population (Rural)	-	1,44,000
6.	Total No. of Eligible couples to be covered (Urban)	-	76,500
	Total No. of Eligible couples to be covered (Rural)	-	24,480
7.	Total No. of Supervisors (Urban)	-	19
	Total No. of Supervisors (Rural)	-	9
8.	Total No. of Co-ordinator	-	1
	Total No. of Asst. Co-ordinator	-	3

References

1. Anita Diamant – A different Indian Epic in The Boston Phoenix Sec 11 May 3, 1983, in interview with Jaya Arunachalam.
2. Hilda Jeffers – Organising Women Petty traders and Producers: A Case Study of Working Women's Forum, Madras, MA Thesis submitted to Department of City and Regional Planning, University of California, Berkeley, November 1981.
3. Helzi Naponen (formerly Hilda Jeffers) – Organising Women Petty traders Paper presented at the Asian Regional Conference on "Women and the House", New Delhi, January 1985.
4. Jaya Arunachalam – Productive roles vs Reproductive roles: Experiment grassroot Health Care Project of Working Women's Forum, Paper presented by Indian Council Medical Research, New Delhi.
5. Jaya Arunachalam – Women in Rice Farming Systems: "Experiment of Working Women's Forum (India) Alternative Employment Options for Indian Rural Women, paper presented by International Rice Research Institute, March.
6. Maria Mies – Housewives Produce for the World Market : The lace makers of Narasapur, World Employment Programme Research, Working paper WEP 10/WP 16, ILO, December 1980.
7. Marty Chen – The Working Women's Forum: Organising the Credit and Change, Seeds No.6, 1983, New York.
8. Nandini Azad – Indian and Foreign Review "Reaching out to Women Workers Through Grassroots Systems" Vol.21 No.22 15th September 1984.
9. Nandini Azad – Completed ILO Working paper No. 10-4-04-18-1, entitled "Improving Working Conditions for Rural Women through Creation of Alternative Employment Options: The Working Women's Forum, Dindigul, a Adiramapattinam Projects.
10. Nandini Azad – The Participation of Rural Women in Development Organisations an Analysis of the Strategies of the Working Women's Forum (India): paper presented by Workshop on Rural Women's Participation and Organisation in Development Madurai – India, 18-22 November 1985.
11. P.H. Reddy and FPF – Working Women's Forum: Experiment in Leadership training that blazes a trial.
12. Robert Chambers – Notes and Reflections on a visit to the Working Women's Forum in South India, Institute of Development Studies Sussex, Mimeographed, February 1985.
13. Sheldon Gordon – The Globe and Mail: "Enriching the lives of Tamil Nadu's Poor".
14. Dr. U. Kalpagam -- An evaluation report prepared by "Solidarity, Strength and Success", Working Women's Forum (India) Points the way.

New Agenda for the Millennium*
- A Charter for Human Security -

Will the Millennium offer an agenda for human security, as a matter of human right, especially from the perspective of man-made and natural disasters?

This editorial's major concern is not only about natural disasters, but more so about disasters caused by human errors that are far more common in the present-day situation endangering hundreds and thousands of lives. The frequent air and train crashes, industrial and chemical calamities, innumerable human imposed disasters, such as construction of dams resulting in the displacement of people from their rights and entitlements, besides cyclone and earthquakes are such illustrations. In addition, to drought prone catastrophes that cause millions of children and adults to die of hunger, starvation or otherwise, are not uncommon but have become everyday occurrences. We hear everyday endless stories of people living in unrecovered shock of ethnic violence per se, as the agenda of religious and fundamental forces end up in large scale terrorist action. Undoubtedly, all these threaten the very existence of human security not only in India, but also in the entire region. The cancerous growth of uncontrolled HIV and AIDS is a growing disaster not only in the last millennium, but also poses a greater threat for the very survival of the younger race and citizens in the future. This is particularly due to the 'sex tourism' promoted as a new strategy of the globalisation and liberalisation processes. India has gone through Kargil War, its disasters and unexpected nuclear tests. People dying in thousands recently due to the super cyclone in the coasts of Orissa, in the inferno at a cinema hall in Delhi, high up in the mountains in landslide disaster and every type of disaster unfolds day after day. While the loners in families are grief stricken, life in misery moves on with memories faded.

To be more specific, India is a classic case of being prone to wide range of disasters, from earthquakes to droughts and floods to high wind and super cyclones having massive effect on the environment, implying larger disaster for the "living poor", as an aftermath rather than those who have lost their lives.

Dwelling on few of these examples both natural, environment or human imposed, one can perceive the complacency on the part of the

---

*The *GROOTS* issue dedicated to the innocent lives lost in disasters - December 2000.

National and International authorities, especially their attention on disaster management, both in efforts of disaster prevention and relief.

In the state of Maharashtra, the 1993 natural havoc at Lattur district was preceded by a flood and then followed by an earthquake. Therefore, it was a continuous disaster prone area as nearly 1,30,000 people in 80 villages and towns in Maharashtra state were affected, 9,500 were killed, over 10,000 injured and rest lost their meagre assets and livelihood and many became homeless and destitutes. Public facilities and services, such as schools, rural hospitals, primary health centres, water and electricity supply were also damaged in varying degrees and became the worst hit.

Unfair international trade agreements have imposed disastrous consequences in impoverishing those slum dwellers living in the neighbourhood of the chemical plant in Bhopal, were thousands died. Many more have become handicapped, particularly blind. This is due to the unfair trade practices of keeping the risks of chemical leakage a secret from the people without sharing such information. Compensation in terms of monetary benefits and proper medical care for them is still awaited from the concerned multi-national company abroad. Yet another unfair trade practice is allowing the flow of industrial waste in some of our perennial rivers, such as "Palar" in the North Arcot district of Tamil Nadu that not only pollutes the purity of water, but also affects hundreds of acres of land, besides seeping into the table as well. Similarly, around Chennai city, due to the domestic waste of the entire Chennai city is being drained into the Buckingham canal, all rivers along its course, including Coovam, Arni and Kuchasthalaiyar rivers are polluted beyond recognition and are rendered unusable for human purposes. Large scale unauthorized digging of wells in the seabeds of Chennai cost have given rise to the danger of pure drinking water getting mixed up with saline water.

The negligent maintenance and non-condemning of the worn out and old aircrafts by civil aviation authorities have proved costly, as seen in the air disaster that have happened several times this year. Similarly, due to unmanned railway crossings, besides lack of proper monitoring mechanisms of rail movements in many places have resulted in several train disasters due to human errors, where thousands have lost their lives.

The rapid deforestation process and exploitation of ground water resources pose greater threat in rural areas where all forests are fast disappearing and the wells are drying up. Thus, it is a strain only on women to walk miles to procure water and firewood. There is marked evidence of this especially in, Dharmapuri district of Tamil Nadu, where such extensive deforestation in recent years has severely affected both rainfall and availability of indigenous forest produce, which was the only source of sustainable livelihood and income for the hill tribes.

Poverty is a complex problem and a big challenge, both at the National and International domain for which no uniform solution is possible, to reduce the pangs of the poor in the developing world whose voices have had no impact on policy makers. Poverty often influences people to take to drugs, accelerates violence and crime. It causes breakdown of families, destroys sociability and induces profound personal threats. Absolute poverty affects over one billion people, i.e., 20 per cent of the population are not able to satisfy even the basic human needs on a regular basis. More importantly the central issue is that 90 per cent of the current growth in population is also taking place only in these developing countries. The uncontrolled population growth is yet another disaster and significant factor in the destruction of eco systems and an additional burden on the remaining resources of the eco systems. Thus, the underdevelopment is interlinked to high incidence of growth of poverty and population. Hence, it is all the more necessary to break the nexus between high levels of fertility, poverty, ill health, illiteracy and environmental degradation in the context of population stabilisation and sustainable development.

In general, the most vulnerable who suffer in these disaster are the poorest sections of the community especially, women, in rural communities, they are mostly small landholders and are landless socially/economically and belong to the category of disadvantaged groups who cannot afford to rebuild themselves. Recently, a report presented at the national level seminar in Orissa on the 'Protection of the high risk children and unwanted motherhood and the offspring' evidently made it clear that the worst forms of exploitation of women occur when disaster strikes. It further brought to light the highly reprehensible issue of child prostitution that the areas of disaster are prone to. It has become a painful reality today that disaster hit areas prove to be 'catchment areas' for picking innocent children and inflicting on them the worst forms of abuse. Such gross child rights violation destroys the future of thousands of young siblings.

More importantly, the glaring and appalling realities today clearly shows that lack of people's participation and very poor governance go hand in hand, leading to innumerable agonies and woes for the people of this nation. It is evidently clear that citizens have little or no stake in the prevention and management of disasters owing to lack of information but on the other hand, the bureaucrats, government and decision-making bodies have the responsibility to ensure that information and relief measures reach the citizen on time.

Struggle of the victims in disasters raises a range of questions to National Governments and bilateral agencies on protection of people's lives and the rights guaranteed during disasters. What can be done to ensure those threatened by crisis of disasters, religious and ethnic violence to have the right to information to safeguard themselves from the disasters? Also what can be done to accelerate steps to increase emergency relief measures on time to reach victims who have survived disasters? Further, all resources allocated do not reach them in time and as such affected areas become hot beds of corruption.

Can the new millennium offer a Charter of Human Security from constraints of disasters to create a world free of conflict, insecurity, poverty and exploitation? Can one make this as People's Agenda for the 21st Century?

Towards Peace Process – A Pathway to Human Security and Prosperity*

The dawn of the new millennium accelerates, the need for a common understanding on the issues affecting the future of humanity in matters of human security, welfare and prosperity. All the U.N. conferences held at the end of the last millennium demonstrated that the U.N. process also endeavours for the same. This was echoed in several world conferences, from 1992 to 1995, initiating a vigorous search process for values, clear, practical approaches of people's initiatives even at the grassroots alerting the international communities to gain momentum towards visualising the dire need for peaceful coexistence.

Despite such drastic efforts, humanity unfortunately not only continues to disintegrate or mutilate into bits and pieces, but it also finds itself in ever disastrous turmoil of terrorism and conflicts. Further, what is happening in Kashmir and Gujarat demonstrates that India and South Asia are no exceptions to such happenings. What do we then do? How are we to channelise the energies of people to stand together to challenge such a disastrous turmoil, with faith and conviction to stand for a peaceful coexistence? How can we impress upon our diverse communities that such an International living conceptualises and assures them the much-needed security? It is equally important to make people understand with the growing population, and the resultant widening, the borders of one nation traverses that of another nation. And in such instances the concept of security does not remain as one nation's security, but becomes a collective security of two nations. When such a concept is visualised with mutual concern, undoubtedly, the aspects of human security and people's livelihoods alone will take the centre stage and not the military or political security. The criteria of security should therefore be within the parameters of where a nation feels secure extending the same to its citizens, to feel safe and secure.

All this and more remind us, that there is an urgent need for a new security paradigm, not only for India and South Asia, it is a global obligatory agenda for international communities that should lead to a global action plan. Currently, the ongoing international and cross border terrorism along the Indian borders, not only creates instability but are also poses a threat to the growth and security of Indian population both in Kashmir and Gujarat. Evidently, such terrorist activities only displaces

---

*Appeared as Editorial in *Groots* in August 2002.

several poor and vulnerable from their poorer habitats to refugee camps.

Diving deeper into the horrible incidents, can we articulate some rhyme or reason for such conflicts and resultant terrorism? Don't we realise it is just lack of respect for democratic values, minority or majority conflicts (like that of traditional Arab-Israeli ones?) authoritarian rule (like that of Taliban, etc.) where women are victimised more, just as products. Why should such gross violation of human rights imposing oppressive actions on innocent people be tolerated? This is just nothing but a clear evidence that there is a 'leadership vacuum', around the globe as most of these so-called leaders suffer from an acute inability to over come the barriers that separate them from each other.

Let us for a moment look to the economic rationale of military spending. Everyone knows it is a wasteful consumption, which is neither aimed at productivity nor towards human development. Undoubtedly in peace times, arms deal/arms trade are even more dangerous/disastrous, stimulating terrorist activities and cross border terrorism disrupting peaceful environments. Common people should be aware of it, unfortunately, they are becoming victims everywhere.

Economically poverty, unemployment and deprivation, always draws young men from poor and vulnerable communities not only to terrorism, but also to pursue dangerous smuggling of arms without consideration for the danger and insecurity involved in it.

We can't ignore the fact that both in the drugs sale and arms deal its the most poor and young people who are being used and exploited. They are ready to enter such dangerous fields as an alternate employment option. Young people adopt such desperate measures, which is a reality, as poverty and hunger are far more difficult to bear. Aggressive youth feel in their dangerous pursuits that even death is preferable.

Nuclear race is yet another wasteful and a dangerous experimental pursuit. Its compulsion is an imposition, by the countries on one another, either a developed or a developing nation. Experiment to date shows that while the nuclear tests were only the privileged pursuits of the big western powers, India and Pakistan, China have followed suit in the recent times. Before making a judgment on all this it is high time that, for sure, we the civil society initiatives have to contemplate, whether to allow the power structures to tread this destructive path and continue in the direction of destroying human kind, or fight our way towards peace process and International understanding.

We have seen that in the recent times that the erstwhile Soviet Socialist regime with its powerful technology base, accomplished and known around the globe as an innovator of several nuclear weapon including atom bombs that threatened the survival of the entire hemisphere for over half-a-million year, have collapsed today only because of its economic failure. The Russians are still struggling to emerge stronger from the collapse, as it will take long time to orient its working population, towards socio-economic pursuits, changing them from their nucleo-technological base. Also, it is time that we realise that a new political class is emerging, promoting and spreading politics of hate, and in their vigorous pursuit of vengeance, they disturb the peaceful nations, turn them into disturbed areas accelerating the human turbulence and turmoil everywhere. Russian experiment elucidates the fact that neither nuclear tests nor arms production would enhance our security. Does an ordinary citizen feel quite secure in such pursuits? Despite all this, year after year this new political class goes in for nuclear tests or arms deal, mortgaging the interests of the poorer nations and further victimising the poor. In fact, such ventures increase the insecurity of the nation on all fronts with such threats of war making people at the grassroots suffer with increased poverty and the nation loaded with debt burden.

People's initiatives therefore have a bounden duty to remind the public often that years of cold war among the powerful nations have only increased their expenditure on armament and further imposed and induced same on the developing nations, to solve even their simple unsolved disputes, through arms interventions. Thus, in the bargain the arms trade has become a profitable deal to big powers, fuelling and fanning smaller disputes among third world countries into open conflicts.

Is it possible to work for a new world order? How can we do so? Today we are not able to solve simple human problems, i.e., our own border issues? This is surprising even in countries like South Asia where people have shared the same culture, language and ethnicity over hundreds of years. This means that the United Nations should make real efforts, instead of making lip service to solve human problems, religious fundamentalism, ethnic conflicts, blocking of arms trade between the north-south and visualisation of a collective security. Until then a new world order will only be a distant dream. Our late Prime Minister Pandit Nehru, followed the path of Gandhiji and strongly advocated ahimsa, policy of non-alignment, and disarmament. Pandit Nehru in his argument has never failed to compare how much of infrastructure facilities could be created to help the poor have education, health measures, etc., instead of producing just one missile in the country.

As of now how can the national governments be brought under such pressure to have wider consultation not only to consult their own immediate political colleagues, but also to have a dialogue with peoples' organisations and civil society initiatives. This can be the golden rule to reduce increasing conflict, arms race, hatred, yielding place to a new world order, of peace, harmony and social development. Will is with the people; can U.N. and the National Governments find the way?

Acceptance Speech
By
Dr. Smt. Jaya Arunachalam, President, Working Women's Forum India)*

As I stand before you in all humility at the intellectual core of the world facing a very highly enlightened community to accept the "International Activist Award 2003" bestowed on me on behalf of the 7,00,000 women of the Working Women's Forum and myself, I express a deep sense of gratitude at the outset to the eminent jurists and the Board of Advisers of the Gleitsman Foundation. But above all to Alan Gleitsman himself for having hand picked me for the award from India, as the President of the Working Women Forum. This great privilege and honour appreciating our long drawn out battle against poverty is indeed an extremely fulfilling moment and is symbolic of the deep commitment of the foundation to adjust and equitable world order.

The history of the struggle of the Working Women's Forum is a saga of poor women's remarkable emergence to leadership from destitution. The path they traversed is a long and arduous one. The conflicts and obstacles they confronted, their war against poverty was not extraneous but from within their homes and in their communities, markets and streets. To establish their rights to their own entitlements was not an easy process. Despite being the most vulnerable and the poorest of social groups, their empowerment process highlights great learnings to tens and millions of women in similar conditions world over.

India historically no doubt is a veritable storehouse of a glorious past and yet its current situation has to be judged by the scorching reality that 41 per cent of its people still live in poverty. The situation at the time when we initiated this movement was that, even after 30 years of India's independence (1978), people were confronted by administrative failures on all fronts and also a vacuum of political leadership and role models. In brief, the country's management could not keep pace with the growing population (and the numbers of the poor) on the one side vis-a-vis the social development agenda and aspirations of the people. The abysmal conditions of higher number of people pushed into poverty resulted in poor women and children bearing this burden, a situation that clearly

---

*Acceptance speech ceremony at the Gleitsman Foundation's International Activist Award 2003 at the Center for public leadership at the Kennedy School of Government at Harvard University.

demanded fresh solutions. Thus, it is this socioeconomic milieu of the Indian nation, that warranted a different style and a new political activism to generate new responsible communities at the grassroots and leadership among individuals for collective action. It was as if a second struggle for freedom was essential (the first during the colonial period) to elicit enormous participation and cooperation of the marginalised poor themselves. To fight poverty through social innovations had become the major strategy.

Working towards these dynamics, one had to mobilise the women at the grassroots, politically into a mass movement with a determination to integrate them into the democratic process.

The motivation has been two fold:

1. To create individual activism and dynamism among the poor women themselves.
2. To create mass awareness among the public.

These strategies helped WWF gradually build up a platform for poor women, prepare them for a long drawn struggle at the outset to confront the obstacles, to establish their and entitlements eventually. With this end perspective, poor women as catalysts moved between villages and urban slums in city squatter settlements, where the poor lived and worked. Creating a collective consciousness in them to fight anomalies of squalor, hunger and to motivate them in large numbers for collective action were all fulfilling endeavours.

The world can't ignore the fact that in the poorest communities the entire organisation or the unit of a family is run from the income earned by women and children. The male income is very low in the poorest families not only due to large scale male unemployment but also as most men in the poorer families are in the grips of alcoholism. Therefore, while choosing the right human resource potential in families, it was in the fitness of things that WWF's strategy concentrated on women as an entry point to social development. This was followed by a new initiative, the arduous task of building up institutions that were responsive to poor women. The critical struggle was to orient poor women to manage such institutions for their own development, their communities and their families. The Working Women's Forum, Indian Cooperative Network for Women and the National Union of Working Women were established with a massive membership of poor women.

As a majority of them were working women, contributing to family income, their access to credit became crucial at the outset to escape from the clutches of moneylenders, whose exploitation leads to their losing major profits from their enterprises. WWF's women members are mostly hawkers and vendors, silk weavers, lace artisans, cigar rollers, incense stick makers, agricultural labourers etc. With credit in their hands women not only had the bargaining power but could also become successful micro-entrepreneurs, diversify their business, acquiring land, housing, trading technologies in the long term and also afford human resource investment for their children (education including girls). With access and control of assets and resources in communities, women became de facto heads of households.

The milestone in 25 years of WWF's existence was that poor women of the WWF have demonstrated to the world that they are bankable, can build up assets, handle resources, take part in sophisticated economic activities, build up institutions and accumulate at the base. A testimony to this is the fact that 3,25,000 poor women now participate in its banking activities controlling and managing the bank leading to profits with 98 per cent recovery, firming up their entrepreneurial ventures.

Further to strengthen their productive roles, they promoted a cadre based reproductive health care advocacy programme, building up a network of advocates in their own rural/urban communities. These cadres hailed from their own class and were able to remarkably strengthen health consciousness of both women and children in the villages; in the squatter settlements of the cities in chanty towns, to utilise the under used government's healthcare facilities. A further learning from this programme was that, female surgery is not the only means to population stabilisation but it is a crucial decision on life's choices for women based on selective contraceptive practices. Women in the Forum established through their lessons that the child bearing role of women be perceived as a social role and therefore they have a right to safe motherhood, to take care of her children, enable decision-making process regarding number of children and in their contraceptive practices, as a matter of her life choice. The programme impacted about 16 lakh (1.5 million) families in Tamil Nadu alone.

Taking up leadership through a political process in their own villages and city municipal wards, they fought for their representation as guaranteed by the 73rd and 74th amendment of the Constitution of India in the village Panchayat and urban local bodies of small towns. They never shirked or failed to go on long marches to draw public attention or create public opinion, against atrocities and injustices against them or for their demands, rights or entitlements for better roads, electricity, water, sanitation, schools for their children, hospital facilities and other public utility services.

Friends, currently the irreversible globalisation process everywhere in all countries of the world affects almost all aspects of human activity. We, in the WWF feel that our focus on poverty reduction efforts has to be intensified with an apprehension lest our women who have come a long way in overcoming to a great extent from their 'Poverty' to be pushed into the trap of poverty once again. We shudder to think that our children would loose their right to normal childhood and become child labourers again. All these are tight ropewalks for us, i.e., between a progressive path we have treaded so far and the conflicting situation we are to face in future, on account of this new globalisation process. Without preparing the largest number of poor in the world (found in India and South Asia) that are found in the developing world to participate in the economic liberalisation, mere imposition of the globalisation process is beginning to push them to the dark corners of hunger and starvation. Without building capacities of the poor or ensuring markets for their products or enhancing their purchasing power, a thrust of the globalisation process will further divide the world inequitably into two parts. One for the poor and another for the rich. I appeal to the enlightened intellectual community to do a fair amount of sensitisation, consciousness rising towards this anomaly to all those concerned.

Secondly, the consequences of war is yet another impediment/burden on the world's poor and vulnerable. This will visibly lead to displacement/disruption of the poorer communities from their homes. The war might be a global war against terrorism, but one cannot ignore the fact that it affects innocent civilians, pushing the world's economy particularly in the developing world back by several steps and its people into persistent poverty. It infringes on the human right of peaceful communities and is a threat to human security displacing more innocents out of their safe habitats to refugee camps.

Moving once again back into the vicious cycle of poverty has several severe consequences and is far more dangerous and disastrous. As a result, millions of poor particularly the unemployed youth, will engage themselves not only in cross border terrorism, but also in their dire desperation will further be induced into the illegal trade of smuggling of arms and drugs.

I conclude friends, by quoting Abraham Lincoln "Malice to none, Charity for all" a philosophy similar to the nonviolent peace pursuits adopted by the Father of our Nation Mahatma Gandhi in India, Martin Luther King in your country, though all of them had been victims of violence themselves. The philosophy preached in India from the ancient Vedas too was "that the world to live as one single family" describing it as "Vasudeiva Kudumbakam" "Our world as one human family". The message of the Working Women's Forum's experience is similar to these ideologies that the world as a global village must move faster towards an equitable new order to meet the demand of the marginalised to become first among equals.

Once again may I express my deep heartfelt sense of gratitude to the distinguished audience before me and thank you for the rare privilege of having chosen the Working Women's Forum (India) and me for this honour.

Thanks to everyone.

Building Better Networks for Human Rights and Human Security: The Social Mobilisation Experiment of Working Women's Forum (India)*

By

Jaya Arunachalam

Introduction

Human Rights - Concept and Origin

The struggle for liberty to secure basic human rights against all social, economic, political and fundamental birth rights have been the most inspiring saga of human history. The concept is an important requirement for a vibrant democracy to function and above all to lead a life of dignity and honour. The issue of human rights has been the corner stone of civilization and humanity's mission of better lives. Such a struggle for human rights through collective activism has led to larger socio-political movements.

"Man is born free, but is everywhere in chains" said Roseau, the French Political Philosopher and architect of Social Contract. He further said it is, "the will of the people - not the force, the basic for governance". Thus was the foundation laid for a vibrant democracy as early as the 15th century in Europe much before the French Revolution. Similarly, Herry David Thoreau another political philosopher in Europe expanded this concept of fundamental freedom as 'human rights' and "civil disobedience" which heavily influenced Leo Tolstoy, Mahatma Gandhi and Martin Luther King - who further developed this concept as a non-violent civil disobedience movement fighting unethical governance of the British in India. During the Indian freedom struggle one of the pioneers of India's Independence struggle Shri Balgangadhar Tilak said, "Freedom is my birth right".

Ever since the formation of United Nations, both the concept of civil liberty and human rights were universally declared and institutionalized. Following this all nations around the globe established human right's commission as National Machinery to protect the fundamental rights of its subjects as guaranteed by respective constitutions. India too was no exception and established one. Former Chief Justice of India and the first Chairman of the Human Rights Commission in India, Shri Ranganath Mishra justifying the functions of the commission, said "As of now

---

*Paper presented at Tokyo at the conference on Human Rights MIT and Chubu Institute 17th and 18th March 2003.

violation of human rights is widely rampant, violation of human rights is in the homes, the streets, the public offices (and) educational institutions." He further said in apprehension, " Promotion and protection of human rights are the only way by which the society can be saved in an effective way. We are degenerating and degenerating very fast, and unless there is first stoppage of the degenerating process and then an attempt for elevation, thereafter, we might lose our status of being homo sapiens and a group above animal life'.

Therefore, right to life and personal liberty is most inalienable and fundamental to human rights as it is the protector of natural law of freedom and justice. Therefore, violation against this Natural Law of rights and privileges, i.e., ones own birthright, when denied leads to protest and revolt in mass upsurge. Unless individuals are guaranteed such inalienable rights he or she can't break forward to find their space.

In India too, the Freedom struggle broke out of social discrimination leading to violation of basic human and fundamental rights in many ways. Therefore, in this context, after Independence the framers of the Constitution incorporated the right to freedom and liberty as the most important fundamental process to human survival automatically, without which the right to live becomes meaningless.

Currently, India is facing new challenges due to political confusions challenging the very roots of democracy at times. While sustaining democracy may be an appreciable effort, at what cost are we sustaining these efforts? Is it also not true that even today more men and women suffer in starvation and many more children go to bed hungry? In fact the South Asian region itself houses large numbers of such ill effects compared to other regions endorsing that it is the poorest of all regions.

UN Declaration of Human Rights Process

Thus political confusion, economic degradation value systems, negative environmental effects on the planets, and the new liberalized policy encouraging market-oriented economics and structural adjustments etc., burdens the poor most. The challenges of poverty and powerlessness threaten human security and welfare, and therefore, spontaneously new forms of mass movements emerged with a new thrust and enthusiasm manifested among the grassroots communities in the late eighties. This happened when the political leadership failed to meet the needs of the poor at the grassroots. This also happened particularly in developing countries where the poor and the women could take up extraordinary leadership. They made their presence felt in various U.N. processes including the U.N. Commission on the status of women and at the various

U.N. Conferences from 1992 to 1995, including the Social Summit at the Copenhagen. Mention has to be made on the particular step made by women's groups and their strong networks that pressurized the U.N. Commission on the status of women to include their concerns in those global conferences. They challenged the U.N. process as so far the poor women's groups have never been accredited by them and therefore this certainly made the presence of poor women's network felt in all the five or six Global Conferences of U.N. process. Further, it was a learning process for the United Nations too, to learn the challenges of poverty in general and the adverse effects on the poor women in particular.

Human Security at the Grassroots

Situation of Poor Women Workers

Let us examine in a chronological manner how denial of such rights ends up in human disasters. The basic and fundamental right of human beings is their fundamental right to work towards gainful employment. But the real challenge we witness everywhere in India is the social hardships imposed on the poor and women, pushing them to extreme conditions of poverty despite hard work for long hours. This is due to the fact that the vast majority of the working population both in India and other parts of developing nations are mainly engaged in informal opportunities of employment without any job security. The unskilled and non-technical workers of this sector are mostly characterized by low wages, living in survival/marginal conditions that further enmeshes them in extreme poverty. The work options of this sector is unprotected, as social legislations were not effective at the grassroots and social security measures, such as maternity benefits for women, were not complied compared within this sector as they have limited work options. This sector further gets enlarged as the effects of globalisation are spreading fast. The current global economic policies, such as unfair trade agreements also have severe implications in altering the livelihood options of poor women, which they have to cope with amidst all odds.

Women's Human Rights

A critical analysis would provide that particularly women workers are poor not by choice but are impoverished in many ways by systematic social excisions. Denial of family's resources at the household level and deprivation of positions of power due to time-honoured traditions of subordination in sex roles further aggravates the situations of poverty. The outmoded cultural practices in India imposed particularly on women, leads to the worst forms of human rights violations, such as 'sati' and 'female foeticide'. Further, the "male child syndrome" in the traditional families leads to large scale "infant mortality" among female children.

Working Children

The situation of working children is pathetic as they are objects of social exclusions at a fairly young age, as poverty pushes them in the labour market prematurely. This results in their exclusion from educational opportunities in their early years, denying their right to a normal childhood.

Land right as a human right

Exclusions from land rights in developing countries not only increase the vulnerability of rural poor but also the root causes of rural poverty. The reason is not only that the custody of land is in the hands of few individuals, also the major complication lies in the non-implementation of land reforms by the national governments everywhere. There are even more instances, of denial of human right options such as freedom to organize, express, threat to human life-security, dignity etc. This is highly reflected in the status and in the treatment of stateless citizens (refugees) who have migrated in emergencies to escape disasters back home.

Endangering Human Security - The Situation in India

Unfortunately, humanity today not only continues to disintegrate and mutilate into bits and pieces but also finds itself in the misery of an ever-disastrous turmoil of terrorism and conflicts. Further, what is happening in Kashmir/Gujarat demonstrates that India and South Asia are the real hot bed of such happenings. What do we do then? How are we to channelise the energies of people to stand together to challenge such disasters, with faith and conviction and to stand for a peaceful co-existence? How can we impress upon our diverse communities that such an international living conceptualizes and assures them the much-needed security in their co-existence? It is equally important to make people understand with the growing population and the globe, and the resultant widening of territorial concept, the borders of one-nation traverses that of another nation, and in such instances the concept of security does not remain as one nation's security, but becomes a collective security of two nations. When such a concept is visualised with mutual concern, undoubtedly, the aspects of human security and people's welfare alone will take the centre stage and riot the military or political security. The criteria of security should therefore, be within the parameters of where a nation feels secure extending the same to its citizens.

All this and more remind us that there is an urgent need for a new security paradigm, not only for India / South Asia, it is a global obligatory agenda for international communities that should lead to a global action plan. Currently, the ongoing international cross border terrorism along the Indian borders, not only creates instability but also poses a threat to the growth and security of the Indian population both in Kashmir and Gujarat. Evidently such terrorist activities only displace several poor and vulnerable from their poor habitats to refugee camps.

Natural Factors Effecting People in Poverty

It is also true that India is a classic case of being prone to a wide range of disasters, from earthquakes to droughts, from floods to high velocity super cyclones whose massive effects are no doubt very disastrous, creating a class of "living poor" than those who 'lost their lives'. These are results of human imposed implications found in the complacency of the authorities in the management of disasters who provide relief to struggled victims belatedly.

The rapid deforestation process in our countries and exploitation of ground water ends up in the fast disappearance of forests, wells and water sources that gets dried up. In terms of human security, this further results in the threat and denial of food security for the growing population resulting in hunger and starvation.

Human Security viz-a-viz Individual Welfare

Poverty is a complex problem and a big challenge, both at the National and International domain for which no uniform, solution is possible so as to reduce the pangs of the poor in the developing world whose voices have had no impact on policy makers. Poverty often influences people to take to drugs, accelerates violence and crime. It causes breakdown of families, destroys sociability and induces profound personal threats. Absolute poverty affects over one billion people, i.e., 20 per cent of the world populations are not able to satisfy even the basic human needs on a regular basis. More importantly the central issue is that 90 per cent of the current growth in population takes place only in these developing countries. The unchecked population growth is yet another disaster and significant factor in the destruction of eco systems. However, while looking for solutions, women become the instruments, as they have to bear file burden of imposition of female surgery to world population reduction measures, also look forward to credit options to carry on enterprises to run the organisations of family, as female headed households.

If concept of human security is equated with basic human needs, it is the anti-people policies that have to be reviewed in terms of global human welfare, such policies often generate far more disastrous consequences in impoverishing the poor, depriving them of even the basic human needs in many poor countries.

The remaining discussions therefore, have to be in terms of human security in relation to individual welfare. All policies have to be reviewed in terms of the socio-economic structures available at the grassroots like the globalisation, land reforms, land tenure, landless and bonded labour, migrants, women's population reduction measures inclusive of health services, violence against women, legal reach and legal resources for the poor. In terms of socio-economic structures at the village level it is found that the rural poor remain exploited amidst wealthy farmers, traders and moneylenders and other power structures. The law enforcement at times bias therefore the poor remain powerless victims as justice in our countries is bias towards the power structures. Therefore we need a strong political will to change this gross exploitation of the poor, to provide justice to the poor and the powerless and also the poor and the vulnerable have to organize themselves in terms of their own human security and welfare. The first stage may be to build a platform and the second stage will be a spontaneous revolt.

A Case Study of Working Women's Forum (India) - A Spontaneous Social Movement

It is in this connection a mention on the experiment of Working Women's Forum (India), an initiative of the social movement of 700,000 has to be made. Women as early as 1978 organized themselves into a grassroots movement in response to prevalent gross violations of women's human rights.

Mobilising Poor Women

To think back on what happened in the early days, WWF never went into the drudgery of collecting women from slums and villages for training them in skills, to find some work for them. At that time, we at WWF were quite cautious, and only strengthened their traditional, existing occupations and this had its own effect. Instead of searching for the poor in our experiment, the poor started mobilizing themselves and reached us on their own in tens and thousands. This contributed to quick outreach to poor women, contributing to Forum's phenomenal growth as a social movement.

Enhancing Women's Social Status

By way of bringing to light the social status of poor women in society not only unmarried women of working class but also the status of those who do not have the sophistication and resources (in the Indian context) to get into legalized wedlock's and, those who lived in common law arrangements in the city slums are totally unacceptable to elites in India. At the same time those who attempted arranged marriages too, had to pay heavy dowries and spend lavishly on marriage ceremonies that they could ill afford. Therefore, such of these women, who are in common law wedlock, are abused in derogatory language in all traditional communities particularly among the poor. Also their relationship as man and wife are equally insecure and women faced desertion in large numbers. WWF was quite concerned about such women mostly, as out of the early 800 initial members two-thirds of them belonged to such category of women. WWF's effort therefore, was to legalise and legitimise these relationships through registration, sometime under Special Marriage Act, if they belonged to different religions celebrating it as a big social event presided over by Governor of States or President / Vice President of India. Such registration of marriages gave women the right to fight for divorce in the court and make compensatory arrangement for her children and herself during times of crisis.

Surprisingly, there were many delightful inter-caste experiments where marriages between high-caste Brahmins and untouchable Harijans, Hindus and Muslims/Christians, also among Christians and Muslims. It was further evidence and an eye opener that poor can't afford the sophisticated caste feelings nor can they get into costly caste networks and it is a learning process to study their own strategies to escape from those unaffordable networks of caste and religion. WWF made wide publicity of such wedding, making it as a gender sensitization effort to fight men in humanity to women and her children. Women from their subordinate position felt they are in equal status, through such wedlock's. Thus, WWF's has effectively tackled the sensitive issue of caste, a common tradition and cause for human rights violation in India.

Combating Female Infanticide, Child Labour and Devadasi Systems

Despite the Hindu Code Bill and several Acts in favour of women, such as Dowry Prevention Act and Bigamy Prevention Act, women's succession to property on a equal basis to men, the messages of these Acts has not reached women living in poorer communities, more so in villages and slums, due to illiteracy and ignorance. The traditional preference of a "male child" leads many families to loose their girl children in foeticides (Dharmapuri branch of WWF) and infant mortalities in some case, but in majority of the families where they survived it has resulted in large numbers of children who had to work for their livelihoods as child labourers (Kanchipuram child bondedness WWF). It was a more common occurrence that adolescent girls were pushed into early marriages and motherhood where their fate became fatal either in mother mortality or in dowry deaths. At the same time, the government sponsored family planning programme in 1977 ran into controversy in many villages and slums, by the mishandling of this programme by the bureaucracy. Casualties of death in male/female surgeries have outnumbered the successes in couple protection rates.

The Devadasi systems (Child prostitution in Bellary branch of WWF in Karnataka), where the girl children have been victims of religious dedication to temples and later facing prey to prostitution was another serious anomaly to be tackled effectively. This evoked the feministic concerns in the WWF, and felt they needed drastic action to save female children from the victimization of religion and culture, besides enhancing the status of the girl child treating her as "Future women".

To prevent child labour, female foeticide, infant mortality, Devadasi system and save women from the crude imposition of female surgery in family planning programmes, thus WWF had to look for new forms of programme strategy. Therefore it was a change from entire character of the state sponsored family planning programme, into a grassroots reproductive healthcare programme spreading the messages through sound methods of advocacy, and pleasant change from control to life choices for women. This new culture of advocacy in the neighbourhoods of slums and villages created a cadre for every 500 families as an advocate of health consciousness who multiplied in large numbers as "network of advocates" in the course of time who not only took up health issues, but slowly advocated holistic gender/class concerns among the women in poverty.

Through a demonstrative experience, WWF was able to bring to light the fact the undervaluation of women at home reflected in the workplaces as well. Unlike in other feministic organisations, in WWF, the conflicts were not the only form of activism but it became a gradual technique or tool adopted, as incidents led to that stage. In WWF, we never allowed conflicts towards a just cause, to contribute to eternal hostility. But they happened on an issue-to-issue basis, where conflicts became a natural phenomenon.

Gender Aware Approach

To quote Dr. U. Kalpagam

"Women engaged in income earning activities and public visibility and moved around freely in public spaces like roads and market places. The restrictions they faced were on account of occupying spaces that the municipalities and corporations felt were obstructing the smooth flow of traffic or areas where the poor have to be kept out of sight. No doubt these women lived in patriarchal family structures and were subjected to some forms of male dominance. Often their decision-making powers were constrained; sometimes they were subjected to domestic violence and verbal abuse from alcoholic husbands and had not much control over their own overworked bodies and sexuality. Peer credit groups that WWF initiated for its micro-credit programme became in the course of time an empowerment group that lent peer support to each woman to handle the varied forms of patriarchal oppression she experienced. Thus, the initial local context of visibility and widespread participation in economic activities were crucial determinants for WWF's micro-credit and empowerment initiatives".

Thus at the outset, the gender question acquired prime place in the WWF. With this ideology in focus, demand for gender equality had become the prime question. Whether in village panchayat, or in fighting caste, religious/traditional barriers or evade customs, and to fight discriminatory wages, i.e., to confront employers/landlords and other power structures like police, municipalities. Therefore, women soon had their way to fight injustice. Everyone had to listen to women. All the women in WWF could do this only with the strength of its cadre based approach. Paul Ekins in his book says, "The numbers mobilised on the road in long marches or in mass, meetings are to demonstrate the injustices by creating a public opinion". Therefore, right from its beginning gender questions gained predominance at the WWF.

Thereafter the "Class" question became equally important when the above mentioned mobilisation strategy became a way of life among the women workers, particularly where they had to struggle on wage questions both in their contract labour work or 'piece rate operations in many of WWF branches in Andhra Pradesh/Tamil Nadu.

Enhancing Women's Capabilities towards Social Transformations—The Right to Decent Livelihood

Being unorganized conglomerations, women workers earnings are so meager and irregular that they hardly make both ends meet. Further their struggle for housing, water and civic-amenities are enormous in the urban slums. Their landless counterpart in the rural areas suffer equally due to underemployment, low wages, sometimes with limited work options to even 45 to 60 days a year. If they happened to be part of drought prone areas (Bidar, Dindigul branches of WWF in Karnataka and Tamil Nadu) it is even worse. Thus, it is more than an annual feature that 'rural poor are on their migrating journey to the already over crowded city slums, in search of new work options and continue to be victims of vicious cycles of poverty.

There women workers of WWF work as weavers of cloth, mats and baskets, cigar or agarbathi rollers, food processors, either work alone or collectively in other branches. They work as agricultural labourers on farmlands or they work for their kith and kin. They are providers for their families; working in service occupations, i.e., dhobis, cooks, sweepers and water carriers, etc. They are an integral part of the production process and contribute to the informal economy. Unfortunately, they have little or no access to fruits of their own labour, nor that of the government's assistance.

While the Forum is a class structure in terms of its membership, it took up mainly gender and caste issues in its initial days of its organising effort. In the urban situation the occupations of vending / hawking being micro enterprises, could not relate to class issues since this urban group was initially an organized one. However, gender (violence) caste (most service workers are untouchables) were on its heights due to the high prevalence of alcoholism, in urban centres. Also most service workers belonged to scheduled castes, and hence the character of the group had been more a solidarity / neighbourhood group at the grassroots initiative, and was working towards leadership effort.

Paul Ekins says, "The clout has come from WWF's ability to get thousands of women out on the streets of Madras in pursuit of their rights, such clout brings practical results: only the most foolhardy policeman or petty official now harasses WWF members for bribes, which was a common place occurrence before."

The activism of the class nature, came up to forefront when WWF organized, agricultural labourers, export workers, piece rate and contract labourers such as cigar, agarbathi and handicrafts, lace and weavers of textiles industry. Here the problems particularly for women are low wages, harsh and exploitative working conditions.

As alternate options of cattle assistance, agricultural workers in the Dindigul branch of WWF in Tamil Nadu have made a remarkable impact in making a real frontal attack on landlords, who had to make revision in the wage by marginally increasing it. While this marginal increase may be the fruits of their struggle, one could not totally claim that this effort in our opinion, had not taken away rural women workers dependence on landlords completely.

Similarly, women lace artisans working in Narasapur WWF's branch rural Andhra Pradesh have been totally neglected by the workers' unions including the Communist Party of India as the work done by women are products made at home, and therefore, branded as leisure time employment.

Similarly, the beedi / agarbathi rolling, fisherwomen's fish marketing activities all have been considered as leisure time activities by male-dominated unions. In fact, fish marketing is a more permanent work than fishing and the fisherwomen's contribution to the families are steady.

In the weaving industry, women as men do weaving, keep out after designing, calling themselves as 'master-weavers'. Similarly, despite a major share of work in many occupations, women's responsibility branded as only low-wage efforts and branded as leisure timework. Therefore, to strengthen a woman worker's bargaining position, against vested interests and to expose the class character of the oppression women go through, WWF thus, decided to register themselves as a trade union in the year 1982 as "National Union of Working Women" that was a turning point in women workers lives. This indeed is a much-felt need to provide a sharper focus to fight the presence of the antagonistic elements in the production process, wherein women had major thrust. Apart from its original grassroots character, now WWF has also acquired additional strength by getting into unionisation process that strengthened women's economic roles.

In addition to this, the health programme physically took care of the health aspect of their productive role both as a worker and her role as a mother. More specifically the trade union offered the micro insurance programme with affordable premium, covered poor women's lives and that of their families against unexpected disasters, such as deaths, illness and property loss. The health insurance took care of women during their entire life cycle from the stage of a girl child to the reproductive age group, maternity benefits to old age ailments as well.

Thus, it was quite important to break through the vicious nexus between patriarchy / feudalistic elements and empower poor women towards leadership, both at home and in the community.

All this was achieved only by relying on the strength of the poor women, both in their numbers, energetic support and could initiate and sustain feministic leadership process. Inadvertently, this effort had strengthened many reform processes towards other women of middle and upper class, (dowry, male violence, property rights and so on).

To be more precise and truthful to oneself, the strategy adopted in the process of building this movement of Working Women's Forum, has not been a sophisticated one but the same indigenous, sustainable effort followed by Gandhiji years before during the struggle for India's freedom. However, despite the strategies being indigenous it has worked, in building up commitment and solidarity among poor women, facilitating other poor women in small communities and neighbourhoods. This commitment of poor women has been responsible that such a small initiative of 800 women, in 1978 led to a massive social movement of 7,00,000 women today.

With the human potential from the grassroots, comprising of low educational levels, but with high common sense and acumen, a model of a credit union, and a women's union was possible within the parameters of poor women's access. Not only has assured poor women food and economic security but also much needed social security. Above all the movement contributed to over all human security and welfare to their families and to their neighbourhoods.

This visible movement of mass upsurge has to be sustained in its future growth. Therefore, conscious strategy of trained/indigenous leaders have been placed in both the urban and rural neighbourhoods. Women members in the WWF, despite being the poorest have not been silent spectators to the happenings. Their lives must have been harshly affected by poverty, cultural, physical and social handicaps. Their commitment to the cause of ameliorating the lives of their sisters in the neighbourhood towards empowerment has been a vital force to make this movement of WWF wider and meaningful. This has particularly been accomplished through several partnership initiative of WWF in the northern parts of India where its methodology and expertise has been transferred to other organisations to work towards reduction of poverty is the much felt areas..

They have the conviction to have greater number of only grassroots women, demonstrating such movements could be alternative to political parties in terms of finding a socio-economic solutions against the perpetuation of discrimination of women could be possible. The movement gathered momentum soon and no longer to provide material benefits to members by access to credit but also widened their scope into areas of human rights, reproductive rights, legal rights, labour rights and other socio-active process gradually evolving itself into a socio-political platform carrying out series of advocacy measures through a network of advocates at the grassroots emerging from the class of poor.

Purpose of the Organisation

Working Women's Forum (India) was initiated in the year 1978 to provide organizational support to poor women workers for visibility/

empowerment to strengthen their socio-economic roles at the grassroots. WWF evolved into an innovative structure that has been more flexible and an easy delivery system to reach the grassroots for the direct and effective participation of poor women reaching in large numbers. Programmes provided are gender sensitive to address the critical needs of very poor women workers through training, employment, health and education and insurance services.

Programmes and Activities in Areas Relevant to the 1Vth UN World Conference on Women and Social Development Please Indicate Country(ies) in which they are Carried Out

Working Women's Forum's success, especially its operation in the Southern and Western parts of India (now moving towards north too) can be analysed in development terms, as growth with equity and distribution, betterment in quality of life, increase in the women worker's visibility/empowerment (through access to credit/employment/ empowerment, support services) resulting in the increase of women's income, consciousness and worker solidarity.

In growth terms, the Forum's member have increased incomes, savings, credit payment accomplishment of 90 per cent implementation of planned health and family planning and insurance services to the most neglected group of women, accomplishing 71 per cent of couple protection rate in family planning alone.

Thus, the Forum's, experiment with poor women leads to its identification that a low cost delivery mechanism reaching large numbers could be an alternate development model, placing empowerment as higher achievement, leading to a movement of women moving beyond material progress.

5

Can Development be the Choice of the Poor?*

Unequal access to credit on the basis of credit worthiness of women in poverty is nothing but a form of discrimination, a discrimination that continues despite the revelation all over the world through feminist studies and surveys that a women worker continues 50 per cent or even more to the family income. Further, our experience shows that even in the credit intervention women entrepreneurs of low income, despite being the poorest have always been credit worthy clientele than other elite borrowers. When once flexible credit is made available to them even at the market rate, they are excellent participants in the credit programmes and have put the proceeds for better use towards asset building. Asset building among these poor becomes so imminent, as most of them feel that the major reasons of their powerlessness is due to dispossession of assets. Hence, despite the phenomenal expansion of the Working Women's Forum in size while maintaining its grassroots character, the credit worthiness has never been compromised by the poor women in the Forum. This was because, poor women took total responsibility to mould their destinies by full participation in all programmes meant for them.

Therefore, this leads to further argument, that while credit is just one component, definitely an important one, the struggle towards emancipation of women to restore their dignity at home, in society, in the labour market and for representation in all the decision-making bodies, i.e., an effort in their larger interest to integrate them into all sectors of human endeavour

*Presented at the Seminar "Emerging Issue and Challenges Facing the Micro-credit Sector at Care India, New Delhi on 17th April, 1997.

is even more important and cannot be compromised. While credit can contribute to the alleviation of poverty at the micro-level in a limited way, its achievement will be miniscule without reforming the macro-economic situation, as an effort to strike at the root of poverty, and "feminisation of situations". Therefore, equal importance has to be given to create an ideological social platform with conducive economic and social environments, where in the poor women can adopt a continuous struggle to confront situation of discrimination, fighting oppressive forces.

Having gone through the experience of working with the poorest, one question that looms large is: Are the poor living in poverty by choice? Evidently, a soul-search would reveal that the problems of the poor are not created overnight, and there are ample examples to prove that, it is a consequence of systematic social exclusions of the poor from policy options or protective measures in their work environment, not only in India but all over the developing world.

Thus, the experiment of ICNW and WWF established a countrywide operation. It has rotated its original capital of a total of 18.2 million rupees into 210 million rupees. This is an evidence that there is tremendous potential for capital growth and sustainability even in the lending programme of poor women's network, if facilitation for their participation at all levels is a pre-condition.

Even more important than economic need, is the compulsion to facilitate women to build up a strong socio-political platform to voice their needs atleast in the affairs connected to them, because, as outside cadres many of us are not permanent actors in their day-to-day struggles. Therefore, to prepare them for a self-reliant, self-management process had become a necessary compulsion with the poor if poverty eradication had to be a serious business.

Further, how can micro-credit be the only solution for poverty, especially when the credit provision comes with exorbitant interest rates and in some cases, with savings as a pre-condition for loaning. As experience shows, this will in our opinion result sometimes in perpetuating the process of money lending, creating a debt burden on the poor and women. A question that we have to ask ourselves, now, especially when the micro-credit process, world over is achieving new dimensions. Further, while all our governments are already immersed in the debt burden, should this new emerging process of micro-credit, be another effort to endorse a system of burdening the poor too, to earn interests for capital funds of north, from the poor of the south?

Only a holistic approach that treats poor women as a rich human resource utilising their innate wisdom and creative methodologies through which they have managed to survive all alone, will result in changing the lives of the poor. This alone will lead to the liberation of powerless, demonstrating that the poor are not problems in themselves, but can be solutions too in the efforts of poverty eradication.

WWF emphasised both at its panel on "Participatory Methodologies" at the micro-credit summit and its participation in other panels, the need towards an emergence of a process, not to stress on the economic benefits per se, but also voice a concern for other critical needs particularly in the developing countries where alongside poverty, cultural barriers and traditional practices oppress women and perpetuate inequalities both at the domestic and community levels.

As an alternate development experiment, WWF adopted its original city experiment with the much-required variation culturally, ethnically and linguistically from the urban slums of Madras to other cities, states and even to remote rural areas. WWF though initiated with only 800 women in 1978, as an experiment of the poor it grew gradually into a mass movement of 4,50,000 women. The leadership came from the women themselves towards building this mass movement by way of their own spearhead teams as critical organisers and not through outside catalysts.

Cadres who are the poorest and the most vulnerable in social standing, came from the ranks of street vendors, pavement hawkers, fisherwomen, dairy women, rural landless, cigar workers agarbathi rollers, lace artisans, women weavers, handicraft workers and so on. Emerging as neighbourhood groups using credit as an entry point that provided them the social security and motivated them towards social change, civic action, access to information and clout to deal with power structures in order to fight for their rights through an entitlement approach.

In a situation, where even the every day survival has become a struggle for the poor due to price rise and various other anti-poor measures in the era of liberalisation, and when the most governments have failed to adopt a simultaneous pro-poor policy to sustain the livelihoods of the poorest, WWF not only stressed the role of Micro-Finance Institutions, to focus on "Micro" finance requirements alongwith other protective measures to help the poor women but drew attention to the "Macro" socio-economic realities in which the poor are placed. In the absence of land, productive inputs, technology or training mechanisms WWF experiment demonstrates that how credit to the poorest can also be a pro-poor strategy in itself to withstand the reform process.

The outreach mechanisms of WWF to reach the poorest through exchange methodologies have been successful in eliciting beneficiary participation in the implementation of micro-credit programmes. The approach could be described as a grassroot initiative most sensitive to the needs of the poor and have resulted in bringing the poorest out of abject poverty. Training for empowerment in WWF has been a crucial tool in providing the poorest women the much required strength to battle against those structures that compartmentalise their lives.

The following paragraph describes the grassroot initiative of poor women and their accomplishment not only in the programme's success, but also in creating a social platform to lobby for their rights.

At a time, when poor women were considered non-bankable women in the Forum established their own banking system known as "Indian Co-opertive Network for Women" – to manage their own credit system. These women at the grassroots were fully responsible for an effective field-oriented policy, determining interest rates, identification of poor borrowers, collection of instalments and even the responsibility of pressurising the default payment thereby, recording a very high credit recovery rate of 95 per cent – a remarkable rate among the "working poor" in the Indian context.

Thus, the experiment of Working Women's Forum (India) is a process of such a integration, ideally combined through a group dynamic process which not only provides collective strength, binding the neighbourhood communities together, it also dealt with diverse needs of the clients, such as business counselling, social support system and solidarity. Providing an alternate strategy for the survival of the poor, the group system served as a training ground to gain clout, share and solve mutual problems. This innovative concept, eventually, not only led to its multiplication in large numbers but also reached multitudes of the poor in a short span of time as a mass movement. WWF and ICWN has been a vehicle of social change where training has made women perceive in their struggles that the process of empowerment is far more important than just material benefits.

The impact study last year shows, that about 63 per cent of loanees used their loans only for business. Earlier before this loan 60 per cent of them were under-employed in wage employment that means Forum has generated permanent employment through micro-credit. Sixty two per cent of the loanees no doubt saved, but their savings is not saved in the bank to earn interest but invested in drinking water requirements of the family, children's education, housing or extention of housing needs, gold, electricity provision, civic amenities or attending to sanitation and drainage needs.

Being one of the largest of micro-level experiments, WWF's experience has demonstrated that even such institutions of the poorest women with low levels of income, can generate growth and human development, if the process is supported sensitively with adequate resources and mechanism, to facilitate cost effective expansion. Breaking several institutional obstacles, women at the Forum have shown that "the poor are rich" not only in their ability to survive against unsurmountable odds, but also in their efficiency to bring about a new accumulation process at the base.

Is Poverty the Choice of the Poor?*

"Are the poor living in poverty by choice?" This is a question everyone of us have to ask ourselves when the entire U.N. system observes the World Poverty Eradication Day on the 17th day of October. It will no doubt be a day of hectic global activity with discussions and talks on the poor who still form 5 per cent of the world's population. Deprived of even the basic necessities of life, they are neither able to change their state of powerlessness nor participate in their discussions of decision-making towards having a better deal of themselves.

The question needs fresh thinking. More and more people become poorer everyday both in developing and developed countries. Is it not a common scene in our daily life that millions of poor are found in the urban centres in all our countries left to eke out a living in the condemned corners of the slums of major cities even without a roof over their heads or a square meal a day?

The process of stabilisation and structural adjustments of the country's economic structures is a real burden on developing countries. The social hardships imposed on the poor due to high level of unemployment, less attention to social sectors and an enmass encouragement of the industrial sectors without a strategy to enhance the income or purchasing power of the poor or of the working class has led to lower levels of living. The global scenario today reveals that neither have the countries of the north found solutions for their problems nor have their strategies in the south reduced poverty or enhanced the status of the poor.

Are these not evidences that demonstrate that the piece-meal approach of planners and policy makers towards poverty eradication has done more harm than good, with the adhoc projects implemented by an imaginative bureaucracy further marginalising the poor?

Evidently, the problems of the poor are not created overnight, but are a consequence of systematic social exclusions faced by these vulnerable communities devoid of policy options, adequate protective measures, welfare benefits or productive employment.

In most urban slums, it is an everyday occurrence that the housing facilities of the poor inhabitants are often relocated from places where they have barely managed to build a viable enterprise. Such enterprises are indeed a major segment of the urban economy and these relocations

---

*Observation October 17th, 1996. – U.N. World Poverty Eradication Day.

not only result in loss of their livelihoods, but also become obstacles to their providing goods and services to the most vulnerable sections, whose purchasing power is also low. This is a disturbance of the vital base of the poor and a hindrance to the establishment of a free and equal relationship.

Concentration of half the world's poor fall only in Asian countries, i.e., out of the 630 million poor world over, 300 million live in South Asia. While the development experts reason that, this poverty of South Asia is on account of an imbalance between population and the resources, it is seldom revealed that such poverty is the result of other consequences too. No one denies the fact that the land to man ratio intensifies rural poverty, but it is equally important to recognise the land rights of the poor, the denial of which intensifies their vulnerability. Human development index in terms of access to water, sanitation, health, and education is abominably low in these countries. Gender disparities are further deepened by the influence of culture, tradition and customs. (even now in the northern parts of India, literacy among women is less than 20 per cent).

Why Network for Women in Poverty?*

The issue of GROOTS bears a special message to draw the attention of UN Status of Women's Commission about the major gap that exists today between the UN Status of Women's Commission and the new grassroot movements and networks in the developing countries. This became more evident when some of the Afro-Asian and Latin American representatives of the GROOTS network (Grassroots Organizations Operating Together in Sisterhood) attended the NGO Consultation on the 14th and 15th March, 1993 at Vienna - preparation for the 1995 Beijing Conference. To the surprise of many like us, only the representatives of the age-old elite organisations that existed in many of our countries from colonial times attended the meet in large numbers. Unfortunately, many of these elite organisations have not percolated to the grassroots, in our respective countries, but continue to move only in the elite circles. However, they all have managed representation major women's bodies of the U.N., since many have their headquarters at Vienna, Bangkok and Geneva in close proximity to the UN headquarters. Such organisations are not only not conversant with the problems of grassroots poor women, but also are not serious to help the poor to come out of their powerless status, and their harsh living and working conditions. They consider helping the poor women merely ads charity and consequently, they know very little about the sustainable development process, which is emerging as an alternative to fight poverty.

Therefore, it will be a lacuna on the part of the UN Status of Women's Commission if it has not become aware of certain facts that are highlighted below. It is time that the UN becomes conscious that its own conferences of 1975, 1980, 1985 have been responsible for this new thrust and enthusiasm among grassroot women's groups all over the world. Even in remote villages, not only many such small women's groups are emerging everyday, but also they have manifested themselves into mass movements in many developing countries. The recent trends show that the grassroot women in many corners of the developing world are more aware of the global situations through their own growing networks. Some of them have even prepared themselves to take up effective leadership roles, both to represent themselves and champion their own causes in the international conferences and global forums.

Thus, visibility being a major problem at the grassroots, all the new grassroot women's networks and movements must take up this challenge

*Extract from the speech at the meeting of NGO at the UN Status of Women's Commission, Vienna – 14th – 15th March, 1993.

and initiate measures to pressurise and draw the attention of the UN Status of Women's Commission and make their new efforts widely recognised. Information regarding the grassroot movements and networks that emerged after the 1975 process must be made available to the UN headquarters at Vienna from all corners of the developing countries. The UN must be made to feel the compulsion to replicate the UNCED process of accreditation, and adopt other means to respect all women's initiatives as equal partners to meet the challenges of poverty and its adverse affect on women.

Public Forum Among 'Devadasis'

The history of Devadasis in India is portrayed differently in different places. During the golden age of India's prosperity when Indian rulers were the great patrons for the art and culture, women artistes, particularly classical dancers and musicians dedicated themselves to religious institutions, such as temples, and called themselves as 'Devadasi' (Women devotees in Servitude'). They do not get into normal wedlock but were presumed to have married a God to whom they dedicate their body and soul.

Evidences are available to show that in certain periods of history that these 'Devadasis' were rich, famous and enjoyed a high social status equivalent even to royal households. However, this system of 'Devadasi' in India gradually deteriorated to exploitative conditions treating these women artistes merely as "Sex workers" (in the words of ILO) leading to prostitution.

The author, Global Coordinator of Regional Development (GROOTS), has taken the initiative to visit Kurdini village, on the 10th of August 1993, in Bellary District in Karnataka, situated 35 miles away from the town. In this village 100 Devadasi households were invited to a Public Forum to express themselves. The facts given below describe the reality of the situation.

According to the details gathered, girls at the age of 7 or 8 are dedicated to the female deity known as Ellamma, a temple in Hospet in Bellary district of Karnataka and are not allowed to marry and run normal family life. Each girl, after puberty can live with anyone who is willing to be with her and can also have a child. The relationship is mostly short-lived and has no commitment on the part of men to share the responsibility of children. Rarely, some men help them financially, invariably these women work either as agricultural labourers or in other wage occupations for livelihood.

The dedication of the girl children is very simple, the girls who are dedicated to a temple are tied a Talisman or a Locket as the symbol of the marriage around their neck and left as they are. The few case studies given below give out the details of the situation.

Kulligamma, who is only 35, says that she was dedicated to the temple when she was 7 years. She said she got into a relationship with a man who was working in an electricity department, but after 2–3 years, he deserted her. He neither provided her monetary benefits nor he took any responsibility for the children. Now she lives with another person and has another child through him.

Kulligamma went indepth to explain the powerlessness of their community and their helplessness which deny them the right for any negotiation with men for any permanent wedlock or security of life. Immersed in superstitious beliefs, elders in the village also threaten these women with all kinds of disastrous effects the families are likely to face, such as frightful curses. It is propagated that women will go mad if they seek a wedlock after they have gone through the dedication ceremony. She also feels that permanent relationships never worked out in their cases as men in reality will not come forward to marry them, considering Devadasis are low status women in the communities. It is always easy for men to have a temporary relationship and desert them when they like. Their preference of a legal wedlock is with women, arranged by their parents.

Anjani Devi is young good-looking lady. She is hardly 26 and was dedicated to the temple at the age of 9 years. She feels they depend on such relationship temporary or in whatever form only to safeguard themselves from other men.

Engamma lives with a man who is having a respiratory problem. He runs away whenever he has an attack of asthma but comes back again. She has to work, feed and protect him.

She was only 8 years when she was dedicated to a temple. She has two boys and two girls and lives with a man who is working in the electricity board. Occasionally, he provides some clothes but never takes any responsibility for the family or children.

Haumakka is 24 and she has three children. In her case, she was ready to marry a man and the man also agreed; but as her parents objected and the marriage broke. The man left her while she was carrying his third child. He has now married another woman. Hanumakka also lives with another person now.

Women reported that it is often a prayer to the goddess when there is any crisis in families that they will offer a girl from the family.

When asked why only girl children are dedicated and not boys, they said that only the girl children have the concern to look after the parents in the old age, and therefore, the practice is that the girl children should be dedicated. In many cases, despite their poor low economic status they have to earn for such men too, who don't feel any compulsion with regard to the family or children – a clear case of male domination.

The whole episode shows exploitation of girl children transcending barriers of class, caste and gender based discrimination just because they happen to be socially girl children, economically poor, organisationally powerless.

Anjamma, who is 31 years of age, was dedicated to Ellamma Temple as "Devadasi" at the age of 8 or 9. Out of her three children, two are handicapped but none go to school. She had relationships with a small farmer in the same village who has 2 acres for himself. After two children, he is married again and now he has two children through the legal wedlock. People do talk about such relationships in public. Many are aware of such affairs of their husbands.

Thus, Devadasi custom seems to be an accepted exploitative system on poor women and girl children in particular.

Interestingly, Anjamma's mother Gangamma who is now 55, earlier having dedicated Anjamma to the Ellamma temple, later courted another man. While first man was a mason (contract worker) to whom Anjamma was born, she refuses to identify the second man, but has four children through him. The second man later married and died probably he has eight children through his legal wedlock.

The mother Gangamma and daughter Anjamma do not live together, owing to various differences. As the discussion was in progress with our group (GROOTS), an older woman, from the village intervened and got angry, protested against marriages among 'Devadasis'.

Further, reporting on her living conditions Anjamma said, that the man courted and deserted her children. Her child became seriously sick one day with high fever and she consulted a doctor. Blood transfusion became necessary. Due to high fever, the child became handicapped, but "the child's life was saved" according to Anjamma "by God's Grace". Carrying on her life as wage earner, Anjamma has to retain her eldest daughter at home for domestic help denying education.

Cursing her fate that all her three children are girls and two being handicapped with no support system, she fears and feels desperate that how long to continue such a livelihood in misery. She prays that such situation should not befall her children. She said that if she had an opportunity to operate her girl child she would not have become handicapped today. Lack of resources prevented her from doing so. She said that she was not getting any help from the government. As a community, they (Devadasis) have no opportunity for any legal wedlocks, and thus, can't proceed against the deserting man for maintenance even for willful desertion. This powerlessness among 'Devadasi' community in Karnataka is a daily struggle. She said "We do not have any respect and social status in society. I look forward to a situation when I will be able to give this legitimacy to my children atleast through a decent marriage or otherwise".

Sharing Poverty or Creating Wealth?*

Background

Powerlessness of the poor and the persistent poverty in all the third world countries demands greater response from the planners, policy-makers and the NGO's communities. A review of earlier planned measures for the poor and the downtrodden shows that suitable strategies have not been devised to enable distributive justice to reach the poor in adequate measures. Whether in regard to resource or service allocation, there is a total denial of equitable distribution reaching the grassroots. Depending completely on government systems for the effective distribution of planned measures has not only resulted in the failure of development programmes, but has also further marginalised the poor. Both a lack of the human dimension in planning measures for the poor and the prevalence of bureaucratic constraints at the implementation level have created stumbling blocks in the development process.

In the recent times, development practitioners and non-governmental organisations all over the world have shown greater concern in development priorities emphasising the need to add the human dimension in the entire development process. They feel that the ideal strategy is to make people's participation a vehicle of change to reach the grassroots.

To understand the concern of the NGOs in accelerating this development process through people's participation, one should understand the informal systems of work opportunities in which the majority of the poor in developing countries live and work.

Informal Sector Working Conditions

Studies by several development experts have time and again indicated how this unorganised labour in the informal sector remains in perpectual poverty and works under conditions of exploitation. They work under harsh conditions for low and discriminatory wagers, and live in squatter settlements in the urban centres, as landless poor in the rural areas working in agricultural operations as wage earners. Most of these rural workers migrate to cities in search of work opportunities after the agricultural seasons are over.

Being unskilled and non-technical in nature, these workers have neither a steady place of employment nor a permanent employer. They

---

*Presented at the Symposium on Access to Financial Services to Women, at the Royal Tropical Institute, Jan. 1991.

move continuously in search of work opportunities, often changing their areas of work and employers. A work of temporary nature of this kind, results in their invisibility in statistical terms. Governments therefore, overlook them for any policy options. While workers in this sector remain as 'Working poor' in 'low paid' occupations experiences from many NGOs experiments show that this sector is a growing sector meeting the needs of poorer communities generating new employment opportunities.

Living in the shadow of the colonial past, Indian trade unions of the organised sector do not lend any solidarity to these informal sector workers. Although dealing only with 10 per cent of the working population, these organised sector unions still object to the recognition of the informal sector workers. Nonetheless, NGOs in India continue their struggle both in organising the poor and fighting with governments and other larger institutions to make them understand the myths and reality of the organised sector and the need to recognise the informal sector workers. Often representations are submitted to governments stating that such colonial models of trade unions have to change their attitude, and the government must also recognise the unions of informal sector workers both for tripartite meetings and for inclusion in labour delegations.

India's Working Population

To understand the inter-sectoral linkages of informal sector workers, a knowledge of their percentage in the total working population in India is very necessary. India has 292 million workers as total working population. Of this, only 25 to 30 million belong to the organised sector. The remaining 267 million do not belong to any formal or informal unions and are unorganised. In this unorganised group, 25 million earn Rs. 250 to Rs. 500 per month. There are about 150 million agricultural labourers, 188 million construction workers, 17 million child labourers and 6 million beedi workers, all these belong to the category of informal sector. While 48 millions of them are under-employed, 89 per cent of unorganised workers are women.

A peculiar situation one faces in this connection is that we do not find anything equivalent to this informal sector work in the developed regions of the world. As mentioned above, non-recognition of the workers in the informal sector results in the non-implementation of social legislations and the non-enforcement of protective measures. Underestimation of the valuable economic roles of these workers certainly results in the slow progress of poverty alleviation programmes among poverty groups.

Despite facing many obstacles of the kind mentioned above, the

Working Women's Forum, an NGO devoted to helping poor women, has taken up on itself the task of mobilising women workers on a large scale. In a massive unionisation process, WWF has gone through immense difficulties. Bringing together the most difficult, disorganised group of workers who had no earlier experience in any formal or informal unions - a real challenge in the early days for the WWF.

Objectives

Following unionisation, the WWF has set itself four main objectives which are closely related to its major strategy of mobilising poor women. Such mobilisation is a strategy for restructuring the socio-political and economic structure at the grassroots.

At the outset, the WWF's strategy of organising workers on occupational on trade lines helped women strengthen their economic roles. Credit was used as an entry point for mobilisation, and women in turn, served as entry points for the development process. Secondly, WWF adopted a flexible innovative informal structure in order to reach a large number of poor women; in turn used the grassroot structure as an effective delivery mechanism for development process. Thirdly, the WWF had adopted a totally women intensive mechanism as 89 per cent as India's working class women belonged to this sector and have ever remained unorganised. Lastly, the WWF addressed itself to the critical needs of these women, (a) through credit, (b) employment generation and (c) training. Thus, all the programme strategies in WWF are meant to enhance the economic status of women and in turn to enhance their decision-making power resulting in effective social development.

Programme Strategies

Thus, the objectives of the Working Women's Forum reveals that poverty alleviation can't be speeded up by charitable overtures, but only a focus on improving economic activities alone can provide a long-term solution. Poor women can be helped to earn more through increase in wages, or earn more by improving their existing low-income skills. All this can be achieved by providing them with credit assistance or working capital, technology, training or other social options.

Formal and Informal Systems of Credit

Therefore, like many formal institutions or governments the WWF did not stop with the provision of credit, as WWF always feels that credit in itself in not enough. Evolving an integrated approach, WWF devotes itself to a principle total development of the most backward groups at the grassroots and results in more tangible gains to the poor women. WWF constantly searches for innovative strategies to reach the poor women in large numbers, also in very short time. At the same time, WWF visualises that it is equally important to intensify the monitoring measures on the end use of credit assistance to poor women. Accordingly, WWF's credit or banking efforts to help the poor, involves series of other responsibilities and never ends with the lending of credit alone. Credit assistance may be to individuals or to group ventures but in WWF it must help generate profits to poor women's effort. It is often necessary to make arrangements for raw materials, skill training and in some cases even marketing; WWF shoulders such responsibilities at times along with credit assistance.

But banking in India still remains a formal system requiring collaterals and securities. It works on the system of collecting deposits invariably from the elites, lending it to other clienteles for a high rate of interest - an operation both to payoff interests to depositors and meet its own high establishments costs. Therefore, this system of banking did not help development process for it is just the reflection of India's colonial banking system, much less to help all sections of society or to meet the needs of the poor. Even the staff and employees of the Government banks are trained only to deal with such formal situations.

The banks were nationalized in India in 1969, with a purpose of reaching the poor, but even after that the banks made no serious efforts to help poverty alleviation programmes. Even the Differential Rate of Interest Scheme introduced to help poor reached only a negligible number poor women at the grassroots. Only about 1 per cent of the total profit of the nationalized banks had been lent to the poor in many nationalized banks. This does not cover even 1 per cent of the poor in the country.

The only other indigenous borrowing system of informal credit option left to the poor are the moneylenders or the 'loan sharks'. This indigenous system is such a disastrous system itself operating on exorbitant rates of interest made the poor enmesh themselves in continued indebtedness resulting in vicious circle of poverty. Nonetheless despite being disastrous this was the only informal option left for the poor to get credit. In most cases the poor pawned their land, house and jewels to such moneylenders in order to borrow for a high rate of interest.

Therefore, large number of social organisations and NGOs like the Working Women's Forum felt the need for introducing other options of informal credit experiments. In the recent times, all over the developing countries experiments are being multiplied in this direction large numbers. WWF being one such experiment an analysis of its credit options through a series of Working Women's Co-operative Societies, will reveal the processes through which they have succeeded in the informal banking experiments among the poor.

Working Women's Co-operative Societies

The WWF's Co-operative Societies not only organised the whole package of service inputs through its informal banking efforts, but also the staff are given basic training to deal with informal credit procedures, in order to reach a large number of the poor in the shortest possible time. To understand the work system in Working Women's Forum, a study of the staff structure alongwith other details of the both the WWF and the WWCS have to be looked into great detail.

Membership

WWF has grown from its small base in Madras city slums to become a multi-state union, with branches in urban and rural areas. Starting with 800 members, the Forum has grown into a massive union of over 1,00,000 members.

Occupations

In the city of Madras, the Forum works with street vendors, pavement hawkers and service specialists (like washer women). It works with landless women in Dindigul, with fisherwomen in the Tanjore coastal area, beedi rollers and match stick workers in the villages around Vellore town. And more recently with women weavers in and around Kanchipuram town.

In Karnataka, the Forum mainly works with agarbathi rollers in Bangalore town, beedi and agarbathi rollers around the Chennapatna villages and with landless women in the Bidar district. In Andhra Pradesh, the Forum works mainly with women lace artisans in Narasapur, and the West Godavari district, and with weavers and rope makers in the villages of East Godavari district. Recently, the WWF has initiated its unionisation work with chicken embroidery workers in the urban slums of Lucknow city and with children of migrant women labourers in the Kanpur industrial town.

Staff and Field Workers of WWF and WWCS

Most of the group leaders, organisers, programme staff, office bearers and members of the Executive, are all promoted from the grassroot membership and are trained to do organisational work. Barring the President and a few researchers, most of this staff are promoted leaders from the grassroot membership. This is the unique strength of the WWF's organisational structure.

The WWF's organisational structure has the ability to avoid elitism and the class and caste hierarchies usually dominant in India. The staff with working class backgrounds have the capacity not only to identify other poor working women and their needs, but also to reach the target group quickly. The most important aspect in the WWF is the promotional possibility of target group members to staff positions.

There are also a few other women staff who are hired from the lower middle class groups for their writing and accounting skills. But most of them belong to the category of single woman, such as the deserted, divorced and widowed. Their own personal life experiences, social oppressions and other struggles have hardened the attitude of these women towards male dominated systems and bureaucratic constraints. This is an additional strength to WWF's administrative units. WWF's policy of promoting such strong group leaders has resulted in a large number of single women among its staff who have become effective role models. They help to shape and spread the ideology of the WWF as spearhead team leaders in new areas, promoting new unions.

Other Social Action and Social Change Programmes

The large scale inter-caste weddings are one of the special strategies employed by the WWF to fight caste and dowry oppressions. Also the introduction of employment generation through the family planning services and work-related training to adolescent girls and the establishment of child workers rehabilitation centres have become essential for the total development of poor rural and urban families. All these form part of the social action and social change programmes of the WWF, besides credit assistance.

Replication and Other Details in WWCS

With cadre and clientele from the same background, the simple credit group model of the WWF is not only strong, but also suited for replication. Thus, the Forum has been able to replicate much faster both in terms of members and areas covered. Further, the Forum has been able to retain its grassroot character throughout its replication and expansion efforts.

The credit operations of the Forum carried out under a separate legal identity (Working Women's Co-operative Society in each state of operation) and are run, operated and audited under the norms of the Government Co-operative department. Each of these co-operative societies, are self-managed units of workers and given the efficiency and volume of operations in those units, the credit for such management goes to those workers alone.

Worker's Management of WWCS

Due to various problems confronted by WWF in dealing with the nationalized banks as mentioned elsewhere in this paper, the Working Women's Co-operative Societies were initiated in 1981 with separate revolving funds. In the Working Women's Co-operative Societies, it is the leaders and organisers of the WWF living in the slum-neighbourhoods help identify, select, guarantee and supervise the end use of loans. They also take responsibility for the collection and repayment of monthly instalments. The most admirable quality of these local leaders is that they take even higher responsibilities, such as providing pressure on default members to make them repay the loans, which is difficult in the national banking systems.

The performance of the WWCS has been uniformly good in all branches, in terms of staff selection, efficiency and training, accurate record keeping and a low percentage of bad debts.

Training in WWCS

An integral part of WWF's operational strategy is its meetings and trainings organised for members and cadres at all levels. The meetings and trainings are of great importance both in giving women opportunities to come out, speak and to share their experiences. The replicability of this type of training is great atleast within a similar cultural context. The level of social confidence and articulation particularly of group leaders, is a proof in itself.

Further, in a year there are 48 training programmes conducted by the Co-operative Societies. 1440 women leaders are being trained by the Co-operative Societies, at the rate of 120 per month or 30 per week in the Madras branch alone. Likewise, in all branches, there are atleast two training programmes every months, i.e., approximately, 720 leaders are being training in each of the branches per annum and a total of about 6480 ($729 \times 9 = 6480$) leaders are trained in all the nine branches.

In order to receive loans, the women clientele go through one day's training to learn to use credit and deal with credit institutions.

The Client Beneficiaries in WWCS

Regarding the client characteristics of the WWCS credit programme about 35 per cent are urban clientele and 65 per cent are rural clientele, it is 100 per cent women intensive. Over 99 per cent are group ventures while a very few individuals are assisted. 56 per cent of the members are illiterate. Seven per cent of them have studied between classes IX to XI, 15 per cent of them have studied upto class VIII and 22 per cent of them have studied upto class V.

Age Group of Clientele in WWCS

Regarding the age group of these women, about 37 per cent of the members are in the category of 22 to 30 years, about 18 per cent are in the 31-40 age group, about 34 per cent are between 41 and 50 years of age, and about 11 per cent are 51 and above. So, the age of clientele ranges between 22 to 50 years.

Entrepreneurial Ventures in WWCS

Regarding the entrepreneurship of these women, 81 per cent of them are retail traders, 16 of them are service specialists and only 3 per cent belong to manufacturing groups. Over 61 per cent of the women entrepreneurs are 'sole traders' over 14 per cent of members have their entire family helping them in their enterprises, and 25 per cent of them have two household members working in their enterprises.

Loan Details in WWCS

While the first loan is invariably Rs. 200, the second loan is between Rs. 400 to Rs. 800 depending upon the increase in trade volume, the repayment capacity and the schedule. The maximum loan the society offers is only Rs. 3000 (Rupees Three Thousand only). All the loans between Rs. 200 and Rs. 2000 are payable by members within 10 months. If the loans for above Rs. 2000 members are given 20 months time for repayment.

Regarding the loans, 99 per cent are group loans and only 1 per cent are individual loans. Most of the members use their loan partly for working capital and partly for the purchase of small equipments. 72 per cent of the women invest in their business. 4.5 per cent of women invest in their equipment. 17 per cent of the women invest on household utensils which are also used for cooking purposes, in the case of food hawkers. 6 per cent of women use the loan to clear earlier loans. A very negligible 0.5 per cent have used it for education and legal expenses.

Operational Details in WWCS

The loans are normally secured by the members on the guarantee of group leaders and the local organisers. The screening of loan applications and the subsequent approval to issue a loan is a long drawn out process in the first instance.

The field officers of the co-operative always visit the work site of the loan applicants alongwith the group leader of the respective group and the organiser who recommends groups in the neighbourhood. After an on the spot assessment of the volume of business, the field officers help women to decide the quantum of loan according to the nature of the trade. Sometimes, this helps to eliminate other types of women from the loan process, e.g., those women who have already received loan through other credit groups, such as chit funds or those who have received loans from the nationalized banks (which can be found in their family ration card), or women who request credit for various non-productive purposes.

Regarding the processing of the loan, in the case of the first loan, it takes nearly a month because of the time that is required for the busy banking staff of the society to make schedules for their field visits and other enquiries. For repeated loans, the time taken for processing is about a week or 10 days.

Most clients of the Co-operative Society are expected to participate in savings programmes. However, in the WWCs savings have never been a precondition to receive financial assistance.

Interest Rate in WWCS

Regarding the interest, while rate is 15 per cent per annum, it actually works out to be only 8.25 per cent as the interest rate decreases subsequent to the monthly reduction in the capital sum. Prevailing rates of interest elsewhere in the country including in other co-operative societies are mostly 18 per cent per annum. DRI loans in nationalized banks charge 4 per cent but they are not given on a large scale. About 13.5 per cent to 17 per cent interest is charged for other loans in nationalized banks and the traditional moneylenders charge 3 per cent to 5 per cent per month (36 per cent to 60 per cent per annum).

Arrears in WWCS

Regarding the arrears in the WWCS, 30 per cent of the arrears are recovered within a period of 3 months. 50 per cent of the arrears are recovered in three to six months time and only 17 per cent are repaid over six months time. Regarding the recovery of the loan, the Forum only applies peer pressure through group leaders and does not use other coercive measures.

Default Rate in WWCS

The total percentage of the loan that is written off in the WWCS is very negligible - just 2.61 per cent. In the WWCS, despite the women being the poorest, failures to repay the loan takes place only when they are caught in disastrous situations like floods or fires in the slums and squattered settlements.

Only 1.25 per cent of the WWCS members are failure as they mostly migrate to other places failing to reconstruct themselves from their losses from natural calamities like floods and fire or from family difficulties, such as death, sickness of children or adults or unexpected accidents (Table 1).

Recovery Rate in WWCS

As expected by WWCS, the loan repayment rates are uniformly as follows:

Madras	98 per cent
Bangalore	98 per cent
Dindigul	99 per cent
Adiramapattinam	99 per cent
Vellore	98 per cent
Narasapur	100 per cent
Bidar	100 per cent

Benefits of Credit Programme to Women

Studies were conducted in WWF from time to time to assess the empowerment process of women workers of various programmes including credit. The studies have revealed enormous facts. The parameters used helped us not only to assess the actual tangible changes in the life style and living standards of members, but also indicated the high level process of empowerment that these women have gone through. The degree of optimism, hope, confidence and courage infused in these women heightened their awareness of the static situation in which they live and make them perceive the desirable changes in their future plan.

Further, the study indicated that nearly 84 per cent of the women were sole contributions to the family income and hence had to bear the economic burden of the families. 92 per cent of women reported that they are able to give their families two square meals a day. All these were the direct results of the WWF's credit assistance after which they could pursue many work opportunities. 76 per cent said that they have relieved themselves of their continuous indebtedness to moneylenders. About 40 per cent of the women have diversified their business or started new but additional business. 89 per cent of respondents reported that they were able to own necessaries of the household. 96 per cent of the respondents said that they have saved their profits in the form of cash and few women reported other forms of investments both movable and immovable, such as livestock. 75 per cent invested their savings on housing and 66 per cent of the women have invested in the renewal or extension of their houses or added civic amenities.

Women's Desire to Upward Mobility

The study further proved that women wanted to move from marginal subsistence level trading to higher options. Very rarely women aspire to move upwards this way. As future plan the WWF proposes to help women achieve their long-term objective towards this upward mobility. These efforts will enable women both to increase the volume of their business earn, to better profits, providing access to productive assets, technology or training. Women also desire to educate and train their girl children to have additional incomes to their families. This is a marked change in the attitudes of poor women and a positive step towards postponement of marriage of adolescent girls, preventing adolescent girls from being pushed into early motherhood. WWF will help and facilitate women to take such positive, forward looking steps and increase decision-making efforts.

Future Plan of WWF

Therefore, the future credit plans of the WWCS points towards helping women to have access to habitable environmental conditions, technological support to their economic activities, improve living standards by better housing facilities, add civic amenities to their houses, drinking water pumps, smokeless choolas and bio-gas plants, help organising of trade co-operative and so on. While the earlier credit option was just to relieve them from their day-to-day struggle of getting out of the debt trap of the moneylenders. The WWF's future proposals are to move towards social development programmes improving the quality of life among the poor women.

Need for Networking Processes

Innovative experiments, such as the WWF are in response to the global need to have a better world for the poor to live in. In its existence of over a decade, the WWF has collected significant experience in empowering poor women towards better working and living conditions. Such experiences have to be effectively transferred to others and help create such models elsewhere in other parts of the world. Therefore, the WWF seeks to train more resource persons who would both carry this process of empowerment/awakening in other powerless communities and initiate similar popular movements through a process of mobilisation, organisation and participation. Also, there is a dire need to initiate this kind of networking process to see that valuable development experiments such as, that of WWF are replicated as otherwise these efforts fade out in isolation. WWF's recent experiment alongwith another global network called Grassroots Women Organizing Ourselves Together in Sisterhood (GROOTS) is an outcome of such desire.

Joint Effort of Groots International and the Working Women's Forum

In March 1990 in Bangalore, in a joint experiment of Groots International and the Working Women's Forum, nearly 22 women representative from 19 countries around the world and 65 of Voluntary Agencies in South Asia met in a global meeting followed by a workshop on Leadership Development with an objective to continue this networking process. This effort generated lot of enthusiasm among the voluntary agencies in South Asia and each one has pledged to themselves to network within their own region with other small and less known voluntary agencies.

The WWF plans a series of such regional networking seminars and workshops among other groups of women in South Asia, South East Asia and Africa and if necessary, in Latin America. This effort of WWF will strengthen the knowledge base on other development effort and will help to build up successful models of development movements, such as the WWF in other parts of the world.

Conclusion

By way of conclusion, it is appropriate to quote from the evaluation report of the Joint Mission of Dutch Development Co-operation on the WWF which recently took place in the month of May. The Evaluation report says as follows:

"...By any standard, national or intentional, the Working Women's Forum (WWF) is a remarkable and successful institution. In terms of numbers, the Forum has more women staff and members than probably any other non-governmental organisations in the world. Even more notably, almost all of the staff are from the same socio-economic class as the membership, that is poor working class women..." (Page 6, II Chapter, Para 1st, Report of the Joint Evaluation Mission of WWF/Govt. of Netherlands, May 24th 1990).

"There is no doubt that the Forum has empowered a large number of women. It offers the women, generally for the time in their lives, an opportunity to share problems and to voice demands. Almost every member, group leader, and organiser will testify that before joining the WWF she did not have the confidence to speak in public, to meet government officials, to deal with traders and middlemen, and more. Indeed, a natural process of empowerment sets in once a woman joins the Forum by virtue of being a member of a local group and of a larger organisation of women..." (Page 15, of II Chapter, Para 2nd, Report of the Joint Evaluation Mission by WWF/Govt. of Netherlands, May 24th, 1990).

References

Arunachalam Jaya - A Decade of the Forum - Working Women's Forum (India), A Movement of Poor Women of Self-help and Social Transformation; published by WWF (I).

Arunachalam Jaya - Credit Needs of Women Workers in the Informal Sector, Case Study of Working Women's Forum (India) submitted by Appropriate Technology International, USA, Sept., 1987.

Arunachalam Jaya - Managing by Value and Vision Lessons from the Working Women's Forum (India), presented at Asian Institute of Management, Manila, Phillipines, April 24th - 28th, 1990.

Azad Nandini - Empowering Women Workers, The WWF Experiment in Indian Cities, published by UNICEF, New Delhi.

Chambers Robert - The Working Women's Forum - A Counter Culture by Poor Women Workers, published by UNICEF.

Chen Marty - The Working Women's Forum; Organising the Credit and Change Seeds No.6, 1983, New York.

Dr. U. Kalpagam - Solidarity, Strength and Success, Working Women's Forum (India) points the way.

Wignaraja Ponna - Women, Poverty and Resources, Working Women's Co-operative Society.

WWF (I) - Periodical, Internal Feasibility Monitoring Reports of Working Women's Forum (India).

- Report of the Joint Evaluation Mission of Working Women's Forum/Government of the Netherlands of WWF Programme in Tamil Nadu, Karnataka and Andhra Pradesh.

Fighting Poverty
Social Innovations and New Coalitions

Panel : 4 Asserting the Power and Influence of the Poor*

The Case of the Working Women's Forum

Is poverty a choice of the poor? Or are they compelled to accept impoverishment? Are they born poor or is it a state of affairs over generations, through exclusions from their rights and entitlements? These are questions that the August Body of the Global Dialogue has to ponder.

For instance in India, the Green Revolution which aimed to induce prosperity through scientific advances proved to be a counter-productive exercise pauperising many of the poorer small peasant households. This was due to the fact that an increased production warranted increased investment which the small and marginal farmers could not afford, unlike the large landholders. Thus, many small landholders lost even their meagre yet valuable possessions to big farmers by way of continuous mortgage. The failure of the Green Revolution and its creation of pockets of prosperity echoes a similar situation in the currently adopted disproportionate reduction of subsidies and curtailing of government investment in the social sectors, carried out under the pretext of the so-called development model in the era of liberalisation, particularly in the developing nations. As a consequence, the needs and responsibilities of the poor are bypassed. This marginalises them further into subordination, a fact which is particularly true for women, thus intensifying the feminisation of poverty and the enduring vicious circle of poverty. In India, 44 per cent of the population still live in poverty, 30 to 40 per cent dwell in congested slums and one-third of the child population work as child labourers, with 89 per cent of women workers working in the informal sector, 290 million adults living as illiterates and 220 million living without any access to drinking water. Here, as in the rest of South Asia, fighting poverty does not mean a simple provision of goods and services but includes a well-planned empowerment process that would be of more relevance to their continuous struggle.

India's socio-economic milieu, and the fact that jobs are scarce, paves the way for an initiation of divergent strategies towards the creation of new opportunities. These could lead to a platform for innovative action-oriented programme strategies to work among the poor, establishing them

---

*Speech at the Plenary Session of the Global Dialogue, Expo-2000 Hanover / Germany – July 25th – 27th, 2000.

as rich human potential. Our experience to date is that the poor and women are undoubtedly the most valuable human resources and that their underutilisation will only lead to a perpetuation of poverty and squalor. Chronic indebtedness, illiteracy and the burden of drudgery of taking care of large families with absolutely no support system to fall back on, compelled the poor women of the Working Women's Forum in the year 1978 to the landmark decision of organising themselves around their neighbourhoods. The Working Women's Forum has thus been engaged for over two decades in a conscious effort to help poor women, through their own initiatives, to enhance their existing skills, acquire new skills and find their own capacities, not only to fight poverty but also to make efforts to help others to sustain themselves in and around their neighbourhood.

Decades of WWF's experience with poor women has demonstrated that, in order to fight poverty, one course for the future is to facilitate or promote self-managed organisations of the poor in building a cohesive and common platform of divergent poverty groups, as the first essential step and a path towards a self-sustaining empowerment process. The tools they adopted for such a coming together (meeting points) was "poverty and powerlessness" as an indicator and "women intensiveness" as the target group approach in a process where class, gender and caste confronted them as major obstacles. In this massive unionisation process, women in WWF resisted authority, discrimination and demonstrated extraordinary leadership roles, uniting the poorest women in solidarity, unfolding themselves into a mass movement of women. They promoted the concept of credit groups as an instrument to end hunger, poverty, squalor and to fight the vested interests of moneylenders. Their innovative delivery mechanism to reach the poor in large numbers contributed to the phenomenal growth of the organisation turning it into a movement in a short time span. The emergence of women group leaders who use credit an as entry point (acting as sole guarantor for each slum household) provided them with an opportunity to demonstrate their leadership in the community. Their contribution to family income, either as sole or equal contributor, assured her alternative leadership in the family, too. Such leadership emerging from the poor and powerless communities was highly committed, particularly to their own people in their own neighbourhoods. They could motivate other members of their communities to challenge adverse circumstances. Women taking control of the banking system - Indian Co-operative Network for Women - brought peer pressure to the members of the co-operative, which in turn resulted in good repayment, enhancement of business opportunities and pooling of their scarce resources for maximum utilisation. Poor women were able to demonstrate that they are not only capable but their institutions and enterprises can grow and they can save, too. 5.4 million rupees of capital funds of the ICNW have now been rotated into 486 million rupees, establishing the sustainability of the poor women's banking network.

Foray for Establishing Employment Opportunities

The availability of credit as one of the options to gain entry into the struggle for success enabled the women to fight tooth and nail against the monopoly of the contractors and merchant exporters in the three southern states of India. They freed themselves from the clutches of moneylenders in the context of lace artisans in the coastal regions of Andhra Pradesh, challenged the malpractices in the material supply by merchant-contractors to the piece rate workers of the beedi rollers of Vellore and established non-farm employment as a means to have better access to markets in the drought-prone areas of Dindigul. In Adirampattinam, a coastal village in Tamil Nadu, the fisherwomen were exploited by the auctioneers at the markets by supplying rotten fish and engaging them in the fish trade with no significant income. This led to the women being caught in persistent indebtedness and poverty. The unionisation efforts of Working Women's Forum (India) assisted the women in overcoming the domination of auctioneers and gave them an opportunity for alternative employment, thereby equipping them to face the threat of moving to other places in search of livelihood.

Organisational Framework to Combat Wage Issues

The provision of organisational support to the unorganised conglomeration of women in the informal sector has abolished child mortgage/bondedness and child labour by strengthening adult employment through wage increases. In Vellore, for example, children are exploited in beedi rolling, while in Bangalore children are employed in agarbathi rolling to work for long hours with meagre pay. In both the places, the young labourers are now attending schools to get integrated into the mainstream. In the case of lace artisans in Narasapur and other East and West Godavari districts of Andhra Pradesh, the empowerment process has helped women to achieve a rise in wages from 3 rupees to 50 rupees. Time and again, the women workers have taken the larger issues to the streets through protest marches and demonstrations, such as the struggle for their land and labour rights. The women beedi rollers of Vellore have used mass demonstrations to enforce the implementation of the government's scheme of equal wages to factory-based workers and home-based workers. Capturing the attention of the then Prime Minister,

Shri Rajiv Gandhi, when he was on his way to attend political meetings, and the subsequent intervention of the Prime Minister's Office, has enabled the women beedi workers to get a raise in their pay from Rs.7 to Rs.35 and recently upto Rs.40, for every 1000 beedies.

Collective Base as an Effective Tool to Fight Social Barriers

The collective base of the women has further enhanced their solidarity through promotion of leadership qualities from the grassroots level. This is evident in the case of women of Bellary, a district in Karnataka, which is well known for its oppression of women in the age old practice of Devadasi. Under this system, a girl is dedicated to the goddess and is allowed to be sexually exploited by anyone. The Forum's initiative has given the women of Bellary alternative employment opportunities and the girls have recognised their right to education. The failure of government measures to reach the poor and alleviate their poverty situation spurred the Forum to action in Kanchipuram, in Tamil Nadu and Bidar in Karnataka. The healthcare project through UNFPA, alongwith credit support, strengthened the employment potential of silk weavers of Kanchipuram. Similarly, in Bidar, yet another drought-prone area in Karnataka, the initiative taken by the women members of the Forum enabled the money earmarked for the poor to reach the target beneficiaries and also promoted empowerment among the women to take up leadership roles.

The concerted efforts of the women of the Working Women's Forum (India) to promote a social platform for social mobilisation has induced awareness in the minds of minority women of Hyderabad and Secunderabad to come out of their closed and isolated worlds and establish their dual role at the domestic front and at the work front. It has also helped them to fight poverty and indebtedness and has unified the women of the informal sector across the barriers of caste/class and gender. The prevalence of casteism in Dharmapuri, a drought-prone area in Tamil Nadu, and the issue of suppression and exclusion of migrant labourers in Bangalore have brought the women to form a common platform to fight collectively the common challenges confronting them in their day-to-day struggle for existence.

Impact of Empowerment at the Grassroots

Educating women through training programmes and role plays has enhanced their knowledge of occupational safety, reproductive healthcare, childcare, educational rights, taking the edge off from the patriarchal male dominated society and the acquisition of leadership roles. The process of creating awareness has resulted in women asserting their resource potential by their significant contribution in the work role and their power to influence attitudinal changes among employers and governments to provide better living and working conditions and welfare measures for the poor.

The on-going experiments of the Working Women's Forum (India) provides ample testimony that, if poverty is understood in the context of developing countries, it is nothing but generations of social exclusion imposed on them and a clear example of an exploitation of class and gender. Therefore, it is time that governments and the growing number of civil society initiatives think of evolving a new culture of facilitation to help the poor and the vulnerable to build up organisation assets. As a means towards productive employment, provide them with a support system to fight exploitation, unfair trade practices and unfair wages, while pushing for welfare services and wide safety nets - in short, for better living and working conditions. This would not only help them to fight poverty but also to participate in the reform process.

Conclusion - The New Economic Order

It is evidently clear that, internationally, we are still just in a process of dialogue and in urgent need of action to fight poverty around the globe, especially in the countries of the North. This is an indication that the countries of the North have not found solutions to their own problems, nor have their strategies reduced poverty in the South. Therefore, the framework for the New Economic Order depends upon how honourably the resources can be transferred to the countries of the South, i.e., on norms that are internationally accepted as the needs of the poor, rather than on the uncertain generosity of the rich nations. Furthermore, poor nations should be allowed to make their own choices rather than be made to accept anything as passive recipients of international aid. Nationally, of course, we as major civil society initiatives are not only fighting out battle but are also making efforts to negotiate with our national governments that we are accepted in an honourable partnership. We emphasise that government assistance should be more in the form of a support system, i.e., a means to an end to sustain a partnership, rather than a provision of handouts to improve the condition of the poor and vulnerable. Above all, our international and national efforts must be to empower the poor, who in turn should experience the change process on their own by way of a self-evaluation process.

Women, Economy, Poverty and Globalisation

Economic reforms are often projected as a panacea for economic progression and economic invigoration, which according to the advocates of globalisation will lead to reduction in poverty levels, squalor and regression. These global reforms though are discernible option, can itself be lopsided in increasing the trauma of the poor; bring down the status of women, if the communities in the developing world are not empowered on the effects of such reforms.

As one observes the direction of globalisation, it is quite skeptical as to what change the globalisation can do to ameliorate poverty, or in altering the status of children and women in the developing world. Economic restructuring may be a grand plan and design to eradicate poverty, but inadvertently the direction of happenings in the globalisation process shows that it works the other way more to ensure the survival of the rich. The products and consumer goods that come out of these new policies even in India takes every right thinking Indian to wonder whether they are here to cater to the 20 per cent of the rich Indian customers or to cater to the needs of the poor? On the contrary, what actually the country's poor pay for the reform process is high rates of inflation and due to governments' complacency to check the same, makes the poor to face a situation of inaccessibility to even basic services such as food, education and healthcare for the poor.

Can there be guarantees from the reform's process that the country's poor can be assured of at least the basic requirement of two square meals a day, a roof to safeguard them over from the rain and sun, decent clothes to wear, clean drinking water, basic healthcare and job opportunities to keep the family going?

Left with an option to manage the households with limited income levels, women are severe victims of globalisation than men as they have to bear the burden and brunt of inflation, increased prices of basic commodities, losing sizeable amount of family income by way of men's unemployment in the family, as they are the households' managers who have to manage the situation of food and other services. Even in workplaces there cannot be a better example of exploitation of women labour particularly in the Export Processing Zones (EPZ). While there is of course every opportunity for increase in women's employment in this globalisation era, not because of any extra concern to improve the conditions of women workers, but it is due to the fact and perception that the women employees are at the outset traceable, would be more subservient to employers' authority, less prone to unionisation activities, almost nil desire for upward mobility and above all more easier to dismiss them under the pretext of marriage and childcare.

In short, the globalisation has never offered women workers any opportunity neither for achieving excellence in their job potential nor in the matter of wages not even in the living and working conditions. Therefore, while it is only an illusive economic freedom that is described by the advocates of globalisation saying that women are expected to enjoy in many job options in present era, the reality seems that they are more vulnerable and hence, opportunities are greater for severe exploitation. The wages that women earn in these jobs are much lower than men. Training and promotion options are always kept at a minimum level. Typically, the trend can be described as women are given work options towards "dead-end-jobs". Thus, but for small percentage of job options for women workers in manufacturing fields, women workers in all developing countries are still part of the informal economy be it in the urban or in the rural scenario. Sometimes, even when women workers are offered new jobs in many places most of them become severe victims of dislocations, as once when they are uprooted from the native settlements, they even lose their traditional sources of livelihood, leading to either feminisation of poverty or prostitution in many countries of East Asia.

If globalisation can remove the economic and social inequality of women by transforming the existing sexual division of labour as part of these restructuring process, enhancing women's status both at home and labour market, then we can attribute some credit to the globalisation process. Otherwise globalisation will leave women where they are or even in the worst of conditions leaving them as victims of 'traditional' and 'capitalist' patriarchy. Further, the disadvantaged positions in which women are placed by Unfair Trade Agreements due to the globalisation process worldwide, to which India is no exception, is an uncompromising solution for job options, as in these agreements feminist perspective is either marginal or almost nil.

Women handle most of the food production activities as subsidized economy, mostly in India and in other developing countries. Therefore, removal of subsidies for food products has not only deepened food security crisis also contributes to environmental degradation as well. We cannot forget that in every region of the world including India and South Asia, it is these women as workers, producers, consumers, mothers and caretakers of families who are the real shock absorbers and bear the disproportionate brunt of both economic transition and economic collapse. A comprehensive gender analysis of the effects of globalisation on women will prove that women workers and children are in the first firing line in terms of economic transition and crisis. Intensified financial crisis in many families in the developing countries provide ample opportunities for domestic violence or desperately leads to prostitution among women. This is an ample proof towards that the ideology of market economy aggravates poverty levels.

The advocates of globalisation have to have real concern by understanding the realities in its full form. They must take instances from the Indian experience as follows there is a clear increases in poverty ratio from 34.3 per cent during the year 89-90 to 40.6 per cent during 92-93 and 45 per cent in the year 2000 during which evidently reforms were intensified. The immediate consequences of the reform could be felt both at the macro levels and community and individual levels. Therefore, the intention of this editorial is not only to highlight the ills and evils of globalisation but also to offer on behalf of women, some suggestions towards betterment and damage control measure, as globalisation is irreversible.

Commercial spree in all spheres of traditional activities, such as fishing and in the handloom weaving has marginalised the poor severely. How are we to make them participate in the ongoing economic reform processes? In many of the coastal zone where fishing is the predominant livelihood option, where women's role as a worker is integrated in the overall family's economy, the rapid proliferation of prawn farms has led to severe salt shortage for the fisherwomen to sun-dry fish that are left over, besides also hindering the access to sea to most fisher folk in and around these areas. Similar is the trend in the handloom industry, where most of the cotton industries are now idled by shortage of raw materials as raw cotton is being exported. This has forced the women to shift their economic ventures towards unfavourable, marginal income generating activities like hawking and vending. There are thousands of instances that are direct consequences of globalisation that cannot be enumerated in this small editorial here.

The advocates of globalisation may argue that these processes may bring in more resources unmindful of the fact that strings are attached to these resources. But most of these resources are spent. Only on the hard sector and hardly anything reaches the soft social sectors. Surplus resources do not necessarily mean economic well-being in reality, it only leads to mismanagement and misappropriation, like for example, the financial crisis in the Unit Trust of India leaving thousands of the investors in the gloom. Ultimately why should the poor always pay such heavy price for the mismanagement of the economy? There should be public hearing and concerted proactive action by people in power to understand the other side of globalisation. Need of the hour is not just bleak responses from politicized unions voicing against globalisation particularly on the issue of retrenchment but a mass movements and education of the people so that the mistakes committed in other liberalised developing economies can be taken as a lesson to be prevented in India.

Long-term measures, such as pro-poor strategies that would ensure delivery of social safety nets to the poor, basic healthcare, food subsidies to diminish the vulnerability of women and children through current trends of malnutrition, prevention of increased incidence of child labour and female infanticide are to be inducted by the policy-makers while structuring plans for the poor. Credit assistance in the form of extension of micro-credit options to enhance entrepreneurship among women, is also one of the avenues that would ensure women to over come poverty and powerlessness. Any innovative systems of micro-credit along with organized social platform in the form of collective effort would facilitate women to transcend the barriers for collective action through their collective consciousness. The vision of the millennium should be rather to offer an agreement of the North and the South on major issues of poverty eradication, assurance to enhance gender relations, concepts of more equal distribution of income, access to equity for all on a global basis. Only such an agreement on resource transfers and time framework would lead to the empowerment of poor working population on their right to food, health, education, shelter, information sharing and fundamental rights as a strategy to fight poverty. As the economic development model that exists today emphasises only the economic growth that finally perpetuated only oppression on poor and discrimination on women. Will it be possible for the advocates of Globalisation to come up with a model that will meet the social demand of poor women to make space for them to move forward, trying to eliminate social biases and enhance economic relations?

6
Status of Adolescent Girls and Their Economic Participation*

Introduction

It is now widely accepted that among the poor of the world, women and girls are the poorest. This directly relates to the systematic subjugation of girls and women so that they are given less food at home, educated less, given lesser attention and care, given more burden, such as household chores and childcare. They work more hours and are paid less or unpaid, yet their work roles go unrecognised and unaccounted in the accounting systems and censuses. Girls and women are subject to more discriminations on account of their gender, socially and economically.

It is this gender discrimination of the girl child from her very birth or even before birth that extends itself to the adolescent girl who is at the threshold of womanhood and she is made to bear the dual burden of being poor and being woman.

Adolescent Girls – Obstacles to Development

The adolescent girls have been neglected thus, far mainly due to the fact that they are viewed as a transient presence to be tolerated, when they attain the status of a married woman and a mother. In fact, her status and role is almost invisible as the girl is considered a liability to be borne by the family until she is given away in marriage to a different family at further cost in the form of dowry. The fact that she is at a formative and impressionable stage in her life and that she is to be nurtured and developed as an individual is hardly understood or appreciated.

---

*From Public Forum conducted among the "Girl Children", October 1996.

On the contrary, due to discriminatory treatment, the emotional and physical well-being of the child becomes crippled and she is led to believe that she is far inferior to her brother and their male counterparts in all respects that really count.

Dharmapuri and Bellary: Two Examples of Discrimination of the Girl Child

The following is an account of two experiences of the Working Women's Forum that demonstrate how the girl child is victimised right from birth. This gives an insight into the depth of the problem that is to be faced while addressing this issue of adolescent girls. On one hand, the girl child is discriminated even before birth by selective female foeticide. On the other hand, in poorer communities where infrastructure for sex determination does not exist, the practice of female infanticide is found. In the tribal regions of Dharmapuri district of Tamil Nadu, where the WWF has been active for the past two years, the Irular tribe which has lost all means of livelihood due to deforestation sees, the girl child as an unnecessary burden on the family. The mothers are therefore, compelled to kill the newborn girl baby by feeding her the poisonous oleander milk. They consider this to be an act of mercy as they are saving the girl from a life of misery.

Alternative options for these women has made a positive impact towards reducing this inhuman practice. Says Ranjitham who is now an organiser at WWF, "After joining as a member of the credit group my mother-in-law and husband forced me to kill my second girl baby. I stoutly refused saying that, now I have a means of income and I can support my daughter"

In the backward district of Bellary, Karnataka, the oppressive tradition of Devadasi system pushes the young girl child at the threshold of adolescence into a life ordained by an age-old custom that prevents her from leading a normal life. She is abused from an early age by men who come in search of work to the village and who later abandon her after she has had a few children. These women often as young as 16 or 18 are forced by social norms to not only support the family of her birth, but also the man she lives with and later his children. Through the training and credit programmes of WWF, alternate employment options have been created for these women and as a result, they are firmly opposing the attempts by their family to push their daughters into this cruel system and are sending the girls to school.

These two examples reveal the deeply rooted patriarchal systems that work against the very survival of women and their existence as equal partners in the society.

An overview of these categories reveals a pyramid like structure with a majority of illiterate, unemployed girls at the base and a minority of girls who are economically active at the apex. In any case, the problems they face are not dissimilar. They are burdened by cultural, social and economic constraints which prevent them from developing their own potential to become rightful participants of the future society.

Anbukarasi is nineteen and comes from a family of nine members. She works in an export garment factory. "I do exactly the same work as the male workers but I am given Rs.20, whereas the men are given Rs.40. When we question, the employers say, after all you are going to use this money for buying 'nice' things for yourselves but the men need the money to feed their family". In fact, she says, the opposite is true. The boys never reveal their actual earnings to the family. They use a significant portion for themselves whereas the girls see their mother struggle day-in and day-out to make ends meet. So there is no question of the girls keeping their earnings for themselves. They give the entire amount to the family.

In the case of Meena, the very survival of her family depends on her income. Meena's mother left her husband a few years back when she could no more tolerate his abuse. Her mother's father supported the family but now he too is dead. Meena and her mother work in an export house. She has a lot of health problems due to the strenuous work that she is expected to do in the company. She had a severe complaint of reproductive tract infection for which she is taking medicines. Even if she wished to take one day off from work her mother starts crying, saying that if she does not bring money there will be no food. This year they also decided to stop her younger brother, who is 15 years old from school. He is now working in a foundry. Meena also feels sorry for her elder brother who at the young age of 20 has to work and support the family. He has to worry about getting his sisters married instead of being carefree like other boys of his age. Meena's prime ambition in life is not to get married to a man who is a drunkard and abuses her like her father did.

In many of the poorer families, it is the compulsion to earn income for the family that curtails the education of the girl. Says Kalaiarasi, "I studied upto class VII but seeing the other girls in our neighbourhood go to work in a leather export company, it was decided that I should stop my studies and go to work. I now earn Rs. 20 to Rs. 40 a day. Kalaiarasi is involved in cutting and stitching together pieces of leather in a shoe company. The men usually do the polishing and finishing "which is a tougher job and women cannot handle that". There is no effort to help these women to train in jobs that require better skills and will offer better pay. The same patriarchal assignment of a transitory role accorded to the girls at home is extended to the workplace as well. The employers feel that the girls get married and leave, therefore, it is a waste of time and resource to train them in better skills. There is no effort either to make their job more permanent or secure. The reason of marriage that is quoted for such a discriminatory practice is often a pretext. The real reason is that due to the unprotected and unsafe working environment, the girls are often afflicted by peculiar ailments. The employers find it much easier to retrench an experienced worker who would demand medical allowances and other long-term benefits and recruit younger women eager for any pay and willing to work with fresh enthusiasm.

At the same time, when it comes to financial matters the girls are quite shrewd. Says Sumathi, "When I earn Rs. 600 a month I give Rs. 400 for the family and keep Rs. 200 for myself, but when I earn only Rs. 300 I still keep Rs. 150 for myself with which I buy jewels, clothes etc.". The sense of pride that these girls have, being economically active is very evident. 9 out of 10 are investing a portion of their earnings in chit funds. Tamil Selvi says, "My life's objective is that I should always be independent and self-reliant and I should support my family and children in future instead of being dependent on them".

In spite of the fact that they are economically active, economic independence is still a distant dream. They are not allowed to participate in the decision-making in the family even in matters that affect their own life and future. These young but strangely mature girls quietly accept their subordinate status at home.

Even when it comes to basic issues, such as food there is a difference in treatment between the male and female child. Says Yuvarani, "We girls keep quiet if we are not given fancy foods. But the boys are not like that, so our mother says to us, your brothers will shout at me if I don't give them this dish so I will keep it aside for them. You are very nice, you will not complain if I just give you rice".

Equal job opportunities are still denied to them. However, capable they may be, it is still the male child's privilege to take over the role of the head of the household. In the case of Anbukarasi, her father died recently while in government service. She was in school final year and was over 18 years of age. But the family decided that the younger brother who is only 12 years old should be the one to get the job and they would rather wait till he is old enough.

These girls are often pained by the blatant preference that is shown towards the male children. They are further expected to bow down to the authority of not just the father but also the brothers. In the case of Nirmala who does not have father, her two older brothers have taken the responsibility of grooming her into a 'proper' girl. They childe her when she comes out of the house when the brothers' friends are around. She is not supposed to leave the house, other than to go to school. The mother feels that her sons are right in advising her daughter on right conduct. Nirmala also feels that they are justified in doing so. She has seen instances of other women who cannot be 'married off' even at the age of 30. These women feel bad because they see other younger girls who are married and have children", she says.

When the question of marriage arises the position of these young girls is very uncertain. Malarkodi is 22 years of age. There is immense pressure on her to get married as she is considered 'old enough' to be married. But she has her own principles. She belongs to the Pentecost community where women do not wear any jewellery. However, prospective grooms want brides who will bring a lot of jewellery as dowry or her parents are expected to give dowry that will cover the cost of jewellery that they would otherwise give to her during marriage. Malarkodi refused to marry a man whose parents demanded that she wear jewellery. But when asked how long she can hold on to her principles in the face of strong pressures to be married, she only smiles.

Anbukarasi says, "The dowry issue that oppresses women so badly can be overcome by inter-caste marriages and love marriages rather than arranged marriages. Her brother married a girl from another caste. Though the parents were opposed to it in the beginning, later they accepted it".

Still, these young women feel that the days when women were silently expected to bear the beatings and offensive behaviour of the husband are long past. "I would never tolerate any such nonsense from a husband of mine"' says Nirmala. They know of many women who have walked out of a difficult marriage and have made a meaningful life for themselves and their children. Everyone agrees that the change in the recent years has occurred due to education and more employment options for women. They discuss these issues on the basis of what they witness around them among themselves. Television is also a reason why girls are becoming more independent says Nirmala. Earlier girls never went out of home but now they go out and get to meet many kinds of people. Their horizons are broadening now, says Yuvarani.

Conclusion

The issue of adolescent girls and their economic participation is to be seen in the broader light of patriarchal norms and values that govern that domestic scent. It is no doubt necessary to enact policies and initiate programmes to address that needs of the girl child, her right to survive, right to equal nutrition, right to healthcare and immunisation, right to equal education and above all, right to equal care and attention.

These psychological, social and economic aspects have to be tackled at every level domestic, community and society – so that the girl child gets her rightful share in the world of the future.

Working Women's Forum (India)- Madras-4 (Health Worker of WWF)

An Analysis of Data Regarding Standard of Living of a Female Child

The Working Women's Forum (WWF) aims at improving the life of women who are financially backward. The WWF reaches out to women in various occupations and provides them an opportunity to change their impoverished life with no hope into a viable dynamic process full of hope. As this state of dynamism is built up during the development of the women, it becomes essential to examine the standard of living, especially in the early years of women when the physical and mental growth is in active progress.

Objective

Interview of family members to obtain data regarding the standard of living of children in general and female children in particular.

Material and Methods

1000 families residing in Madras, Vellore, Kanchipuram, Dindigul, Adiramapattinam, Bangalore and Narasapur were interviewed. The families were randomly selected in the above places. A member of the family was interviewed using a questionnaire and the data have been analysed.

Observations

Among the families interviewed, there were 2970 children of whom 53 per cent female children.

Education

Money spent for school and tuition fees was 24 per cent for a female child than that spent for a male child. At the same time, the female child could spend less time in preparing lessons at home. This may be the effect of the proportionate time spent in household chores. These chores were considered a part of the female child's education necessary for their future responsibilities during the later year.

Primary level education was given only to 25 per cent of the female children with an idea to give them just enough knowledge to read and write which would be necessary for day-to-day life.

Food and Nutrition

Of the families interviewed, 71 per cent priority to food and nutrition for boys. The remaining 29 per cent said that equal distribution was made between boys and girls in the household. By tradition, less importance is given to the nutrition for girls. They either consume less food or in most cases the leftovers.

Due to economic status, the poor quality of the food in the rule, as certain items like milk and eggs are considered a luxury. It is distressing to note that when quality is beyond the reach of most of them, food itself is beyond the reach of the female child. This is due to the fact that preference is given to boys traditionally, leaving the female child to survive on the leftover.

Clothes

Sixty-nine per cent of the families spend more on boys while 31 per cent said there was equal distribution. Many of the female children had one-half of the body scantily clad while the other wet half of dress was drying up. At the same time, the male child had a choice of wearing three or more sets of dresses. The reason offered for this disparity was that men go out to work and as such this provision was necessary.

Medical Treatment

Seventy-four per cent of the families tend to concentrate more on boys who are the potential bread-winner. 26 per cent stated that equal attention was given irrespective of the sex of the child. It is a fact that while social workers concentrate on population control in general, the rural people concentrate on controlling all facilities for the female population alone.

Workload

Ninety per cent of the female children coupe to study with a view to share the household chore. They are also engaged in looking after the younger siblings of the family. These responsibilities become an essential part of life, especially after puberty is attained.

Entertainment

Question was diverted at eliciting information regarding factors like nature of spots, sleeping hours, provision of pocket money for their children.

Seventy-three per cent gave more importance for the male child, while 27 per cent stated giving equal importance for both sexes. The male child is able to spend time on outdoor games while his sisters are engaged in some household chores. Female child has to go to bed late and rise early to carry out the household chores while their brothers go the bed early and rise up late in the morning.

Sixteen per cent distributed equal pocket money among their children. Still there was preference in families for the male child.

Property

A gross injustice was the rule when the distribution of property was questioned. Despite the enactment of the law for equal property rights, 81 per cent of the families ensured that the boys inherited the property.

Conclusion

The following salient observations are made from the review data:

(1) There is an under-estimation of the work capacity, ability and talents of a female child. Even the mothers who in the earlier years were in a similar trend to deprive their daughters of the facilities preventing them from having any lofty aims.

(2) By depriving the female of adequate education, it is ensured that the female child becomes more dependent on their parents in the earlier years of life and on their husbands in the later period. These children walk through the stages as a daughter, daughter-in-law, mother, mother-in-law undergoing the tension attributed to the various stages and ensure that their female off springs also go through the same experience time in end out.

(3) Nutrition necessary while passing through the phases of puberty, pregnancy and post-pasturation are not provided for by their own mothers.

(4) There is curb on extra-curricular activities of a female child especially on attaining puberty.

The finger points to the parents who are responsible for the inadequate facilities accorded to the female children in the society. A social reawakening can appear on the horizon only when spirit of WWF reaches out to these people and guide them on to an optimistic dynamic way of life.

Concerns on Special Protective Measures for Women Workers*

Introduction

With increasing alcoholism and unemployment among men, it is the income of women and children alone that carries many families through. The major obstacles that poor women go through are dispossession of productive assets, local hierarchies, elite domination and continuous indebtedness. Despite unfavourable, harsh working conditions women as a workforce face "invisibility as a serious handicap to their work. Their economic role is undervalued, their produce is considered cheap, but their contribution had been crucial to family income. Women workers thus carry a double load of drudgery of both working at home and outside.

Productive Measures in for Women Workers

1. *Employment*: With reference to protective measures in the case of rural workers, both among those who work as plantation labour and agricultural workers, there are large number of legislations enacted by the Indian Parliament, but enforcement will be difficult since employers played clever tactics. Employers always try to employ less than the stipulated number of workers whenever law stipulates that over a certain number of employees employed in workplaces such plantation are found, welfare measures are compulsory. For example, if the stipulated number is mentioned as 30, the employers always employ 29 members and still escape from enforcing any protective measures.

2. *Maternity Benefits*: With reference to maternity benefits, it is always stipulated by the employers that the workers have to be permanent and put in atleast 200 days of man work or so. Workers are at the same time are not given that many days of work, just to keep out of stipulated number of days, preventing employees becoming eligible for maternity benefits and so on. Therefore, again, it is in the hands of employers who play such malpractices.

3. *Night Work*: With reference to night work, for women workers India and other developing countries have been a party long before to one of the resolutions of the ILO Employment Conference, preventing women to do night work. However, in the modern situation, where women are fighting for equal opportunities and for defending their rights, they have to accept to do night work if it is going to be a lucrative situation,

---

*Presented at the ICEM World Conference, South Africa - 2001.

women workers will be the loser. Wherever transportation and other protections are given, there is nothing wrong for women to participate in the night work because of the high wages and overtime benefits given to men and women seldom get opportunities. It is also true that women have been working for longer hours than men but they are paid much less and are not even considered for overtime.

4. *Other Welfare Measures*: It is also true that many women do not have rest shed wherever they work. They are not given time to look after their small children and sick child and are not considered for casual leave even during sickness and discomfort. On the contrary, they are required to carry heavy loads in plantations and employer in plantations have always been very in sympathetic to women workers. It is also true women employees do not have rest shed, separate changing rooms, separate toilet facilities, childcare facilities, though these are theoretically spoken of by employers, but are practically non-existent. It is also true that we have to pressurise the government for a special law with reference to maximum of load that women can carry. At present, there seems to be no legislation for this and therefore, it has to be enacted.

5. *Health Hazards*: Also there are laws protecting health hazards, but in the case of chemical supplies in agriculture, it is never enforced. We are aware that many pregnant women undertake to work in chemical supplies in agriculture and rural areas which affect their reproductive capacity. There is also no law preventing this.

6. *Sexual Harrassment*: Women also go through a lot of sexual harassment from managers and other supervisors. However, even though there is a law that woman can always complain, for fear of continuity of job, women never come out and complain.

7. *Need for Strong Union Among Women Workers*: The only answer is a strong union for those women workers, which will pressurise the government to enforce such legislations regarding maternity leave, payment of allowance during maternity leave, payment of bonus for maternity, the provision of creche facilities at the place of work and time off for feeding of infants.

8. *Situation in India*: This is specially important. In India, there are about 292 million workers, out of whom only 25 million workers are organised. 6 million of these organised group belong to central trade unions and the rest of the 19 million workers belong to states and indigenous unions. The remaining 267 million workers do not belong to any organisation; 25 million of these workers get Rs. 250 to Rs. 500 per month. Rest get only Rs. 60 to Rs. 300 per month. 48 million of them are unemployed. 150 million are agricultural labourers while 18 million are construction workers; 17 million are child labourers and 6 million being beedi workers. But 89 per cent of the 267 million workers are India's women workers belong to this unorganised sector.

Women Workers – Priorising Health and Occupation Safety*

Being the major component of India's working population women workers form 89 per cent of the total workforce, most of whom belong to the informal sector. Due to growing industrialisation in India, women workers currently face serious problems of occupational health and safety. While lakhs of accidents take place every year and thousands of workers die, poorly maintained statistics rarely highlights this reality. It is presumed that more than 60 accidents take place per thousand workers, i.e., 8 times more than what is happening in the industrialised countries. The situation is growing worse day-by-day.

It is well known that several categories of workers suffer from various diseases which are directly caused by the production process that they are involved in. This arises from dust tobacco inhalation, humidity, temperature, chemicals, cement, construction materials and so on.

Women suffer from respiratory disorders due to working in sawdust in the case of agarbathi workers. It is also common among the beedi rollers in the North Arcot districts of Tamil Nadu. Sometimes, working in sawdust leads to blood cancer, likewise working in tobacco, i.e., the beedi workers get into diseases that deteriorate them slowly leading to disability of limbs and become crippled at an early age. Children and adults working in hazardous occupations like the match workers and in the cracker factories, work in very unsafe conditions and expose themselves to excessive heat and dangerous chemicals like phosphorous without adequate safety precautions, leading to occupation related diseases. Few examples that we give below are from the women workers concentrated heavily in the informal sector and unionised by NUWW.

Among the Narasapur lace makers, the constant use of needle and crochet requires bending down and looking sharply into the object leading to eye problems, also, blindness in some cases. They also get into spondilitis (neck pain), a major hazard associated with this kind of work.

Equally in electronic industries, eye straining is a typical hazard and mostly affects women who are largely engaged in this industry, also in computers, gem cutting and so on. In the construction industry, it is mostly the women who participate by going up on the scaffolding steps. Not only they have to work in cement, but some of them also work in brick kilns standing near the furnace even during the scorching sun. Such

*At the ICEM World Health & Safety Environment Conference Geneva, 5th – 7th May 1998.

humidity in these industries lead to respiratory diseases. When women work in these hazardous industries, if they happen to be pregnant, they face a threat of spontaneous abortion and severe health consequences.

The Sivakasi Municipal town of Tamil Nadu in India is known for its match and fireworks production. Child workers are employed in these industries, presumably 60 per cent of the workers are child workers. Working conditions in these factors are extremely unsafe and hazardous.

Children have to work long and hard hours in hazardous chemicals. Inadequate ventilation, dust from the chemical powders and strong vapours spread both in the storeroom and other places in the factory are just enough to explain the hazards. (These highly explosive materials cause frequent explosions and fire, killing and disabling hundreds of workers). Apart from this, children are brought from far of villages which are 20 kms away from factories. Children have to wake up at 4.30 a.m to reach the factory for work at 9 a.m., in the evening these children below 14 years reach home only at 10: 30 p.m. There have been major accidents during the transportation of these children in the early hours of the day, towards which, employers have given very little attention. National Union of Working Women (NUWW) has made a small study of these children match workers to help a visiting ILO official, it is enclosed here.

The chronic poisoning by working in chemicals have direct effect on human tissues and they affect the internal organs like liver, kidney, lungs, brain, stomach and so on. The women who work in leather industry where they have to use chemicals for tanning of leather get into sensitivity / allergies, rashes, extensive superficial skin damage, cough, breathlessness leading to asthmatic attacks, fit and so on. Women workers breathe in unconsciously the industrial substances that is often found as cause for cancer.

To tackle the demand for introduction of safety and occupational measures in industries, the employers employ less than the stipulated number whenever law stipulates that over certain number of employees work, occupational, safety and welfare measures are compulsory, if the stipulated number is 30 the employers always employ 29 members and still escape from enforcing any protective measures.

With reference to maternity benefits, it is always stipulated by the employers that the workers have to be permanent and put in at least 200 days of work or so. Towards this end, workers are treated casually and not given continuous work and if the workers have put in 180 work days they do not become eligible for maternity benefits. Therefore, such malpractices by the employer lead to disastrous consequences as women workers get neither employment nor maternity benefits.

With reference to night work, for women workers in India and other developing countries, it has been so that they seem to have been a party long before to one of the resolutions of the ILO Employment Conference, preventing women to do night work. However, in the modern situation, where women are fighting for equal opportunities, defending their rights everywhere, they have to accept night work, a lucrative situation, if women workers refuse, they will be the losers. Wherever transportation and other protections are given, there is nothing wrong for women to participate in the night work as it brings them high wages and overtime benefits. All these opportunities are given to men while women seldom get opportunities, even though women do put in longer hours than men, they are not only paid much less but are least considered for benefits like overtime.

It is also true that many women do not have rest sheds where they work. They are not given time to look after their small children and are not considered for casual leave even during sickness and discomfort. On the contrary they are required to carry on heavy workloads everywhere, separate changing rooms, separate toilet facilities, childcare facilities, though these are theoretically spoken of by employers, seldom exist practically towards the benefit of women workers. Unions have to go a long way to pressurise the governments for a special law with reference to maximum of load that women can carry. At present, there seems to be no legislation for this and therefore, such legislations become imminent.

There are of course laws protecting health hazards, but in the case of chemical supplies in agriculture, it is never enforced. We are aware that many pregnant women undertake work in chemical supplies in agriculture in rural areas, which affect their reproductive capacity. There is also no law preventing this.

Women also go through a lot of sexual harassment from managers and other supervisors. However, even though there is a law that women can always complain, for fear of being fired, women never come out and complain. Ordinarily workers are not fully aware of the sources and causes of occupational injuries and diseases. They are made to believe that many of these injuries and illness are necessary components and inevitable constituents of their work. Besides, they think that any solution to these problems would entail high degree of technical expertise and large financial investments.

This thinking and approach needs to be radically changed and the beginning to be made by the workers themselves. And the workers need to have the knowledge of the risks and hazards at their workplaces.

Experiences across the world shows that the occupational, health and safety issues are far more important, assuring the workers a confidence to continue their work culture. However, organisations like NUWW continuously collect such concrete information, such as occupational, health and safety measures, educate the workers, organise struggles making them aware and drawing the attention of government/employers. To supplement our work and to create better environment for workers, what is more important is an attitudinal changes among the employers and government to provide better work conditions and welfare measures for women workers. The author hope this August body will take all these into consideration.

References

Jaya Arunachalam : A Decade of the Forum – Working Women's Forum (India) A movement of poor women of self-help and social transformation; published by WWF (I).

Jaya Arunachalam : Credit Needs of Women Workers in the Informal Sector, Case Study of Working Women's Forum (India) submitted by Appropriate Technology International, USA, Sept. 1987.

Jaya Arunachalam : Managing by Value and Vision Lessons from the Working Women's Forum (India) presented at Asian Institute of Management, Manila, Philippines, April 24th – 28th 1990.

Jaya Arunachalam : Sharing Poverty or Creating Wealth? Access to Credit for Women's Enterprises, presented by Royal Tropical Institute, Netherlands, 7-9 January 1991.

Azad Nandini : Empowering Women Workers, The WWF Experiment in Indian Cities, Published by UNICEF, New Delhi.

Azad Nandini : "Creating Bases of Women's Solidarity"; A Study of the Grassroots Credit Groups of the Working Women's Forum (India) submitted in partial fulfillment of the requirements for the degree of Doctor of Philosophy in Anthropology in the Graduate School of Syracuse University, August 1987.

Chen Marty : The Working Women's Forum; Organising the Credit and Change Seeds No.6, 1983 New York.

Chambers Robert : The Working Women's Forum – A Counter Culture by Poor Women Workers, Published by UNICEF.

Nicro Schrijver and C. Pavlien Vanden Temple : Solidarity Against Poverty – A Socialist Programme from Hollan Published by Evert Vermeer Foundation.

Sara K. Gould : "A Working Guide to Women's Self Employment" prepared by Economic Development Administration of the U.S. Department of Commerce.

Wignaraja Ponna : Women, Poverty and Resources, Working Women's Cooperative Society.

Report : A Case Study "Women's Access to Credit in the Dominician Republic" Published by UNIRTIAW.

Building A Culture of Advocacy*

Preamble Towards Advocacy

Prevalence of widespread illiteracy, acute morbidity, high maternal and child mortality in addition to time-honoured cultural values that promote or practise female foeticide at the grassroots are the trends in South Asia, more importantly in India. Therefore, both physical and social environment for women and girl children leave much to be desired towards enhancement of their economic and social status. This is more or less so in all the developing countries as well. Hence, in our cluster of priorities, an emphatic need based, sound advocacy methodology should form the prime strategy to convert everyone towards a human-centred approach in population policies. As mentioned in the beginning, in the entire region, gender gap is very wide in education, health services and quality of life. The poorer families are greater victims of this gender gap. Even in normal households, men and boys eat first and women and girls eat what is left-over, which reflects very much on the life expectancy of women and girl children.

Change of attitude towards population reduction is not so easy. To quote an example, in 1977, a drastic methodology of population reductions measures pursued by Government of India supported by strong political leadership received a severe jolt and left an unsavory impression among the general public. Therefore, a strategic people-centred voluntary effort to convert the people themselves through a change process is the best way to achieve better results in realising the ICPD message at the grassroots.

While looking for alternatives, its time that we recognise the growing network of grassroot social movements, private non-government efforts, civil societies, that can strengthen the livelihoods of the poor and democratise systems and energise communities to generate income and acquire assets. Therefore, their partnership is very important. Methods of advocacy requires different strategies among different people. This is particularly relevant to India and the other countries of South Asia where people are multi-cultural in character. The motherhood of women is still be considered as a social role for the family, communities and in the country. Such women's unequal status in traditional communities affects even their right to a safe motherhood. Therefore, it is imperative to spread the message of the platform of action of ICPD in providing affordable

*Presented at UNFPA Headquarters, New York. 14-17th June 1998.

reproductive health care, through building up a new concept and culture of advocacy at the grassroots, where the anomalies are more common than any others.

Women Workers – Victims of Exploitation

Increasingly women are forced to cater to unstable markets, imposition of wage valuation by dominant patriarchal cultures pushes women to a position of subordination, subject to discrimination of class and gender not only at home, but also in the labour market. Further, the conditions of the women workers in this sector are characterised by low wages, low capital investment, labour intensiveness, exploitation and malpractices that push them into traps of indebtedness and intense poverty situations. Most of the women in the unorganised sector are forced to work outside home and augment family income. Yet, apart from shouldering economic responsibilities of the family, home and children are part of her social responsibilities too. While there are umpteen number of social legislations enacted by the Indian Parliament, still it requires strong advocacy measures to make our governments ensure their stringent enforcement at the grassroots.

Denial of education facilities to women not only reflects in their low employment status, but also results in their poor health and that of the large families for which women are held responsible. The children become the sole responsibility of a women in her role as a mother. Very seldom the father takes up responsibility for children. Now the time therefore is for women to demand a responsible fatherhood as much as a concerned motherhood. Women cannot become full partners in the social and economic development of any country until they get over this age-old gender discrimination. Time to time, WWF conducts participatory workshops among its cadres of grassroot women. During the course of these workshops, women identify the various problems that they face in their day to day life and the struggle process that they undergo for their very survival. The strategies that emerge as methods to combat these oppressive structures are then comprehensively presented and disseminated widely to create better awareness among women.

Role of WWF—A Growing Social Movement in the three Southern States of India

In the context, WWF's experiment in South India is an effort engineered by the community health workers themselves to voice the needs of the poor women who have hitherto been denied even the basic healthcare. It is a endeavour of convergence of all services to poor women and children at the grassroots as a major strategy both to enhance women's economic and productive role. And to reduce frequent pregnancies, safeguard their reproductive role and promote the concept of safe motherhood. Therefore, integrating several programmes to take care of women from birth to reproductive stage and even beyond, towards a safe and sensitive post reproductive period too is the hallmark of the programmes in WWF.

More importantly, it is the adolescents who face increasing risks of unprotected sexual activity making them susceptible to STDs including HIV and AIDS that pose great health risks to them. Further, this segment are also the victims of high maternal and infant mortality, as a consequence of early marriage and subsequent child bearing. All these risks together have the greatest toll on the lives of young women.

In order to combat the multifarious problem faced by this largely neglected adolescent group, WWF in its health advocacy strives towards better adolescent, health through the following measures. By creating a safe and supportive environment through distribution of contraceptives and by educating their parents, mothers in particular on issues of reproductive health. Their awareness is enhanced on reproductive and child issues through peer group education and IEC meetings in the communities. Thus, WWF's focus is on skill building of the adolescents who are mostly school drop outs towards bringing about economic self-reliance which would in turn delay their marriage and subsequent motherhood responsibilities.

WWF programmes reaching the poorest does not merely offer short-term solutions for alleviating poverty but tackle the structural reason behind it in order to break the vicious cycle of poverty, indebtedness and ill-health. This is achieved through a holistic approach of delivery of financial services and through addressing the whole gamut of reproductive health issues. Such a multi-pronged strategy alone can sustain the impact of improved health and economic status of the communities which will ultimately help in bringing down the fertility rates voluntarily. (See Case Study I)

The Third Phase of Partnership between UNFPA and WWF (1998-2003)

The third phase of the health project of UNFPA/GOI/WWF partnership has integrated even many more aspects and is a multi-faceted human resource development programme initiating from micro-credit orientation, health advocacy to social action measures.

The programme of WWF involves a large number of cadres of grassroots women from the poorest families, from the urban slums to rural landless and is a low cost model. It is suitable for replication in other developing countries. Therefore, it is no exaggeration to say that WWF as a social movement of people with strong women's network is a social platform for the poor to carry on their conflicts and confrontation through a struggle process to achieve their goals through sound advocacy methods.

Gender Sensitivity – Important Areas of Operation of WWF's New Phase

An extremely gender sensitive programme, it touches many sensitive areas that are in direct need of WWF's advocacy. While in the village of Dharmapuri, cadres of WWF work to put an end to the heinous crime of female infanticide, where the very survival of the girl child is threatened, in areas of Bellary, sexual abuse of the women and girl children are rampant among the Devadasi Communities, the need to advocate for alternative means of survival assumes paramount importance. In several other urban areas with abysmal living conditions where adolescent girls are pushed into early marriage and motherhood, health cadres of WWF are entrusted with the responsibility of enhancement of age at marriage and the need for economic empowerment. The programme covers wide areas of urban slums of Chennai where 1.8 million people live and in the city of Hyderabad in Andhra Pradesh and in Bangalore town, and also areas of shanty towns like Bellary in Karnataka, Dharmapuri in Tamil Nadu. The programme impacts a population of over 10,00,000.

Choice of Dharmapuri in Tamil Nadu is a strategy to check on female foeticide and infanticide widely prevalent among the tribal population. Integrating a strong education and advocacy programme resulted in making those families understand that it is the human right of every girl child to survive in the world as much as male children. In Bellary, the girl children at the age of 7 years are dedicated to female goddess in temples, subsequently allowed to survive through prostitution or Devadasi system (see Case Study 3). A disastrous cultural practice treating girl children not as a human species but more like cattle. Women here in this area have severe health problems through multiple sex partners, also suffer from many infections, such as RTI/STD.

Interpersonal Communication in WWF

Women lack basic healthcare, need strong advocacy and advise against these cultural practices. Government has many welfare programmes in this area which have little or no effect on them. Only an interpersonal communication programme through local cadres of WWF emerged as an alternative and could counter the fear and misconception, infusing confidence against such myths of culture and traditions in this area. A recent study conducted among the women of Bellary revealed that 92 per cent of the women in the pre-reproductive and reproductive age suffered from various degrees of RTIs and sexually transmitted diseases. 69 per cent of them also reported incidents of sexual or physical abuse at the hands of their clients. Sexual exploitation of girl children is widely prevalent, of which 90 per cent of them had not even attained their puberty.

Similarly, introduction of this programme in the urban slums of Hyderabad town, dominated by Islamic minorities, WWF finds that there is little or no awareness on contraceptive practices barring few families who know about methods like tubectomy. Therefore, the new project plans a sound advocacy strategy that combats the most traditional or cultural practices that are oppressive structures on women, towards a change process. (See Case Study 2).

WWF Cadres – Network of Advocates

Such an unconducive social environment warrants a multi-tier system of advocacy wherein the grassroot health cadres of WWF take up advocacy measures, inform and educate their own community towards creating an enabling environment that brings about a more gendered and humane systems or policies in population planning. The dynamic cadres of WWF at the grassroots are a "network of advocates" in the community in convincing the clientele on their reproductive health concerns.

Inter-linkages of Women's Empowerment and Reproductive Health*

Introduction / Priorities

If one looks at the history of the world, it has been demonstrated over and over again, that women even in the worst of circumstances have not only brought children into the world, but also have cared for them as best as they could even in poverty or otherwise. Therefore, to make child bearing safer for women, even in the most remote areas is far more important in our priorities of reproductive healthcare, as mothers are the most important in any primary healthcare system.

However, the time has come for us to dialogue and debate about the capacities of individuals, to exercise their conscience with respect to their own decision-making, to decide freely and responsibly the number and spacing of their children and to have information, education and the means to do so. It is even more important that women have the right to make decisions regarding reproduction, free of discrimination, coercion and violence as visualised by the human rights concerns.

Holistic Approach

As experience reveals, the question of the reproductive health of women is inextricably interrelated to other issues, such as gender equations and the affordability of a sustained means of livelihood. The complex link between all these factors not only within the domestic front, but also in a wider social context together determine the status of women's reproductive health. Very often, the steep difference between the various policies that have been framed for improving the health status of women and the results that have been achieved at the implementation level. This is because of the failure to recognise and make provision for wider range of issues that are interconnected and having a direct bearing on the social status of women.

Setting / Environment

Undoubtedly, both physical and social environment in all developing countries, more so in India where patriarchal culture is dominant, promotes unequal status or social condition that affects women's health status as well. The poorest women in the country are the most vulnerable, they are powerless politically as well as legally, dependent economically, living in

---

*Speech Delivered at the UNFPA Headquarters at the meeting of NGO advisory Committee, 1996.

marginal survival conditions. Women as workers have to fight for survival in exploitative working conditions. They work longer hours than men, but their work is mostly unpaid in many places and totally undervalued. In most informal sector occupations, they have to go without maternity benefits, maternity care or insurance, that affects them adversely and is responsible for many cases of maternal mortality.

Target Group / Women

With the differential access that men and women have in the control of power and resources leading to an inequitable gender and power relations between the two sexes, it becomes crucial that women's empowerment be addressed critically. Only in a gender balance and gender just social environment, we could hope to see a positive change in effecting reproductive rights of women into a reality. If one takes the example of women among the working population (agricultural or construction workers), the complexity of their work is such that they have to perform all routine domestic duties in make shift homes, that adversely affect the health situation resulting in high infant mortality rates. They often live in unhygienic and sub-human conditions with no water or sanitation facilities. In this context, the effort of organising the marginalised and unorganised segment of the workforce with particular reference to the women workers assumes greater significant since they form 89 per cent of the total workforce.

Violence Against Women

Yet another issue of grave concern that needs to be addressed immediately is the problem of violence against women. There are almost umpteen number of cases of rape and molestation of both women and girl children being reported. With the fear of facing otractization and the ridicule of society, many more of such cases go unreported. With the effect, it has on the reproductive health of women and girl children as it is directly related to issues, such as illegal abortions, this has to become a priority issue for not only the social activists and women's groups but also for the law enforcement agencies and medical community. When there is increasing focus on the reproductive rights of women, this grave human rights violation needs to be addressed.

A Total Development Approach

To effectively tackle these multifarious problems that address these productive, reproductive and community problems of women, multi-pronged strategies will have to be adopted. On the productive front, variables like micro-credit assistance are important to strengthen their economic capacities to get them out of indebtedness and abject poverty. To enable women carry out their biological roles effectively, reproductive and child health programme should cater to the entire gamut of reproductive health issues right from the human rights issue of female infanticide to the health of adolescent girls, to that of the mothers and elderly women in the community. More significantly, it has to tackle the MCH and occupational health needs of women workers, by both educating them on health and safety measures as workers, and health care provision as mothers towards better health status. The community roles of women have to be strengthened through social action process, i.e., lobbying with the government and other institutions for better and improved living and working conditions to achieve an enhanced quality of life.

Yet another segment of the population that are reflected are the migrant communities as well as those families that have been displaced during the process of urban slum resettlement. These communities have to be reached not only through provision of healthcare services, but also by supplementing health programmes with skill or vocational training to generate employment opportunities.

The adolescent employment has to be strengthened to give impetus for many working children to escape oppressive and deplorable working conditions. They must be provided with alternative means of livelihood alongwith provision of non-formal education.

Significantly, enhancing women's political participation at the grassroots in panchayat and municipalities becomes important. Such participation of the grassroots women alone will throw out hundreds of leaders to confront anti-social situations in their own neighbourhood and create a socio-political platform for themselves.

In a country like India, where we are so much dependent on the government for the delivery of health service, there are many remote areas where the programmes are not only weak but also non-existent. For instance, to make child bearing safer for more women even in remote villages, it is imperative that the traditional birth attendants must be trained and whenever needed. This attempt will leave atleast train traditional birth attendant in the remote corners of the country instead of nil services. Equally, the community health workers have to be encouraged and equipped adequately to attend on pregnant women and even handle child birth so they can be useful in rural areas. Normally, a community worker always limits her knowledge to minor ailments and first aids or adopts shortcuts to healthcare by suggesting quick allopathic remedies.

She must therefore, be trained in preventive health care systems and other related health issues including environmental sanitation, personal hygiene etc., which would benefit the adolescent population better.

Adolescent Population

The rate of infant mortality of girl children and more significantly the prevalence of the practice of female infanticide in the rural areas and female foeticide in the urban areas (where there is a greater availability of medical infrastructure by way of devices for scanning) is reflective of the status accorded to the girl children in our society. The discrimination which starts even before birth continues to be perpetuated at every stage of her life right until death. The significant practice in traditional families, where even today men and boys get more attention than women and girls, is reflected adversely in the life expectancy of women.

The fact that the infant mortality rate is much higher among girl children indicates that the nutrition and development needs of girl children are far too inadequately met with, thus affecting the healthy growth of the female children. Their ailments are least monitored through medical intervention and comprehensive/preventive measures, like immunisation, environmental hygiene, provision of safe drinking water, spacing of child birth and so on that can really save girl children. Whether it is being given a lesser share in food, the burden of domestic work, being stopped from school to take care of younger siblings, lesser opportunities for developing her potential or being pushed into early marriage and motherhood, the disparity is so glaring a process that it is evident at every stage.

The gender gap in terms of the number of girl children attending school is so wide in our educational system, that it more often ends up in young girls being pushed into early adolescent marriage, a practice that affects social/economic participation and deny the guarantee of equal rights and freedom to women. As a vicious circle, such denial of educational status to women not only re-elects in their low employment status, but also in the poor health of large families for which again women have to take responsibilities. Studies have shown that women with higher educational accomplishments not only had better opportunities and less number of children, but also sometimes they even opt for late marriages.

More importantly, it is the adolescents who face increasing risks of unprotected sexual activity making them susceptible to STDs including HIV and AIDS that pose great health risks taking toll of their lives, very early in life.

In order to combat the complex problems faced by this largely neglected adolescent group, our health advocacy methods should strive towards better adolescent health services, create a safe and supportive environment by counselling parents, mothers in particular on issues of reproductive health care. Their awareness should be enhanced on all aspects of reproductive healthcare, through peer-group education, both among rural poor and urban slum communities. Among the poverty groups, focus should be on skill building of adolescents if they happen to be school drop outs to bring about economic self-reliance in order to delay their marriage, motherhood and other responsibilities in their early adolescence.

Suggestions Towards Enabling Environment

The prevalent competitive spirit among the government and voluntary community health workers sometimes are cause for concern, but such spirit must play a positive role in enhancing the quality of healthcare system aiming to promote the cause of "Health for All" concept in their own neighbourhood and communities. Governments must take efforts that their Doctors and ANMs are oriented towards the same and appreciate the role of voluntary health workers in a given community in the larger interests of the clientele. In fact, in many primary healthcare centres instead of working about their not being able to fill in the posts of several employees due to non-availability, they can certainly make use of the services of low cost voluntary health workers who would certainly provide an effective link between the healthcare systems and the community at large.

Human-Centred Development

A reflection of the new thinking after the series of world conferences has been that all plan of actions and programme formulations (from local, regional, national and international level) need to be a "Human-centred Process". Since an individual's well-being is a multi-faceted one, a multi-dimensional approach based on an integrated and comprehensive pattern is the need of the hour. Further, the same has been the emphasis of the Post-Cairo advocacies that include advancement of basic rights of women, men and young adolescents and to safeguard their right to sexuality and reproductive healthcare allowing reproductive choices. Most importantly, access to improved and appropriate healthcare has to incorporate aspects of gender sensitivity and well-being of human kind, which includes even mobilising resources towards the achievement of all the above mentioned objectives. Such integration of population concerns into a comprehensive approach towards reproductive health rights not only reduces female responsibility, but also enhances the male responsibility as well, looking into the healthcare of women even beyond their post reproductive period.

Advocacy

Our major concern now is to create a conducive social environment through a multi-tier system of advocacy. If the cadres of advocacy do not emerge from the community themselves, it will be a Herculean task to disseminate the message of ICPD to the grassroots. Equally, the cadres have to be oriented and empowered to take up the mission of disseminating such information and education in order to bring about a change in the attitude and mindsets of the communities at the grassroots. It is these volunteers alone who can infuse gender sensitivity in the service delivery systems promoting quality in service, more importantly and by constantly reminding the government and the policy makers of their requirements, to reinforce a change in policy, programmes and legislations that are either inadequate or even detrimental in addressing the needs of the poor in general, women and adolescents in particular.

"Network of Advocates"

Thus, creation of an enabling environment to bring about more engendered human systems, policies and population planning depends upon our vision and task to build up a network of advocates in each community, to convince their clientele on reproductive health concerns which alone can transform the micro activism of the grassroots cadres to macro policy options.

Emerging - Informal Sector

"We take care not to be undermined from outside. Why should we not take care from within"?

Sardar Patel*

Histories of social movements when analysed are always reflections of the struggles of women and men bearing the philosophy of justice and fairness towards those victimized and suppressed.

Intimation of Working Women's Forum's (WWF) too has been a necessity and a turning point at a time when India was going through severe vacuum of political leadership. This was well reflected when even after 30 years (since WWF movement was initiated in 1978) of Indian Independence in the year 1978, there was no physical evidence of any change towards betterment in the lives of the poor in the country.

Women among them were the most vulnerable, as world's army of illiterates, were found only among women in this country. Women have had the shortest life expectancy then, something like twice less than that of men. The persistence of dowry, making women victims of abuses, desertion, bigamy and even murder. Almost 50 per cent (in 1978) of country's masses being poor, their day-to-day sustenance are an abysmal demonstration to sight. Increase of beggars, living as homeless on the platforms, further mass migrations from villages in search of new work opportunities, made the slums of the cities swell and overflow with people. Equally the rural masses were at the mercy of the landlords not being able to alter the bonded conditions of employment, they had to continue their sustenance on patron-client relationships, low wages that to in cash or kind etc. Women were to work mostly as unpaid labour or for a marcel of food. Therefore one could imagine, that the conditions of colonialisation could not have been different than this. People started losing faith in the political leadership, particularly the romance of the "Independent India" and their expectations of their retuning to past glory and vision for their families was lost.

There was general resentment among the public particularly among the poor as they felt that this new political class is responsible for shaking up the political system that stood on just and ethical pillars laid by the founding fathers of the Constitution and freedom fighters.

Around that time, things were also deteriorating in India's counterparts in South Asia too, as all these countries have achieved

*Presented at Gandhi Labour Institute 16th – 17th May 2003.

freedom around the same time.

Everywhere political leaders have their own selfish agendas, moving away from service motive to the people at the grassroots.

Further the 60's marked the pauperization of peasantry by sheer exploitation by the landlords or the new rich. Indifference of bureaucracy in addition to the corrupt practices of the political class simultaneously yielded to the rise of new civil liberty initiatives.

The failure of the political class and the leadership vacuum compelled many of us to reintroduce the concept of Mass Leadership. I came out of the Congress party in disgust to visualize the future of leadership in India.

In search of leadership and mobilization strategy, the initiation of WWF was thus a spontaneous initiation and demonstrated to the new political class (after independence) how the socio-economic milieu in India require divergent strategies to generate mass movements and leadership rather than stereotyped leadership that clings on to chairs and mikes in vacuum addressing empty halls.

Though non-political, WWF demonstrated more a class based intervention of all vested interests - caste and gender situations were taken up as and when the need arose.

Objectives

To demonstrate women's contribution to the family and to the national economy and enhanced value of women's economic role vis-a-vis to do away with such an impression that women's role is only an extension of their household duties.

To reach only poorer households in order to reduce poverty among women in the slums and rural neighbourhoods.

Structure

Towards this aim, drastic structural change in the pattern of organization has been evolved to facilitate the poor women to participate at all levels.

This bottom up structure not only facilitated their participation, but also improved the poor towards their decision-making and leadership roles.

Further this was a strategy to help them to easily identify other poor, bring in more and more of them into the fold of the organization.

Above all it kept the organization out of elitist control. They went to the extent of promoting, themselves as supervisors, office bearers and staff from their own class.

Group Process

Undoubtedly the neighbourhood group of 10 or 20 women, a small unit at the grassroots was thoughtfully evolved as a manageable outfit in which women learned all the principles of collective management and action. Though as a credit group, their interest was in trade and business only, gradually these women took up other issues that affected their day-to-day concerns at the grassroots, and started mobilizing other women in the neighbourhood for collective action towards achievement. Of their needs and requirements.

Such consciousness raising efforts of women in particular, became an absolute necessity in the existing discriminatory, patriarchal structures towards a new social order with female values, governed by principles of autonomy and solidarity among themselves.

The Need

Therefore it is with a commitment and urge to deliver at least some kind of vital services to poor women in poverty that the original idea of providing small micro loans to women vendors / hawkers were initiated in the slums of Chennai and rural areas. Taking advantage of the nationalization of the Indian Banks in 1969 by the then Prime Minister, this micro loan service delivery to the poor became possible in 1978. The WWF's was initially giving the first loan of Rs. 200 now it has increased thousand in another scheme Rs. 400 was given initially, now it is Rs. 1200. The loan disbursement was 1 crore, now it has increased to 11 crores. Earlier there was only the LIC scheme, now there is LIC I, II, Sakthi Security and Sakthi Health. Maximum loan was only Rs. 3000 before, but now it is Rs. 20000 and orders are awaited for giving upto Rs. 50000.

Conceptual framework of class, caste and gender

Undoubtedly we at the WWF, have gone through enormous struggles in structuring this movement, particularly in an adverse social or physical environment for women and female children. At a time where everything has been controlled by traditions, patriarchal cultures, where women's equal participation, in the society has been totally limited. In this process, women's socio-economic status has not only been degenerating day by day, but has denied women access to power, resources, even fundamental privileges and human rights. The issue of such a widened gender-gap was reflected in education, employment, social or community participation, in fact, in total human existence.

Thus, women's participation at all levels ran into rough weather due to the fact that the enactment, enforcement and legal interpretations of social legislations in favour of women were in the hands of male-dominated institutions and were administered by hardcore patriarchal fundamentalists, where women had very little to say.

Therefore at this point of time, the effort to bring total participation of women at all levels needed a drastic, revolutionary approach even here at the WWF. In all aspects of their living and working conditions, women's issues and gender questions had to be addressed seriously, The caste / class issues were taken up as and when women had to confront the same.

State of Assetlessness to Accumulation

When it was, an issue of ideology of the Forum to lead the particular target group towards a permanent struggle process, one can't think of a short-lived projector-project approach. Therefore, we had to think of a permanent strategy that would help them in their day-to-day life and work, i.e., a strategy to escape moneylenders, negotiate or bargain amidst middleman, with cash in hand, or educate their children, or relieve themselves from the illiteracy they suffer, acquire a technology to reduce their drudgery from their manual labour operations, purchase small piece of land or make small home of their own. In fact to move away from a state of assetlessness to become asset holders, i.e., a permanent change process towards quality of life. Towards this process, credit thus strengthened their group dynamics, increased their collective consciousness and paved the way not only for collective survival, but also led to a state of sustainable existence towards their total livelihood security. Studies further showed that women through credit intervention, could move from marginal or subsistence level to trading, from trading servicing to manufacturing and production, steadily towards growth orientation in economic ventures.

Mobilizing Poor Women

To think back on what happened in the early days, WWF never went into the drudgery of collecting women from slums and villages for training them in skills, to find some work for them. Therefore, we in WWF were quite cautions, and only strengthened their traditional, existing occupations and this had its own effect. Instead of searching for the poor, poor started mobilizing themselves and reached us on their own in tens and thousands. This contributed to quick outreach to poor women.

Enhancing Women's Social Status

By way of bringing to light the social status of poor women in society not only unmarried women of working class, but also the status of those who do not have the sophistication and resources (in the Indian context) to get into legalized wedlock's and those who lived in common law arrangements that are unacceptable to elites. Even those who attempted arranged marriages, had to pay heavy dowries and spend lavishly on marriage ceremonies that they can't afford. Therefore such women, who are in common law wedlock, are abused in derogatory language in the traditional communities even among the poor. Also their relationship as man and wife are equally insecure and women faced desertion in large numbers. WWF was quite concerned about such women mostly, as out of the early 800 initial members two-thirds of them belonged to such category of women. WWF's effort therefore was to legalise these relationships through registration, sometime under Special Marriage Act, if they belonged to different religions celebrating it as a big social event presided over by Governor of States or President / Vice President of India. Such registration of marriages gave women the right to fight for divorce in the court and make compensatory arrangement for her children and herself during the times of crisis.

Surprisingly it was a delightful inter-caste experiment where marriages between high-caste Brahmins and untouchable Harijans, Hindus and Muslims/Christians, also among Christians and Muslims. It was a further evidence and an eye opener that poor can't afford the sophisticated caste feelings nor can they get into costly caste networks and it is a learning process to study their own strategies to escape from those unaffordable networks of caste and religion. WWF made a wide publicity of such wedding events making it as a gender sensitization effort to fight man's in humanity to women and her children. Women from their subordinate position felt they are in equal status, through such wedlocks.

Combating Female Infanticide, Child Labour and Devadasi Systems

Despite the Hindu Code Bill and several Acts in favour of women such as Dowry Prevention Act and Bigamy Prevention Act, women's succession to property on a equal basis to men, the messages of these Acts has not reached women in communities, more so in villages and slums, due to illiteracy and ignorance. The traditional preference of a "male child" lead many families to loose their girl children in foeticides and infant mortalities in some cases, but in majority of the families it has resulted in large numbers of children who had to work for their livelihoods as child labourers. It was more a common occurrence that adolescent girls were pushed into early marriages and motherhood, where their fate became fatal due to mother mortality or as dowry deaths. At the same time the government sponsored family planning programme in 1977 ran into severe controversy in many villages and slums, because of the mishandling of this programme by the bureaucracy. Casualties of death in male and female surgeries have outnumbered the successes in couple protection rates.

The Devadasi systems (child prostitution), where the girl children have been victims of religious dedication to temples and later falling prey to prostitution was another serious anomaly to be tackled effectively. This evoked feministic concerns and needed drastic action to save female children from the victimization of religion and culture, besides enhancing the status of the girl child treating her as "Future Women".

To prevent child labour, female feoticide, infant mortality, Devadasi system and save women from the crude imposition of female surgery in family planning programmes, thus WWF had to look for new forms of programme strategy. Therefore it was a change from entire character of the state sponsored family planning programme, into a grassroots reproductive healthcare programme spreading the messages through sound methods of advocacy, and pleasant change from control to life choices for women. This new culture of advocacy in the neighbourhoods of slums and villages created a cadre for every 500 families as an advocate of health consciousness who multiplied in large numbers as "network of advocates" in the course of time and not only took up health issues, but also slowly advocated holistic gender / class concerns among the women in poverty.

Through our demonstrative experience, WWF was able to bring to light the fact the undervaluation of women at home reflected in the workplaces as well. Unlike in other feministic organisation, the conflicts in WWF were not the only form of activism but it also became a gradual technique or tool adopted as incidents led to that stage. In WWF we never allowed rightful conflicts to contribute to eternal hostility but it was only on an issue-to-issue basis, where conflicts became a natural phenomenon.

Gender Aware Approach

Gender question acquired prime place at the WWF, with this question of gender equality in action whether in village Panchayat, or in fighting, caste, religious/traditional barriers or evade customs. Also, when discriminatory wages were paid to confront employers / landlords to make power structures like police, municipalities listen to the grievances of women and soon women had their way to fight injustice. All these women in WWF could do only with the strength of its cadre based approach, and the numbers mobilised on the road in long marches or in mass meetings to demonstrate the injustices by creating a public opinion. Therefore, right from its beginning gender question gained predominance at the WWF.

However, the "Class" question became equally important when the above mentioned immobilization strategy became a way of life among the women workers, particularly where they had to face struggle on wage questions both in their contract labour work or piece rate operations in many of WWF branches in Andhra Pradesh / Tamil Nadu.

Enhancing Women's Capabilities towards Social Transformations : Experiments from the Ground

Being unorganized conglomerations, women workers earnings are so meagre and irregular that they hardly make both ends meet. Further their struggle for housing, water and for civic-amenities are enormous in the urban slums. Their landless counterpart in the rural areas suffer equally due to underemployment, low wages, sometimes limited to even 45 to 60 days a year. If they happened to be part of drought-prone areas (Bidar, Dindigul) it was even worse. Thus, it is more than an annual feature that 'rural poor' are on their migrating journey to the already overcrowded city slums, in search of new work options and continue to be victims of vicious cycles of poverty.

They work as weavers of cloth, mats and baskets, cigar or agarbathi rollers, food processors, either work alone or collectively. They work as agricultural labourers in farmlands or they work for their kith and kin. They are providers for their families; working in service occupations, i.e., dhobis, cooks, sweepers and water carriers, etc. They are integral part of production process and contribute to the informal economy; unfortunately, they have little or no access to fruits of their own labour, nor that of the government's assistance.

While the Forum is a class structure in terms of its membership, it took up mainly gender and caste issues in its initial days of its organising effort. In the urban situation the occupations of vending / hawking being micro enterprises, could not relate to class issues since this urban group was the initially organised one. However, gender (violence) caste (most service workers are untouchables) were on its heights due to the high prevalence of alcoholism, in urban centres. Also most service workers belonged to scheduled castes, and hence the character of the group had been more a solidarity / neighbourhood group in a grassroots initiative, and was working towards leadership effort.

The activism of the class nature, came up later when WWF organised, agricultural labourers, export workers, piece rate and contract labourers, such as cigar, agarbathi and handicrafts, lace and weavers of textiles industry. Here the problems particularly for women are low wages, harsh and exploitative working conditions.

As alternate options of cattle assistance, agricultural workers in few families in Dindigul branch of WWF have had, remarkable impact in making a real frontal attack on landlords, who had to make revision in the wage by marginally increasing it. While this marginal increase may be the fruits of their struggle, but this effort in our opinion, had taken away women workers from the dependence on landlords.

Similarly, women lace artisans working in Narasapur, rural Andhra Pradesh have been totally neglected by the workers' unions including the Communist Party of India as they are work done by women at home, therefore, branded as leisure time employment.

Similarly, the cigar / agarbathi rolling, fisherwomen's fish marketing activities all have been considered as leisure time activities by male-dominated unions. In fact, fish marketing is a more permanent work than fishing.

In the weaving industry, women work as their men do weaving, keep out after designing, calling themselves as 'master-weavers'. Similarly, despite major share of work in many occupations as women's responsibility they are only low-wage efforts and branded as leisure timework. Therefore, to strengthen women worker's bargaining position, against vested interests and to expose the class character of the oppression women go through WWF decided to register themselves as a trade union in the year 1982 as "National Union of Working Women" that was a turning point in women workers lives. This indeed is a much-felt need to provide a sharper focus to fight the presence of the antagonistic elements in the production process, wherein women had major thrust. Apart from its original grassroots character, now WWF also had acquired an additional strength by getting into unions that strengthened women's economic roles.

In addition to this, the health programme physically took care of the health aspect of their productive role both as a worker and her role as a mother. More specifically the trade union offered the micro-insurance programme with affordable premium covered poor women's lives and that of their families against unexpected disasters such as deaths, illness and property loss. The health insurance took care of women during her entire life cycle from the stage of girl child to reproductive age group, maternity benefits to old age ailments as well. The premium death claim for an accidental one was initially Rs. 5000, now there are two schemes, one scheme of Rs. 25000 and another of Rs.50000. In the case of natural death, earlier it was Rs. 5000 now it is Rs. 5000 or Rs. 20000 depending on the scheme.

Thus, it was quite important to break through the vicious nexus between, patriarchy / feudalistic elements, and empower poor women towards leadership, both at home and in the community.

All this were achieved only by relying on the strength of the poor women, both in their numbers, energetic support and could initiate and sustain feministic leadership process. Inadvertently, this effort had strengthened many reform processes towards other women of middle and upper class. (Dowry, male violence, property rights and so on.)

To be more precise and truthful to oneself, the strategy adopted in the process of building this movement of Working Women's Forum, has not been a sophisticated one but the same indigenous, sustainable one followed by Gandhiji years before during the struggle for India's freedom. However, despite the strategies being indigenous it has worked, in building up a commitment and solidarity among poor women, facilitating other poor women in small communities and neighbourhoods. This commitment of poor women has been responsible that such a small initiative of 800 women, in 1978 led to a massive social movement of 7,00,000 women today.

With the human potential from the grassroots, comprising of low educational levels, but with high common sense and acumen, a model of a credit union, and a women's union was possible within the parameters of poor women's access. This has assured poor women, food plus economic security but also the much needed social security. Above all the movement contributed to the over all human security and welfare.

This visible movement of mass upsurge has to be sustained in its future growth. Therefore, conscious strategy of trained / indigenous leaders have been placed in both the urban and rural neighbourhood. Women members in the WWF, despite being the poorest have not been silent spectators to the happenings. Their lives must have been harshly affected by poverty, cultural, physical and social handicaps. Their commitment to the cause of ameliorating the lives of their sisters in the neighbourhood towards empowerment has been a vital force to make this movement of WWF wider and meaningful.

Sustainable Integration of Microfinance and Education in Child Survival, Reproductive Health and Hiv / Aids Prevention for the Poorest Entrepreneurs*

Fighting Poverty - Global Agenda

The current dialogue towards a new economic order depends on how much we get into pragmatic innovation, simple implementation strategies for reduction of poverty. When this is said it is with reference to one billion people, who are not able to satisfy even their basic needs on a regular basis and still constitute 20 per cent of world's population. Our strategy should be not only to formulate sound employment policies to fight poverty, interlinking the same with sound healthcare programmes but to strengthen their productive roles towards improving their quality of life. We cannot ignore the fact that a sound healthcare system among the poor, will also facilitate to check the uncontrolled population, that is mostly taking place in the developing countries where the majority of the poor live and work.

Credit and Social Change

Amidst the informal systems of work available for the 'working poor' in India, we cannot forget the fact that the female workers outpace their male counterparts. These women form as much as 89 per cent of India's working population outside the formal trade union. Having realised that the workload of these poor women increases with increase in poverty in addition to their responsibilities to their families with their meagre income. Working Women's Forum a social movement, and a spontaneous initiative of poor women, emerged in the year 1978 in the slums of Chennai adopting divergent strategies to fight poverty and squalor.

Operating itself at the outset as a gender based intervention to fight caste, class biases, WWF through micro-credit intervention demonstrated the valuable economic role of poor women, as equal or sole contributor to families. Organising them on trade lines further proved their greater contribution to the production process but it was not an extension of the household activities.

A drastic structural change planned as it was with an objective to reach the poorest of households in large numbers, bringing in more and more of their classes into WWF's fold aiming at poverty reduction, WWF concentrated on employment generation, particularly for women in urban

---

*Presented at the Micro-Credit Summit, February 15-19th, Dhaka, Bangladesh, 2004.

slums and rural areas where the poor lived and worked. The organisational structure facilitated the poor to participate at all levels of the worker's union. Response being remarkable, as the movement helped to facilitate the poor in decision-making not only for themselves but also for their families and their neighbourbood, soon resulted in throwing up more and more new and spontaneous leaders from their own class, visualizing their future prospects through collective vision and action. There are more than 1,12,000 groups today in WWF though it was initiated with 800 women, covering over 7,16,000 women in the 15 branches of the three Southern States. The credit outfit of WWF the Indian Cooperative Network for Women has reached about 3,65,000 members through micro-credit options, helping poor women to achieve sustainable livelihood. Together WWF/ICNW have reached nearly 3,415 villages and 2,078 slums.

Need for Health Intervention to Strengthen Employment Options

Related to this is WWF's cadre based Reproductive Health Care Programme that had build up a strong network of advocates in their own rural / urban poorer communities. These cadres hailing from their own class, remarkably strengthened the health consciousness of poor women / children (including HIV/AIDS) in villages, squatter settlements and chantytowns utilizing the existing, healthcare facilities of the government. Further learning from this programme is the establishment of reproductive rights of women asserting that the child bearing role is a social role of women and therefore are entitled to health care facilities both as a mother and a worker. Crucial to the programme was the enhancement of the decision-making power of women, even with reference to number of children and contraceptive choices. The programme impacted nearly 16,00,000 families (1.5 million) accomplishing 72 per cent couple protection rate in the poorest communities, providing employment to 960 grassroot health cadres spread out to 720 slums and 340 villages. The initiation of a social security programme for poor women impacted, maternity benefits and insurance cover to over 4,00,000 women for life, disability and health aspects.

Currently, ongoing globalisation and the restructuring of economic policies aggravates the intensity of poverty among the poor through mounting price rise, non-availability of services and commodities, deprivation of income particularly among those who have no access to productive assets like land and other variables pushing the poorer families several steps behind to extreme poverty. Instead of allowing poverty to assume gigantic proportions the fighting of poverty through a multipronged strategy becomes necessary. Access to Micro Credit towards occupational facilitation, integrating the same with other aspects such as skill training, healthcare, becomes appropriate.

HIV/AIDS - Victims - Women and Children

Related to this question is subject of our presentation today, HIV / AIDS at the workplace as it affects the worker during his / her productive years. The discussion therefore, should focus on the survival strategies of those workers engaged in a variety of occupations both in urban and rural areas. HIV / AIDS is a global crisis, an impediment to the reduction of poverty and a drain on the human resources, destroying their capacity to be productive and useful. This critical issue requires both a developmental and a healthcare approach. HIV / AIDS is not only a problem mainly among the migrant working population where urgent preventive measure is an inevitable need, but it is said that the face of AIDS is that of women, as they are the easily susceptible victims and have to be saved from the disaster. Women get into this category because they lack information on the disease and are not aware of the various preventive measures. Besides lack of decision-making in sexual matters, many young women are pushed into HIV / AIDS by cohension, rape and induced sex by older, stronger or rich man. This is because of the prevalent large scale political, economic processes in the gender politics, that place women in the high incidence category of HIV / AIDS particularly developing countries.

At the outset, female children have to be saved through intensive medical monitoring interventions and comprehensive medical care. This is particularly so in areas where child prostitution is highly prevalent. Besides, they are the most neglected human resources who don't get nutritive food or care for their ailments. Besides lack of immunisation and the abysmal environmental hygiene, surroundings, lack of provision of safe drinking water, all this and more remain as obstacles to save the girl child.

The current scenario worldwide indicates approximately 19 million people are infected with HIV, each day infecting 6,000 people. Many new infected are said to be among the age group of 15 to 35 years i.e. in their prime youth. Out of the 33.4 million people affected in the world, 90 per cent of whome are living in the developing countries and about 2 million of them are still not aware that they are affected.

Human-centred Approach - Employer's Concern

HIV / AIDS in dire workplace results in the consequences and the productivity of the worker is completely destroyed. Here it has to be the responsibility of the employer to provide medical facilities as it would be costly for the workers to meet the expenses for HIV treatment. It must be the humanitarian concern of every employer if the worker becomes completely invalid. They have to make alternate income facility to the worker's family particularly towards the education and future prospects of children. Besides education, when both parents die of HIV/AIDS, the employers in consultation with the local communities have to arrange for adoptions too. There are an estimated 20 million children who are AIDS orphans today. Therefore, the ethical and moral duty of the employer and the community is an urgent need to invest in childcare centres, adoption centres and schooling for these children. As the status of service delivery institutions particularly in the healthcare area are in deplorable conditions affordable and qualitative and culture specific comprehensive healthcare for men and women of all ages (these affected by HIV/AIDS) has to be organised by the employer. In fact the employer should treat the epidemic of HIV/AIDS as an occupational hazard when it affects the worker in his productive years and treat it as occupational safety process.

HIV / AIDS Victims - Micro Finance Services

Here, Micro Finance Services becomes very important to help the victims in the initial days to promote alternate employment. Income generating skill training may help tide over the initial crisis. The focus should be on skill building among the adolescents, who invariably happen to be school drop outs because of AIDS affected parents. This will help to bring the much required economic self-reliance among the AIDS infected people, particularly those who are facing innumerable social exclusions as victims. They are considered as outcastes, untouchables by their own family, children, friends and society at large. Our experience to date of such discriminations, places the vulnerable groups, to face enormous challenges pushing them to a state of further vulnerability, poverty, starvation and hunger and in many cases there had been extreme cases of suicides as well.

Enabling Environment - WWF's Cadre based Approach

In order to involve the HIV infected population to start some occupations, the WWF's integrated intervention to link reproductive health-care in addition to micro-finance has helped the victims particularly the infected people. WWF has taken into consideration the productive capacities particularly physical and mental state of the affected ones in which they are found, as an ideal base into micro-finance operations. Evolving a participatory and need based policy structures at all levels maximizing the client participation resulted in both prevention and rehabilitation methods of HIV suspected and affected victims. Such micro-finance activities provided the much required facilities to start, expand small business, increase income, improve access to food, nutrition, healthcare and send their children to school.

Mass media campaigns, visual trainings / orientation in the field not only created awareness among the general and affected victims but also resulted in the identification of HIV/AIDS victims, helped the cadres to take care of both referral and delivery of medical care at appropriate time. For instance, in the district of Bellary, a backward / drought prone district of Karnataka, WWF's organisational ability brought the Devadasis community, (women who have become victimised due to the degenerating cultural practices leading to female child prostitution on a common ground.) under its organisational framework, providing them micro finance services and healthcare, and empowerment, few of these women victims could breakaway from these exploitative tradition, and pursued other alternate employment options. In fact, these children and women who had been in the line of prostitution for ages had been the most high-risk group in terms of HIV infection and required both prevention and rehabilitation measures.

Thus, the Working Women's Forum's cadre based enabling environment, helped dissemination of information / education and could bring about a change in the attitude and mindset of such communities at the grassroots. It is these networks of cadres who infused gender-sensitivity in the healthcare service delivery systems promoting quality in service. More importantly reminding the government and the policy-makers of the requirements to reinforce a change in their policy programmes, legislations that hither too had been inadequate. In addressing the needs of the poor women and adolescents, WWF's forethought and vision to build up such a "network of advocates" in each community to convince their own clientele on the much needed, reproductive healthcare concern, transform, the micro-activism of these needed grassroot cadres to macro-policy options in many places.

Legal Protection - Government Policy

The Indian Government as in the US and Philippines does not have legal protection or laws against discrimination of HIV/AIDS victims, to protect their employment rights. In fact, a recent High Court ruling in Mumbai said in so many words, "It is not the disease which is wiping the persons, but the discrimination." In fact, the Mumbai High Court directed one of the insurance companies to give permanent employment to a HIV positive woman who was thrown out by them. Further ruling that employers cannot dismiss victims from their jobs on the grounds of their

HIV status, as it is in violation of their fundamental rights.

The ILO (International Labour Organisation) in collaboration with Lawyer's Collective in India has drafted a legal code towards a future bill to be presented in the Parliament, but this has not been done yet! The draft mentions not only the rights but addresses the stigma and discrimination, need for dissemination accurate information about HIV, also the need to preserve the confidentiality of the same. However, there is a large gap in the law that needs to be bridged in order to ensure the confidentiality of the AIDS victims, denial of which is the main reason of stigma and fear of the epidemic in the country. Therefore, our goal should be to pursue a mandate towards sustainable human development worldwide through an effective multi-strategic approach to meet this global crisis (HIV / AIDS) that is devouring humanity, through variables like economic empowerment, provision of micro-finance and healthcare delivery. This partnership can be found in the growing civil society initiatives trade unions, co-operatives and Non-Governmental Organisations.

Micro-credit programmes can really be a framework to vulnerable sections, and help meet their needs even in most difficult circumstances. Lack of access to credit has been the discrimination of the poor, that has been well countered by Micro Finance options globally. This will hold good to those affected and infected by HIV/AIDS problem too, as today the HIV/AIDS communities are the most discriminated. To quote Mrs. Bill Gates "India hangs in balance so far as AIDS is concerned". She said the biggest problem in fighting AIDS in India was in fighting awareness and social stigma. "Social stigma is still an enormous issue, but pockets of people are speaking out, and it is fundamental to back them," she said.

References

1. An ILO Code of practice on H1V/AIDS and the World of Work - ILO, Geneva.
2. ICEM, HIV/AIDS workshop Johanesburg, South Africa - Dr. Jaya Arunachalam's Paper.
3. Legislating an Epidemic HIV/AIDS in India - The Lawyers Collective, New Delhi.
4. AIDS in India - News letter of the National Aids Control Organisation - Women and AIDS - Issue and Concerns March 1995.
5. Rashtra Mahila - Newsletter Vol 3. No.45 July 2003 - AIDS Death.
6. Draft legislation on HIV/AIDS for consultation on HIV/AIDS and the world of work 12th to 13th December 2003 at New Delhi, India.
7. A Resource Manual on HIV/AIDS for training of education offices of the central board for workers education. - Prepared by ILO in collaboration

with VU Giri National Labours Institute under the project Prevention of HIV/AIDS in the world of work: A Tripartite Response - Supported by the US Department of Labour.

8. HIV/AIDS - A National Emergency Cost Effective Emergency Measures for
   Aids Prevention - Rtn. Dr. K.L. Jacob, MBBS, Ph.D.
9. UNDP / HIV / AIDS - Elizabeth Reid - Director HIV and Development, New York.
10. Recommendations on HIV / AIDS National Human Rights Commission.
11. HRM - HIV - Human Resource Management Rapid Assessment Tool for HIV / AIDS Environments, Management Science for Health 2003, USA.

7

Fifty Years of Democratic Survival – Time for Retrospection*

India completes 50 years of freedom this year. Our founding fathers sacrificed themselves at the bedrock of national struggle, ensuring a formidable strength and conviction, hoping that India would move solidly forward with confidence and courage into a changing world. Their vision of modernity was not of India forgetting its ancient roots but to cherish such storehouse of values, utilising the same as a backdrop of moral force behind every step that the country took to move forward.

The 50th anniversary of India's Independence brings memories of glorious moments when great women and men dominated the political scene of the country. Their outstanding services and sacrifices, as patriots enabled the nation to get this cherished freedom. They expected their descendants to value this freedom with patriotism and spiritual concern and follow their footsteps for the public good. But such values seems to be on the descend these days.

A country like India that has been guided by principles and values of non-violence, peaceful and harmonious co-existence, inspiring even the other countries of the world, that are chained in the grips of violence and disharmony. As India celebrates its 50th anniversary of political freedom, it is a strange coincidence that having been inspired by this Indian experiment, more or less all countries in the entire South Asian region barring Bangladesh have not only shackled the bonds of colonial rule,

*Appeared in "GROOTS" as Editorial of India's 50 years Independence Special issue – August 1997.

but also celebrate their Golden Jubilee of Independence. All these countries, India too, can be proud that they all have sustained democracy, but at what cost? Have these countries moved towards economic freedom of all their citizens? While sustaining democracy may be a laudable effort, is it also not true that even today more people suffer in starvation and many children go to bed in hunger? This region still houses the largest number of illiterates in comparison to others, endorsing the fact it is the poorest of all regions.

If it was a question of governance, our visionaries believed in a parliamentary and democratic system despite the challenge that India posed, with its huge size, population and cultural diversity. Their vision of socialism and democratic ethos, was nothing but a commitment to the freedom of individuals and to uphold their dignity. Such a constitutional guarantee, conferred on every adult of the nation, through Adult Franchise ensured the participation of every individual citizen in the decision-making process through the voice of representation.

But as the nation celebrates 50 years of Independence, of course all of us are aware that there will be a lot of funfair, ceremonies and celebration honouring the freedom fighters with rich shawls, sound and light programmes on the freedom movements everywhere, motorcades of tableau and the like. But, when it comes to reality, it is totally miserable to think of the declining years of this nation plunging itself into obscurity.

Day after Day one Feels Whether this Nation and its Governance has Either any Sense of Dignity or a Place of its own in World Polity

At the present time, there are evidences of the visible collapse of party systems and democratic standards that are the essential pillars of democracy. Day after day political parties get divided into several bits and units. Functionaries of legislature and parliament do not represent people's agenda or their aspirations. But today, these high level decision-making bodies are witnesses to not only such imposition of individual agendas, but also to the unruly behaviour of their members, adjourned hour after hour, without transacting any serious or useful business. The bureaucracy remains totally paralysed and are victims of complacency and the country survives only on judicial and media activism. A painful state of affairs which none of the founding fathers would have expected 50 years ago. The entire political system has come to a grinding halt with all the political parties breaking up and are on the disastrous decline. Politicians are mainly interested in establishing a single pattern solution, countries around themselves, instead of functioning collectively to strengthen democratic credentials guided by common vision and objectives.

Politicians have to be blamed for bringing the country to a "brinkmanship" and instability. Chaotic conditions, class hatred, indiscipline, erosion of cultural and ethical values, rise in communalism, casteism, religion and linguistic chauvanism are into the forefront of public and political life. Corruption eats away all our national resources and mounting burden of violence and terrorism are resulting in the disintegration of this country. The founding fathers of this country will be turning in their graves, if they are aware of the disharmony and disunity that disturbs and threatens the nation's very survival.

To quote Kallil Gibran, the great poet of Middle East, as he describes the rule of Emirs, and their unwise governance that dominated his times in Middle East countries says, "Thefts were legalised, oppression was supported by authority, crushing of the weak became commonplace. Thus, the greed of the humanity grew". His quotes are but very relevant even today.

History reveals the fact that freedom from colonial rule was not an easy affair, but it imposed imperative compulsions and heavy responsibilities on the Indian masses. There was voluntary propulsion among people belonging to different caste, class, ethnicity, tradition and culture, to come together making secularism as their watchword, necessitating to work together despite strong differences towards peace and harmony for the cause of 'Mother India'. In contrast today, there is collapse of moral values and patriotism or nationalism have become words of ridicule and old belief. The nobility of sacrifice and service have been abandonded, yielding place to selfishness, materialism and greed. Today, the Indian masses remain confused about their political choice.

On the issue of poverty alleviation and economic development, when the new nation was left in the shadow of colonial exploitation, the founding fathers thought of co-operative development as a vehicle of social and economic change. To build up a nation that has suffered years of exploitation and to assure quality of life for millions, an achievable reality was the main national agenda then. This agenda is much obscured in today's poverty alleviation programmes as they are lopsided and hardly ever reach the poor.

The very objective of the reservation policy formulated by the founding fathers was to make it a tool to assure equality among the unequals, i.e., to provide the oppressed and backward classes their rightful place in the society. The vulgar misuse of such reservation policy by our present day politicians by inflaming communal and casteist passions everywhere, has resulted in the contrary. Neither their reservation has really reached the backward classes nor have their exclusion from the society been prevented. Their reservation policy today defeated its very purpose by excluding the meritorious in the field of education and had brought down the quality of scholars in the nation. As we approach the 21st century the country, is producing third rate scholars who cannot be marketed or stand the challenges, when placed in competition in the international spheres.

The media today being in the hands of large number of private operators and multi-nationals, there is nothing but effort to thrive by portrayal of negative information turning the villains into charismatic leaders. Such a distorted activism in the media has only led to replacement of national leaders by the film stars who are leaders of luxury, doing more dis-service than service to the people of this nation.

The liberalisation of the economy demonstrates neither gain nor benefit to the people of this nation that still has 41 per cent of its population below poverty line. The globalisation of restructuring economic needs to be brought to an environment to build up growth with equity. The advocates of globalisation have to be sensitised that their reform policies have to be different for the poorer countries from that of the rich. Alongside, the national policies too must facilitate a liberal investment in human development to enable greater and equal participation of the poor. Universal access to basic services like health, education, drinking water, nutrition are today's imperatives for healthy human development. Will India atleast before it celebrates its Platinum Jubilee, 25 years later, be able to provide the much required social activism by taking these as priorities on a war footing and show the way to other countries of this region?

While it is a painful reality, that we have lost fifty vital years of useful national development, can the speed of liberalisation come down to a moderate level? Can there be an indication that the economic policies are neither pro-rich nor towards marginalisation of the poor by free distribution of doles, subsidies, clothes etc., in the name of poverty reduction? Will it be possible to convince the advocates of liberalisation, to stop their effort in creating two different worlds, one for the vast majority of the poor and other for the handful of rich?

These are questions left to those in governance and the respectable members of civil society to ponder over especially during the 50th year of our democratic survival.

50th Anniversary of India's Independence*

On this 50th year of India's Independence, it is time for retrospection of various anomalies of the past and formulate proactive strategies to combat the future crisis for the betterment of the poor, who still form 41 per cent of the countries population. As this country is passing through an era of market forces having a stronghold on the Indian economic situation, governments capacity to accord greater priority to the social sector expenditure is diminishing year after year. To quote the human development report – 1997 on India by UNDP, "During 1992-95, the average utilisation rates of earmarked social sector funds was little over 44 per cent during the 8th plan outlay". These statistics only vindicate the vehement protests made by several peoples organisation and civil society initiatives that bring to light large-scale wastage and leakage of resources on the one side and leading to morbidity of funds on the other.

Today the very task of identification of the poor and their dwellings is much obscured due to the outdated and bureaucratic procedures adopted by the state governments, collectorates and local planning bodies. While the census of India once in a decade, throws light on the socio-demographic profile of country, at the local level the remuneration procedures and statistical updation are lopsided giving unreliable and imbalanced data on the prevailing condition. To quote an example, the task of enumerating and classifying the number of slums in the important cities like Madras, Hyderabad, Bangalore etc., carried out by the corporation and metropolitan authorities reflect very little on the actual realities in the field. Either the notified slums are non-existent or do not measure upto the definition of being termed as slums. Often the resources extended by the external funding agencies are never targeted sharply at the dwellings of the poor and the results is siphoning out the funds earmarked for the poor to other non-poor areas and their priorities.

Even the basic task of denotifying those areas that have sufficiently improved their levels of living is not done, this is because the government depends only on the over-ambitious bureaucrats who try to sustain a long list of slums that are not slums any more as the inhabitants live in lavish style with fan, refrigerator and TVs. They do this only to attract social investment from funding agencies into poverty eradication programmes. In their effort to mobilise funds for their districts, the

---

*At the meeting of the 50th Anniversary of India's Independence held on 21st July, 1997 at New Delhi.

institutions of the government fail to respond to the immediate crisis in which the real poor are suffering in hunger and poverty. The result is the emergence of more and more dwelling of the poor and resettlement columns in various parts of the city or its outskirts, that has for decades never reached the attention of government records.

On the issue of resettlement, the slum dwellers are often thrown out from the heart of the cities to the outskirts to facilitates construction of corporate houses, business enterprises and metro railways etc. While on one side, the country has to struggle to achieve housing for the millions of the homeless and those living under sub-human conditions, municipalities and corporations in the name of development are on a eviction spree and are having the houses of the poor bulldozed everywhere to make the cities beautiful for inviting multinationals. Since most of such relocated areas are far from workplaces like markets, schools etc., making the life of the poor more miserable without even drinking water or other basic civic amenities. Thus, the chances of integrating the evicted people into the ecological niche of the society remains remote. This is nothing but a reinforcement of the fact that all the planning and policy making bodies have become nothing but a formality and no serious attempt is paid to the issues concerning the poor. Thus, the poor in any city or village of this country still remain a vulnerable segment of the society and are the first objects or targets of destruction and disintegration. Can thought be given to this atleast on this 50th year of India's Independence.

This apart, the situation in the health sector is also serious, where no efforts are made towards preventive health while the existing curative healthcarc system are unaffordable to the poor. Anti-poverty programmes have also failed to recognise the strong nexus between poverty and health issues. This has led to the calamity in the lives of millions who are already imprisoned in poverty.

There is an urgent need to initiate a process that results in complete change of attitude of the bureaucracies to change the ways in which they have traditionally been operating and induce behavioural and attitudinal changes in tune with the changing times. This will result in substantive improvement on various aspects of public administration with particular reference to poverty eradication aspect and improving the lives of toiling millions.

The author thinks after 5 decades of attending on to the development issues atleast now there is a need for evolving new ways of identifying the poor, build capacities to manage the resources earmarked for them whereby the resources are properly targeted and utilised to reach the poor with more effective delivery mechanisms. Making goods and services especially in the health and employment sector within affordable limits of the poor are critical needs.

Action Plan for Commemorating 50th Anniversary of India's Independence*

As India completes 50 years of freedom, our thoughts go back to our founding fathers who have sacrificed their lives at the bedrock of the national struggle for India's Independence hoping that India would move solidly forward with conviction and courage. Their vision of India moving towards modernity was not forgetting our ancient roots but to cherish such storehouse of Indian values using the same as a moral force behind every step that the country would take forward. We salute them and pay our regards to those martyrs on this occasion.

Despite 50 years of independent governance in India, we are all well aware still 40 per cent of India's population remain poor and are found in the condemned corners of urban slums and in remote rural areas. Unfortunately, the current scenario does not present a picture of prosperity in the country but pushes more and more people into poverty even without a roof over their heads or a square meal a day, especially in the major cities, in remote villages.

The current process of stabilisation and liberalisation of country's economic structures are a real burden on the poor imposing insurmountable social hardships on them with no space to move forward. The growing unemployment situations are given less and less attention by the government, as the social sectors programmes become a mere casualty. The current strategy of the governments towards an enmass encouragement to industrial sector alone, without a component for skilled training programme, or ways and means to enhance incomes or the purchasing power of the poor, and the working class, not only results in further deterioration of poor masses, but also leaves very little scope for the participation of the poor in the reforms process. This only demonstrates the piece meal approach by the planners and policy makers towards poverty eradication and implementation of the social sector programmes. The number of projects implemented by an unimaginative bureaucracy in the government further marginalises the poor.

The issue of poverty eradication, therefore, needs fresh thinking and our political Action Plan in this year of Golden Jubilee should lead to new efforts of transformation, providing importance to social sector programmes and in an effort of this all of us have to transform ourselves

*Speech at Committee Meeting of the 50th Aniversary Meeting of India's Independence Aug, 1997.

into a new class of social and political activists transcending barriers of caste, gender, ethnicity, class or North/South divisions. The poor can no longer be treated, as clients but have to be treated as comrades. The poor need solidarity and not our sympathy. The need of the hour is social and political activism at the grassroots throwing innumeral social education programmes in every village and town. All our congress workers have to become political and social activists in action.

Therefore, the need of the hour is an action plan in this year of Golden Jubilee of India's Independence, a plan with few more innovative programmes apart from our regular honouring of freedom fighters or engaged ourselves in poor feeding. It is said so as after their honouring of the martyrs and poor feeding, our Congress workers forget their political consciousness and activism and are back to the walls for several months. Congress workers, thus have to keep in touch with the masses in one way or other all through this year. Our Golden Jubilee action plan should be commemoration of our grassroot work, to begin our effort to build up a socio-political platform as it was done in the days of freedom struggle.

1. Organise the unemployed workers at the grassroots on occupational lines and help them as much as possible in their economic activities forming small co-operative initiatives.
2. If there are stray economic activities pursued by the poor families at the block level, it has to be strengthened with local resources forming group initiative.
3. Empowerment, training, orientation of the organised group should include the spreading of the ideologies of the 110 year old achievements of the Congress Party and the golden era of Congress rule where major decisions like 20 Point Programmes and National Technology Missions that have been the landmarks of Congress governance benefiting the poor, women mainly. This forum of Golden Jubilee initiative should be widely used for educating youth and the coming generations on the achievements of the 50 years of India's history especially in Congress regime.
4. In many areas, this golden jubilee initiative should lead to an asset building effort of the poor people living in the destitute conditions around which a Congress initiative can grow at the grassroots more as a political platform for the party.
5. Groups at the block level or in major cities should comprise atleast a cluster of 40 to 50 families either in the slum neighbourhoods or in the rural areas where large number of rural poor live in destitutional conditions.

While some initiatives can come from the party, (if possible) and if arrangements of organising activities could be attempted to encompass all sections of the society more as non-political efforts ensuring the participation of the general public even funds can be mobilised otherwise too. Such emergence of new initiatives will lead to social mobilisation, building up an effective social and political platform for the Congress Party. The immediate action plan to formulate such clusters as the Golden Jubilee initiative of India's Independence, will certainly leave behind such celebrations a spirit and an action, as "Mandals" or "Mandrams" at the grassroots as grassroots political platform for the Congress Party in future.

40th Anniversary of India's Independence 1987*

Deviating from the colonial past, we are an Independent Nation today as free citizens with freedom of expression. While we have achieved only the political freedom, we are still far away from the much needed economic freedom. Heritage of feudalism and colonialism still hangs on India's poor, who face obstacles at every stage for effective participation in all development programmes. During these 40 years after our political freedom, we have given very little or no attention to human resource development and equitable benefit distribution – a process that is most effective to achieve human dignity contending or assuring a quality of life for every individual. Despite widespread calls and concerns for increased people's participation in development, there are many obstacles hindering the emergence of any such a genuine effort. Our collective realisation today must be to realise that our development need today is only development of people alone.

As all of us are aware, vast majority of the targeted poor suffer in oppressive situations as workforce, and are victims of social handicaps, suffer in hunger and poverty. One out of these targeted poor, half of them are women, 60 per cent are illiterate, 60 per cent are below the poverty line, 75 per cent of them live in rural areas. If one takes 100 households in a rural area, easily 30 to 40 households are found as landless or possess only marginal holdings pledged and mortgaged. Further, they are unorganised, under-nourished, unemployed and under-employed, invariably highly indebted, vulnerable to all kinds of diseases, suffer from lack of confidence and are easy prey to exploitation, and form the long suffering mass of this country. They live in places with no electricity, either filthy or no sanitation, in far away and isolated areas where no transport system can reach.

Lack of productive asserts, local power hierarchies, elite domination and conflicts among the poor themselves are the major obstacles that impede the progress of the poor.

The answer to all this lies in an enmasse social mobilisation of these people to evoke their real and true participation in the development programmes of the nation. It may not be easy as it is a long drawn-out process. But through a fullfledged support to social action groups to educate and organise them, can to an extent, bring them to a stage of growth towards fulfillment. Therefore, for the next 10 years, the ruling

*Speech at the 40th Anniversary of India's Independence 1987.

party should engage itself in social mobilisation, organising movements of magnitudes in which targeted poor have to be taught to decide, control and empower themselves at the grassroots, train themselves for new responsibilities of leadership, participation, management and new orientation through a process of conscientiation.

Women alone form 50 per cent of the poor, living in sub-human conditions of starvation and squalor. Theirs is a recurring story of incomplete human existence in this country. Economically, it is the most disheartening feature that the women workers' contribution to community and country is totally invisible. The recognition in their own right for such a contribution is totally denied. Women's work is under-valued and under-estimated. Even if it is a women headed household run by a deserted woman or a widow, their work is always considered cheap, flexible and disposable labour, and as workers, they have no bargaining power. Undoubtedly, development in rural areas demand a great deal from these rural women both in the production process and in family care.

Thus, National Governments have to support emerging social organisations of magnitude with grassroot character. New effective delivery mechanisms have to be innovated to reach a large number of poor quickly. And an alternative leadership pattern must emerge for social development like those envisaged by Gandhiji and Martin Luther King to lead the poor to fight powerlessness. We cannot forget that it was the civil rights movement that brought the Black Community in the U.S.A. nearer to power and occupy at least few key positions.

In the next 10 years, as immediate measures we will have to be concerned about indecent slum neighbourhoods and squattered-settlements where no human habitation is possible. Our plans have to adopt processual approach and not the blueprint approach, where organisation of poor must be involved both in planning and in the process of implementation of the projects that benefit them.

After 40 years of this political freedom, we now have to turn our attention to a kind of non-elite leadership that alone would bring in the new social change. The new social development must lead to halting of deforestation, provide clean water to the community, promote the full involvement and strengthen the women in the development process defend the rights of children, foster self-reliant professional organisations, adopt appropriate human technologies that would utilise available resources to develop cooperative methods for production and decision-making awaken communities to their true potential by awakening every individual.

In other words, we have to put the priorities of the poor first, work only with the poor, promote leadership from below and exercise a clout to make the poor get their rights. This is essential for the sake of tens of millions of the oppressed and the poor in India, and effort that emerge as a model, should inspire similar other movements in other parts of the developing world just to struggle for a better life.

Vision of Rajiv Gandhi*
A Golden Era in Gender History of India
1984 to 1988

"A society can be judged by now well half our society progresses and if they are to progress half the talent, and energy cannot be ignored. Women should be allowed full freedom and action". Rajiv Gandhi NAM 1985, New Delhi.

With the demise of the young visionary, Sri Rajiv Gandhi, we see a great loss to the movement and momentum for social change process in this country. Rajiv Gandhi was a firm advocate of secularism, poverty alleviation, development of women and mobilishing youth for progressive actions. For one so young, Rajivji was a farsighted visionary to lead this country to the 21st century. During his tenure as Prime Minister, we have watched for the first time various policy pronouncements and programme measures aimed at the development and empowerment of poor and women.

In terms of women empowerment and grassroots leadership, he brought in a percentage allocation for women at the panchayat level for the first time on the national scene. Sex ratio figures registered an increase towards women, age at marriage arose to 18.4 years; life expectancy for women improved; the largest scheme for women covering all schemes for women was planned for, in the form of a Perspective Plan for Women.

In the recent years, we notice a stagnation of gender issues so intensely advocated during Rajivji's term in government. A leader committed to science and technology, it was during his tenure, several technological missions were promoted. He was totally convinced that harnessing science and technology is the only way to remove poverty and its drudgery among poor. Women's study centres in universities received a fillip during his time so was the training and sensitisation of functionaries and administrators in the government on gender issues. Professionalising women programmes; incorporating women's concerns into the census – all such issues received a great thrust and guidance from the young leader, Rajivji.

As champion of women's empowerment, Rajivji was well aware of the multiple burden of women as a crucial obstacle to their development. To quote Rajivji, "It is really at the grassroots at the daily level that the discrimination must be removed".

---

*Extract from Policy paper presented to Rajiv Gandhi Foundation.

His concern for the environmental degradation was also related to the sustenance of human life as well as the needs of poor women, such as fuel and fodder.

No less important was his emphatic pronouncements on the need to develop the 'future women', i.e., the 'adolescent girl' or the 'girl child', who otherwise is a victim of neglect and discrimination.

His period of rule in India led to the recognition that to develop adult women, attention has to be paid to the education, socialisation and health of the "girl child". It was only during Rajivji's regime, the campaign on the girl child was first initiated, leading to the SAARC declaration of 1990, as the year of the 'Girl Child'.

In his endeavour to fulfil his dream and vision to position India among the front ranking nations of the world, Rajiv Gandhi realised that the shackles of tradition, the barriers of communalism/regression must be broken by long-term goals of systematic elimination of gender bias in all aspects of life and society. Rajiv's era was the golden age of programmes and promulgations in the General History of India, leading to long-term actions accelerating gender justice and development towards the millennium.

Corporate Responsibility: New Directions*

Introduction

I am extremely happy that the seminar works on the doctrine of trusteeship formulated by the Father of Nation, Mahatma Gandhi. All of us are aware that his doctrine of trusteeship had a vital bearing on the economic situation of the country not only at the time of British exploitation, but also now. Gandhiji arrived at this doctrine as a synthesis of Plato's Philosophy of European economic thought, Tolstoy's concept of bread labour, John Ruskin's "Unto this last" and above all from the ancient scriptures of India like Gita and Rig Veda. While Tolstoy conditioned the labour confirming the dignity of work culture, Ruskin's Doctrine is more a condition to the employers that the treatment of workers be more humane, where he even goes to the extent of saying that the employers are not only responsible for the workers' basic needs but also their cultural needs, thus highlighting the principles ingrained in our ancient scriptures. The Rig Veda describes this doctrine of trusteeship that the entire world's property belongs only to God as, "Isa Vasyam Iyem Sarvam", further confirming that the human family is God's own family. "Vasudaiva Kutumbakam".

Expansion of the Doctrine of Trusteeship

In his doctrine of trusteeship, he necessitates subordination of the individual good to a social good advocating that the birth of an individual is in vain or useless, if it is not useful to the society. Accordingly, such a social environment alone conditions the behavior of an individual. Neither living in seclusion nor excluding the society is possible in an egalitarian / righteous society. Such a close relationship between society and the individual heralds the ushering of a new era of socialistic order for which there is no alternative. Though he may not be appreciative of communism as a political philosophy he was highly influenced by Engles, who believed that men make history themselves and they do so only in a given environment, which conditions it.

This new social order visualises a distinct social necessity, not of private property or of class distinctions bereft of exploitation. He further said that a person of possession however rich he may be should consider himself as a trustee of all wealth, which he inherits. He will be permitted to

---

*Speech at the Seminar of Citigroup and Partner's in change on Oct 1st 2003 Taj Mahal Hotel, Mumbai on Gandhi Jayanthi Celebrations.

retain a small percentage of this for his personal use and spending of the rest of it will be determined not by himself but by social necessity. Unlike the capitalist owner, the trustee has no right to misuse the wealth, as he likes, only a portion of it is entitled to his free personal use like what is necessary for his own existence, the maximum being determined not by himself but by the state. He further said in his doctrine that under the socialist dispensation, his entire capital will be confiscated. Therefore, the underlying idea is that the property is only an incident of production, but does not belong to him as a birthright and therefore, its use must not be controlled by any individual. More positively, the social necessity determines the management of proceeds in keeping with the egalitarian ideas of social justice.

Even in the matter of trust ownership according to the doctrine of trusteeship it cannot be exploited for private benefit. These are however directed by schedules of rights and obligations as mentioned in the doctrine and Gandhiji was quiet liberal in dealing with the owners of private property. Before he applies the socialist dispensation of confiscation of the surplus, he gives a chance to the wrong doer to improve himself, that is, he tries to do away with the wrong before he deals with the wrong doer, showing him the right course. Even as early as that Gandhiji's prediction was to avoid larger accumulation of capital in few hands and pauperization of masses. Therefore, he desired more a change in the hearts and minds of the owners of the property before he gets into the next action. The word "trusteeship" he felt cannot be misconstrued to reduce the capital of an employer to a manager of trust property. But the press and others drastically questioned Gandhiji, if owners of property refuse to be trustees what would be his next action? He said that if the trustees fail to accept the schedule, voluntary deprivation of their position through the state with a minimum exercise of violence is the only action. In Gandhiji's dream, the trustee will be a new man who will be able to restore democracy through a doctrine of equality of opportunities.

Dignity of Poverty

Similarly Gandhiji felt that there is a dignity in poverty and personally he preferred to be in a hut than being in a rich man's place. A poor man according to him is not ashamed of poverty, as he works for his daily bread and there is much to learn from him because everybody has to work (and imposing on them a voluntary poverty) so that mind and body can be sound. He along with other colleagues did believe in the cooperative way of life, as the secret of co-operation is that the members must be honest and realise the great merit of cooperation guided by a definite goal. According to Gandhiji, without character there is no cooperation; also the success of cooperative movement cannot be measured by the number of cooperatives formed, but on its credibility. He severely warned the working population to imbibe the work culture instead of cursing the poverty.

The Initiation of Working Women's Forum (India)

Following Gandhiji's footsteps and guided by his philosophy, the Working Women's Forum (India) was born in the year 1978, with 800 women workers as its members and the Indian Cooperative Network for Women Ltd., in the year 1981 with 2500 members. Today, Working Women's Forum (India) covers over 7 lakh poor women in 15 branches spread across 3 southern states of India. Likewise, Indian Cooperative Network for Women is catering to about 3,28,284 poor women members in 15 branches in 3 southern states providing the micro-credit option, helping them build sustainable livelihoods and empowering them in all aspects. Together, WWF and ICNW reach out to poor women in 3,031 villages and 1,675 slums.

Problems of the Working Poor

The women workers in the informal sector, both in the urban and rural areas more are less face the same kind of oppressive situation. The series of economic problems that women confront in this sector are abysmal living conditions, exploitative and harsh working conditions, low and discriminatory wages, invisibility and powerlessness, disposition of assets and landlessness, monopoly of moneylenders and middlemen resulting in heavy indebtedness and impoverishment, low skill levels / technology / productive inputs, caste inferiority, male dominance and isolation and physical weakness due to large families. The situation was more an imposition of poverty on themselves rather than being poor themselves.

Structure and Decentralization

Formulating a totally innovative structure, integrating poor women at all levels of decision-making within the organisation, WWF entrusted the key responsibility of the administration of the organisation and the bank training to internal cadres from their own neighbourhood communities. This paved the way for major chunk of the organizational business to take place in the field. Participation of poor particularly "The working poor" paved way for access to credit, marketing, socio-economic and political responsibilities, resulting in the remarkable empowerment of the poor.

Health as a Mother and as a Worker

WWF's healthcare programmes conceptualises the dimension of human-centered approach and takes care of women from birth to adolescence to reproductive age group to the post-reproductive phase. The reproductive healthcare programme has covered over 16,00,000 families in Tamil Nadu through 960 grassroots health workers spread over 720 slums and 340 villages. Basically, the healthcare programme implemented by WWF was to straighten the productive role and protect them from occupational health hazards both as a mother and as a worker. Access to health insurance and other social security needs became the integral part of this programme for the working poor.

Unionization - towards Rights and Entitlement

Later, formulating itself as a trade union for women workers, it took up the issues that affected them, like malpractices in wage payment and material supply in their wage employment options, particularly to save the lace artisans, beedi rollers and women weavers. Its task became significant in reducing child labour and child bondedness, by establishing child labour rehabilitation and vocational training centres. Uniting women in solidarity, the union further helped women to take leadership to fight for their rights and entitlements through organised rallies, protest and demand marches.

WWF's Partnership with other NGOs

Working Women's Forum has partnership programmes with the NGOs working in the backward districts of Orissa, Maharashtra and Kerala. As initiators, of a grassroots global network called GROOTS, WWF has effective networks with organisations working at the grassroots globally. Partnership efforts with the banking institutions outside the country (RABO bank and Royal Netherlands Embassy and the Citibank) has ameliorated the conditions of hundreds and thousands of working poor women.

Its sister concern, the Independent Commission for Peoples Rights and Development, ICPRD (New Delhi) works in the poorest states of Central India, Jharkhand, Bihar, Orissa, Madhya Pradesh, Chattisgarh and Uttranchal to build coalitions of the poor, building capacities and transferring technologies - having had 760 NGOs participate in its activities in 21 states. Particularly in the states of Maharashtra, Orissa, Bihar, Uttaranchal and Kerala, strong bonds of partnership I have already been established.

WWF - Citibank Partnership

Describing the enduring partnership of Citibank and Working Women's Forum in the year 1998 August as it happened, two high-ranking officials Ms. Anita and Ms. Uma from the Citicorp Bombay visited WWF with the object of exploring the possibilities of initiating their community support programme between Citicorp and WWF and extending the same for the first time in South India. The team met the President and understood the organizational structure, which is a totally decentralized process, also learned the area of it's functioning. The team visited the market vendors in an area meeting and had a wide ranging discussion with the leaders and members who have benefited from the credit and other programmes. The problems figured were mostly male alcoholism, abuse and violence against women and the team learned how through personal empowerment, the poor working women adopted various strategies to counter the situations that confronted them in their neighbourhood. The local Citibank officials also joined us and learned about the growth and history of this movement and its impact on the lives of poor women. The Citibank team appreciated WWF's pioneering efforts and were particularly impressed with the 24 hours banking concept and simplified and easy to operate procedures. In the WWF, priority was given to the members and their daughters being provided employment in the Forum. An overview was also provided with regard to the training programme that focused on gender equality and social empowerment of women.

After that officials from Citibank visited the Kanchipurarn unit of WWF, had interactions and discussion with the members of WWF in many villages. The women appraised the team on the difficulties they faced as producers of silk; a slump in the silk industry not only because of the high cost of raw materials, but also due to the lack of markets. A similar situation was faced by other handloom weavers and the women weavers in Andhra Pradesh unit. WWF women weavers suggested that the Citicorp partnership can make an intervention if desired to help them by supplying cheaper raw materials and taking up marketing of their products through buyer and seller meets.

The other major issue that came up from the discussion before the visiting team was the child-bonded labourers in Kanchipuram in many weavers' families. While many children were already redeemed from bondedness through the effort of WWF and were put back in schools or made to assist their own parents, there are many more children who still remained pledged and whole conditioned have to be attended to. The Citibank and WWF team assured them that something would be done through a process of consensus. The meeting was followed by visiting the households of silk weavers. Later, the same year the Citibank WWF partnership was officially launches at a press meet on the 4th October 1998.

Programme in Detail

The core elements of the Citibank community support programme in India are financial advisory services, technology transfer, marketing advisory services and direct grants from CAF America to NGO partners towards WWF's partnership. Citibank appreciated the use of micro credit as an effective empowerment tool. The Citibank community support programme emphasizes this commitment, not simply through cherub book philanthropy but with active employee volunteerism to ensure its effectiveness and sustainability, particularly in the direct marketing support, opening new chapters in the lives of many poor women weavers. On and off, WWF's staff were sent to Mumbai to attend the management training programme conducted by Citibank.

During the Phase 1, that were provision of rotating capital for technology support, business diversification and entrepreneurship development to Kanchipurami silk weavers, lace makers and agarbathi makers. Training in new looms and designs brought in better productivity among the weavers. Micro loans have benefited women to bring about economic security in their lives. In physical terms, Citibank and WWF partnership has touched higher echelons women in Chennai and among the women weavers in Kanchipuram through micro credit provision. During the Citibank Phase II partnership, many of the women who were only weaving in borrowed looms on high rent became owners of the looms. In fact, women weavers in their strong gender struggle have been able to establish a lead and gain membership in the male dominated government weaver's cooperative and marketing societies and today their prestige in the community and neighbourhood has gone up many fold and is very much appreciated. The rotating corpus will strengthen many more women in the future, particularly in Bidar, Dharmapuri, Bangalore and Narasapur; especially, in Bidar where the women are prone to under and unemployment due to severe and periodical drought. Childcare rehabilitation centres and service homes run in Tambaram has provided dresses to the children during festival time and have made the children enjoy the delight of these festivals. Drinking water infrastructure facility has been made available. Uniforms to many children who cannot afford to buy these uniform has been a great support.

Training workshops supported by Citibank for grassroots trainers as resulted in the production of excellent training materials in three languages as also audio visual aids – both acting as further catalysts to unleash the empowerment process in more poor women.

Poor to Participate in the Globalisation

In the era of globalisation, where the markets have a mind of their own and the working opportunities often are the domain of the privileged lot in the community, the poor and the deprived are left to themselves with little or no support system to compete in the world market. Remedy for such a scenario is the holistic partnership of Citibank's collaboration with WWF. Indispensable assistance of Citibank has helped the women to have greater access to credit, access to speciailsed skills, designs, information towards quality products and finally access to markets.

Insurance and Social Security

Living in shackles of poverty, women find it very difficult to make both ends meet especially in a era of rising prices and dwindling living standards. In such a scenario, the social security options and insurance is a luxury as far as poor women are concerned. Citibank has volunteered in this sphere and has brought about the much needed social security coverage for poor women, particularly those facing discrimination, desertion and other vulnerabilities at the time of joining WWF.

To bring about holistic provision of banking and training services needed for adequate building infrastructure becomes imminent. While earliest standing bilateral partners of WWF came forward to extend support for the purchase of land, Citibank, although young in years of partnership stood strongly by WWF in realising its vision of need based infrastructure for banking and training. This was certainly a milestone in the history of Working Women's Forum (India) Mr. & Mrs. Raymond witnessed the structure in person.

Conclusion

Therefore, we are happy to place all this before this August body that the Citibank / WWF partnership is not only about provision of financial, technical, micro credit, marketing support, but also the honoured visits of the dignitaries of Citibank to the Working Women's Forum, providing an opportunity to share these salient features of the experiment mutually. Thus, Citibank really makes history, its members are truly conditioned by the corporate philosophy meaning that it has to work for the needy particularly in a given country where they operated and benefited.

Elections - Is It A Social Contract?*

Elections in few states of India are on now, and within a year there will be general elections in all the states. Hence, it would be a worthwhile effort to do a real soul-searching analysis. Today, the governing principles among parties and politicians demonstrate whether they have any regards for morality or ethics.

Party Systems, Gandhian Values and Electoral Success

Electoral success in a parliamentary democracy rests largely on two aspects. Firstly, on the existence and sustenance of political parties and recently on the strength of the values and the character of the candidates who represent the people of the given constituency. Unfortunately, both these aspects in the Indian electoral system are fast disappearing. Immediately after independence, the father of the nation Mahatma Gandhi tried his best to bridge the gap between ethics and politics. He laid stress on the means used by the political parties and their candidates. But, what's being witnessed today is very different from what was expected!

Is there a real election system in many parties? No! We see that many of them go without elections, for years or forever. Is it possible to understand the real objectives of political parties today, as they are based mainly on caste or religion and are neither secular nor democratic? Our party system has degenerated to caste politics. What could be the agenda of political parties? They have their own agenda promoting self-centred political leaders clinging on to power. The growth and privilege of fundamentalism in the recent times in our country destroys the very secular fabrics that we were assured of in the country.

Criminalisation, Money and Muscle Power

Criminalisation of politics has become the order of the day. Such political degeneration not only made the administration of criminal justice a mockery, but also undermined the character of candidates with money and muscle power. Gone are the days when political parties who had heritage playing a greater role in the governance of the country, than having a sound party system to participate in the elections with a reputation of service records. These parties could use the citizen's support mechanism as a 'lifeline' assuring success to their candidates respecting democratic value. In fact, the secret of their success have been an effective manifesto expressing their desire to selfless service to the nation guided by principles of ethics and morality.

---

*Appeared in Groots as editorial Issue 16 - Vol. IIV / Oct. - 2003.

This destroys the electorate's dreams and expectations of their candidates' selfless service to the nation with ethical and moral values. Thus, this is the reason why our electoral verdict these days appear more indecisive and confused with no majority to anyone. Also, it is proof that electorates cannot be taken for a ride forever and the electorate's turn back to them to disappoint those candidates whose reputations are doubtful and subject to question in their local areas. So more often Indian elections lead to hung parliament & assemblies. What is being witnessed today is different from what was expected.

Insensitivity of the Elected Representatives

Does India maintain any such discipline in its party system today? Do they represent high standards of morality? It is a forgotten chapter that now the framers of the Constitution visualised a charter to the general elections to assume democratic office. How they committed themselves to such policies, to uphold the nations honour and democratic values? It was an ambitious charter directing governance to usher a new social order based on equality and justice ensuring probity in public life.

Undoubtedly a political charter such as this has been given to our elected representatives of the country, slowly had given an opportunity to the emergence of a new political class to our surprise and dismay. Gradually this class with unlimited powers and privileges in the parliamentary assemblies in addition to access to wealth and other resources have become rigid-power structure in themselves. Thus, our representatives in their "power-clad new avatars" have not only left the Gandhian values far behind, but also adopted class / religion and corruption in its place proving themselves worse than the colonial ruling class of the yore. They returned to their feudalistic values and caste networks.

How Elections are a Foul Play?

Gross violations of human rights of the tribals, dalit women and other marginalised group have come to stay permanently. In fact India's pluralistic traditions have never ever severely threatened as of now. Naxals have gained upper hand among the poor, not because of any other reason, but because of the communal attitude of civil and police authorities. The candidates today, collect enormous money in the name of the party by fair or foul means, without any accountability on their election expenditure. Therefore, election to many politicians is a one-point programme to amass wealth. Thus, unfortunately what we witness today as political scenario are the reflections of our elections and the candidates we have chosen.

Our elections are nothing but a bundle of nefarious activities of the political parties who indulge in threat, violence, false impersonations and intimidation on voter as part of the electoral process. Besides, the growth of fundamentalism everywhere undermines the very secular attitude India enjoyed immediately after independence.

Reflection of Business in Parliament

What is the reflection of business in our Assemblies and Parliament today? Having elected themselves, certainly not with the good will of the electorate, but with money and muscle power they have no sensitivity to people's issues. They are indifferent to what is happening around them. They are unaware of the increasing number of vulnerable people in poverty, not due to shortage of food in the country, but because they lack purchasing power. On the contrary, with the elected office in hand they have the most converted influence, i.e., the political influence, an influence that can distort and manipulate every thing under the sun including law. For instance, there the priority would be to do away with the Urban Ceiling Act, i.e., facilitate urban elites rather initiate a real pro-poor land reforms infavour of poor peasantry in the rural areas. The woes of the farming community everywhere is not only due to the crisis of the vagary of the monsoon but as the recent media report present there are more suicides among the farmers as their lands are appropriated by multi-nationals these days in the name of liberalisation. This is a major threat to livelihood and the survival of the lowest of the social groups at the grassroots. Further a rich town dweller is more important to them to get a ration card without much effort, while the poor slum dweller has to struggle for one or more days together. All this happen because the majority of our elected representatives shun visiting either urban slums or his poor constituents in the rural areas. They are totally ignorant of a value, known as probity in public life in its place. They will be showering the contractors and businessman with opportunities to amass wealth in their own interest. They are totally indifferent to mass displacement of the poor, dalits and tribals thrown out of the habitats to facilitate development project, an agenda to do away with the poor in favour of the rich. Such is the agenda of the majority of the elected representative with utter disregard to basic human need of the marginalised poor of the country. The mounting unemployment on the educated young among the new literates is yet another major problem for the governance because the dejection and the depression among the youth will lead to more dangerous consequences as they would be attracted by the undesirable and anti-social elements. Living in squartered settlement the poor are the ones who are highly enthusiastic in the elections, they are the surest of the electorates who vote unfailingly. Do they get their due for their exercise of unalienable right of voting?

What is the Alternative?

When the election system fails the governance also fails because the attention of elected ones is more to keep themselves in power by any means rather than look at the needs of the people. Therefore, in a secular democracy there must be a demand from the electorates to those perspective candidates, a demand for a "Peoples Agenda". Before the elections educate the voter on who should be brought to power who are not in the elections. Elections are inevitable in a democratic system of governance, however evil and imperfect they are. There is still a faith that there is ample scope towards corrective measures, as proactive we will have to continue in such faith we live in. In the word of British elderly statesmen Late Mr. Winsten Churchill on democracy, "Democracy is a bad form of governance" but "all others are worse". That is political wisdom.

Index

D

E

F

G

H

N

V

W

Y

Z